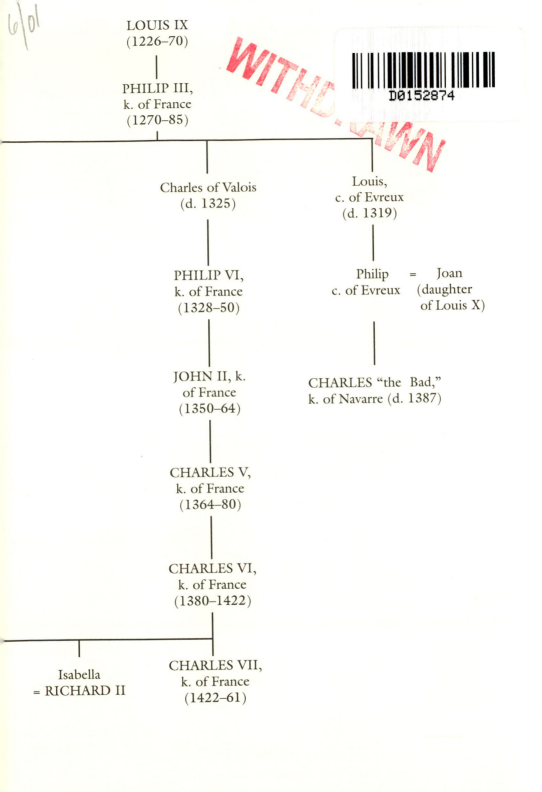

LOUIS IX
(1226–70)

PHILIP III,
k. of France
(1270–85)

Charles of Valois
(d. 1325)

Louis,
c. of Evreux
(d. 1319)

PHILIP VI,
k. of France
(1328–50)

Philip   =   Joan
c. of Evreux   (daughter
of Louis X)

JOHN II, k.
of France
(1350–64)

CHARLES "the Bad,"
k. of Navarre (d. 1387)

CHARLES V,
k. of France
(1364–80)

CHARLES VI,
k. of France
(1380–1422)

Isabella
= RICHARD II

CHARLES VII,
k. of France
(1422–61)

JOHN ABERTH

CONFRONTING

FAMINE, WAR,

PLAGUE, AND DEATH

IN THE LATER

MIDDLE AGES

From the Brink
of the $\mathfrak{A}$pocalypse

Routledge
New York   London

Published in 2001 by
Routledge
A member of the Taylor and Francis Group
29 West 35th Street
New York, New York 10001

Published in Great Britain by
Routledge
11 New Fetter Lane
London EC4P 4EE

Printed in the United States of America on acid-free paper.
Designed by KS at Sun & Vine Design.

*Contents page: One of the many angels depicted on the tomb of Alice de
la Pole. (Courtesy Royal Commission on Historical Monuments in England.)
Chapter openers: Illuminations from the Burckhardt-Wildt Apocalypse.
(Courtesy Conway Library, Courtauld Institute of Art.)*

Library of Congress Cataloging-in-Publication Data

Aberth, John, 1963–
  From the brink of the apocalypse : confronting famine, war, plague, and
death in the later middle ages / by John Aberth.
    p.cm.
  Includes bibliographical references and index.
  ISBN 0-415-92715-3
    1. Great Britain—History—Lancaster and York, 1399–1485. 2. Apocalyptic
literature—History and criticism. 3. Disasters—England—History—To 1500.
4. Great Britain—History—14th century. 5. Famines—England—History—To
1500. 6. England—Civilization—1066–1485. 7. Hundred Years War,
1339–1453. 8. Black death—England. I. Title.

DA245 .A24 2000
942.04—dc21

00-038263

For Laura,

> "Chiare fresche et dolci acque, ove le belle
> membra pose colei che sola a me par donna."

CONTENTS

And when he had opened the fourth seal, I heard the voice of the fourth living creature, saying: Come, and see. And behold a pale horse, and he that sat upon him, his name was Death, and hell followed him. And power was given to him over the four parts of the earth, to kill with sword, with famine, and with death, and with the beasts of the earth.

—Apocalypse of St. John the Apostle

CHRONOLOGY

1307	Death of King Edward I of England. Succession of his son, Edward II.
1315–22	Great Famine throughout the British Isles and Northern Europe.
1327	Deposition and death of King Edward II of England. Succession of his son, Edward III.
1337	King Philip VI of France confiscates the English duchy of Aquitaine in retaliation for Edward III's harboring of a condemned Frenchman, Robert of Artois. War is declared between England and France.
1340	Edward III formally assumes the title of king of France.
1346–47	English victory at Crécy in northeastern France. After a year-long siege, the port of Calais falls to the English.
1348–49	The Black Death arrives in Europe. By the end of 1349, the disease has spread throughout England and the British Isles. Edward III and his council issue the Ordinance of Labourers, fixing wages to the level they had been before the plague, in 1346.
1356	English victory at Poitiers. The French king, John II, is taken prisoner by the Black Prince.
1360	Treaty of Brétigny between England and France. Edward agrees to renounce his claim to the French throne and release John II of France, in return for an enlarged duchy of Aquitaine held in full sovereignty and 3 million gold crowns, or £500,000.
1361–62	Second outbreak of plague in England.

1367   Victory of Edward, the Black Prince, over Henry of Trastamara at Nájera, Spain.

1369   Third outbreak of plague in England. Resumption of war between England and France.

1370   Famine in England.

1374–79   Fourth outbreak of plague in England.

1381   Peasants' Revolt in England. Thousands of rebels, led by Wat Tyler, convene on London, where they demand an end to serfdom before being dispersed. Simon Sudbury, archbishop of Canterbury and royal chancellor, is beheaded by the rebels on Tower Hill.

1390–93   Fifth outbreak of plague in England.

1396   Truce to last twenty-eight years declared between England and France at Ardres near Calais. The truce is sealed by the marriage between Richard II of England and Isabella, the French princess and daughter of Charles VI.

1399–1400   Deposition and death of King Richard II of England. The king's cousin, Henry of Bolingbroke, is crowned as Henry IV.

1400   National outbreak of plague in England.

1407   National outbreak of plague in England.

1413   Death of King Henry IV of England. Succession of his son, Henry V. National outbreak of plague.

1415   Resumption of war between England and France. English victory at Agincourt.

1420   Treaty of Troyes between England and France. Henry V is made regent and heir to the French throne and marries Catherine, daughter of Charles VI. National outbreak of plague in England.

1422   Death of King Henry V of England, on August 31. King Charles VI of France dies two months later, on

October 21. Henry's ten-month-old son, Henry VI, succeeds as king of both England and France.

1423   National outbreak of epidemic disease, perhaps plague.

1424–25   Dance of Death painted on the walls of the southern cloister of the cemetery of Les Innocents in Paris. Henry Chichele, archbishop of Canterbury, builds the first "double-decker" transi tomb in England.

1426–29   National outbreaks of epidemic disease, perhaps plague. Joan of Arc raises the English siege of Orleans on May 8, 1429, reversing English advances in France. Charles VII, son of Charles VI, is anointed and crowned king of France at Reims on July 17.

1431   After a five-month trial on seventy counts of heresy presided by Pierre Cauchon, bishop of Beauvais, Joan of Arc is burned at the stake at Rouen on May 30. Henry VI of England is anointed and crowned king of France at Paris on December 16.

1433–35   National outbreaks of plague and famine in England.

1436   English abandon Paris. John Lydgate returns to England to translate the Dance of Death at Les Innocents into English and re-create it in the north cloister of the Pardon Chuchyard at St. Paul's Cathedral, London.

1437–38   Famine throughout northern Europe.

1438–40   National outbreaks of plague and famine in England.

1445   King Henry VI of England marries Margaret, daughter of Réné, duke of Anjou.

1453   English forces are defeated at Castillon in France and the English commander, John Talbot, earl of Shrewsbury, is killed on July 17. The Hundred Years War is over. King Henry VI suffers his first bout of insanity.

1455   The War of the Roses, a civil war between the Lancastrians, or "Red Rose," led by King Henry VI, and the Yorkists, or "White Rose," led by Richard, duke of

York, opens with the battle of St. Albans on May 22.

1456　　　　After a retrial authorized by Pope Calixtus III, Joan of Arc is exonerated and the verdict of 1431 is nullified on July 7.

1460　　　　Henry VI is captured by the Yorkists at Northampton on July 10. Richard, duke of York, is made heir to the throne but is killed at the battle of Wakefield on December 30.

1461　　　　Edward, earl of March, son of Richard, defeats Lancastrian forces at Towton and is crowned king of England as Edward IV.

1463–64　　　National outbreaks of plague in England.

1467　　　　National outbreak of plague.

1470　　　　Henry VI is restored to the throne of England by Richard Nevill, earl of Warwick, the "kingmaker."

1471　　　　Lancastrians are defeated at Barnet and Tewkesbury and Edward IV reenters London. Henry VI is murdered in the Tower. National outbreak of plague and the "stich," perhaps pleurisy.

1473　　　　National outbreak of the "flux," probably dysentery.

1475　　　　The "French pox," perhaps gonorrhea, afflicts King Edward IV's soldiers.

1479–80　　　A particularly severe national outbreak of plague in England.

1483　　　　Edward IV dies. His brother, Richard, duke of Gloucester, is crowned king as Richard III. Edward IV's adolescent sons, Edward V and Richard, duke of York, disappear in the Tower of London.

1485　　　　Richard III is defeated and killed at the battle of Bosworth on August 22. Henry Tudor is crowned king of England as Henry VII. The War of the Roses is over. Outbreak of the "sweat," probably influenza, in London and East Anglia.

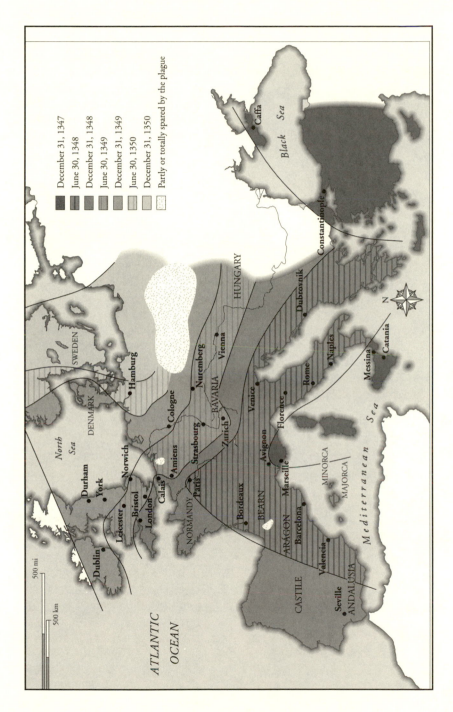

The path of the Black Death over Europe.

The counties of England as they existed during the Middle Ages.

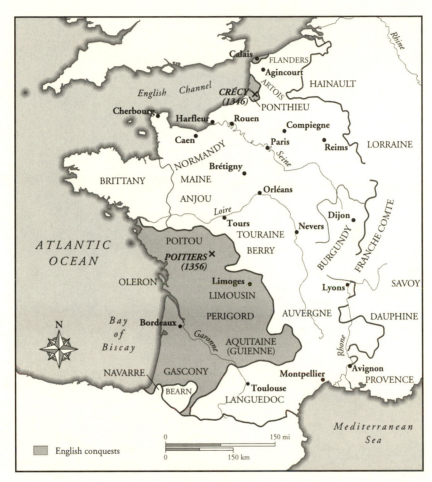

Calais
FLANDERS
Agincourt
HAINAULT
ARTOIS
CRÉCY ×
(1346)
PONTHIEU
LORRAINE

English Channel

Cherbourg
Harfleur
Rouen
Compiègne
Reims
Caen
NORMANDY
Paris
Seine
MAINE
Brétigny
ANJOU
Orléans
BRITTANY
Loire
Tours
TOURAINE
Dijon
Nevers
BURGUNDY
FRANCHE COMTE
ATLANTIC OCEAN
POITOU
BERRY
POITIERS ×
(1356)
OLERON
Limoges
LIMOUSIN
Lyons
SAVOY
AUVERGNE
DAUPHINE
PERIGORD
Bay of Biscay
Bordeaux
Garonne
AQUITAINE (GUIENNE)
Rhone
Avignon
PROVENCE
N
NAVARRE
GASCONY
Montpellier
BEARN
Toulouse
LANGUEDOC

Rhine

Mediterranean Sea

English conquests

0   150 mi
0   150 km

France after the Treaty of Bretigny, 1360.

Calais

FLANDERS

AGINCOURT ✗
(1415)

ARTOIS

English *Channel*

Crécy

PICARDY

Cherbourg

Harfleur

Rouen

Compiegne

Caen

Reims

NORMANDY

Paris

Seine

CHAMPAGNE

BRITTANY

MAINE

Orléans

Domremy

ANJOU

Loire

BERRY

Chinon

Tours

NEVERS

DUCHY
OF
BURGUNDY

TOURAINE

Nevers

POITOU

Poitiers

BOURBON

TERR. OF FRENCH KING

Limoges

LIMOUSIN

ATLANTIC
OCEAN

DAUPHINE

Bordeaux

AUVERGNE

N

Bay
of
Biscay

AQUITAINE

GASCONY

Garonne

Rhone

Avignon

ARMAGNAC

Toulouse

LANGUEDOC

PROVENCE

BEARN

TOULOUSE

English conquests

Loyal to the Duke
of Burgundy

0   150 mi

0   150 km

Mediterranean
Sea

Rhine

France on the eve of the victories of Joan of Arc, 1429.

PROLOGUE

In the same year [1347] in the month of September, a great mortality and pestilence began . . . namely that near Greater India in Eastern parts, in a certain province, terrible events and unheard of tempests overwhelmed that whole province for three days. On the first day it rained frogs, serpents, lizards, scorpions and many venomous beasts of that sort. On the second day thunder was heard, and lightning flashes mixed with hailstones of marvelous size fell upon the land, which killed almost all men, from the greatest to the least. On the third day there fell fire together with stinking smoke from the heavens, which consumed all the rest of men and beasts, and burned up all the cities and castles of those parts.

—*Chroniques de Flandre,* 1348

Thus Louis Heyligen, a musician in the service of Cardinal Giovanni Colonna at the papal court of Avignon, describes the cataclysmic arrival of plague in a letter appearing in an anonymous Flemish chronicle. By 1348 this disease, which was to become known as the Black Death (a term used by later historians to refer to this particular outbreak), found its way to Western shores. Within the next two years it engulfed nearly the whole of Europe, striking down nearly half its population, and returning again and again throughout the rest of the century and into the next. Among the victims was Heyligen himself, who died in July 1348.

Even before the plague, however, bad weather and bad harvests brought devastating hunger to northern Europe during a Great Famine that lasted from 1315 until 1322. Shortly thereafter followed the start of a destructive conflict between England and France, the so-called Hundred Years War, that would rage intermittently from 1337 to 1453. And above all, there loomed the image of Death, ever present and unconquerable, a constant figure in much of the art and literature of the later Middle Ages.

Is it any wonder, then, that late medieval men and women believed that the Apocalypse, the end of the world, would soon come to pass? Heyligen may be forgiven if he describes the origins of the Black Death in language borrowed from the Revelation of St. John. Compare his words, for example, with Apocalypse 8:7, when, after the seventh seal has been opened:

> the first angel sounded the trumpet, and there followed hail and fire mingled with blood, and it was cast upon the earth; and the third part of the earth was burnt up, and the third part of the trees was burnt up, and all green grass was burnt up.

Such apocalyptic language surely came to mind when observers were tasked with describing so great a disaster as the plague. Gabriele de Mussis, an Italian chronicler from Piacenza, announced the advent of the pestilence by evoking St. John's vision of seven angels pouring out seven vials of God's "poison" upon the earth. Like Heyligen, Mussis also told of a "thick rain" of serpents and toads in the East, namely in Cathay (China), while in India there were earthquakes and a rain of blood and stones from the sky. An anonymous account from the monastery of Neuberg in Austria echoed these Eastern portents with a tale of a "deadly rain" of serpents and "pestilential worms" in the land where "ginger comes from." Jean de Venette, a Carmelite friar in Paris, wrote that in August 1348 a "bright star" appeared in the west just as the sun was about to set and sent out rays of light over the city. In Messina, Sicily, according to Michele da Piazza, a black dog "carrying a naked sword in its paw" bounded into the midst of a group of citizens just as they were about to form a procession to ward off the Death.

But perhaps the strangest sign of all to herald the plague was that recounted by a monk at Meaux Abbey in Yorkshire. "A short time before the pestilence began," he writes, a "human monster" was born in Kingston-on-Hull who was "divided from the navel upwards and both masculine and feminine, and joined in the lower part. When one part ate, drank, slept or spoke, the other could do something else if it wished." The monster (probably a conjoined twin) lived only to eighteen, as one half "died before the other, and the survivor held it in its arms for three days."

Europeans spoke in equally apocalyptic terms about what would come after the plague as what came before. John de Rupescissa, a Franciscan visionary who contracted the disease in 1348, saw the great mortality as prefiguring the coming of the Antichrist. In 1349, rumors circulated in Rome that the Antichrist was at the moment "a most beautiful child," age ten, who was "so well educated in all branches of knowledge that no one now living can equal him." In the medieval view of millennial history, Antichrist was the leader of all that was unchristian, who would reign for a brief time before the final victory of God's forces and the Last Judgment at the end of the world. Typically associated with the seven-headed beast of the Apocalypse, the Antichrist was a terrifying figure but, ironically, a source of comfort as well to medieval Christians because his appearance meant that their tribulations were about to end. According to the famous twelfth-century visionary Joachim of Fiore, Antichrist would usher in a new age, the Age of the Holy Spirit, during which peace would reign after his defeat. Both the friar Jean de Venette in Paris and John of Reading, a monk at Westminster Abbey in London, saw signs of this new age in the fact that children born after the plague had fewer teeth than their elders.

Perhaps the most detailed explanation of what would follow plague during the time of the Antichrist flowed from the quill of John Clynn, a Franciscan friar from Kilkenny, Ireland. Repeating a prophecy that had been circulating in various forms since the mid-thirteenth century, Clynn predicted that for fifteen years after the plague there would be one world faith (presumably Christian), a time of peace and prosperity, and the rise of a race of men without heads. Alas, Clynn did not survive the pestilence to see if his premonitions would come to pass.

Visions of the Apocalypse thus proliferated during the later Middle Ages. The plague was perhaps the most dramatic, but by no means the only, crisis that convinced men that the end was nigh. During the Great Famine of 1315–22, men from the north of Europe saw heavenly signs, such as comets, showers of scarlet light resembling blood, and a lunar eclipse, all of which betokened disaster. John of Bassigny, a self-proclaimed "prophet" from France, foretold that his country's defeats to the English at the battles of Crécy and Poitiers during the Hundred Years War were but a prelude to a reign of peace before the arrival of the Antichrist.

England too was rife with apocalyptic visions. During the 1380s especially, many Englishmen were so dismayed by a series of disasters—including recurring pestilence, declining fortunes in war, a Peasants' Revolt in 1381, and an earthquake in 1382—that they predicted the year of reckoning to be not far off. An anonymous poet was inspired to trumpet these signs to his audience as "A Warning to Be Ware":

> The Rysing of the comuynes in Londe,
> The pestilens and the eorthe-quake,
> Theose threo thinges, I understonde,
> Beo-tokenes the grete vengaunce and wrake

That schulde falle for synnes sake,
As this Clerkes conne de-clare.
Nou may we chese to leve or take,
For warnyng have we to ben ware.

The Rising of the Commons in London,
The pestilence and the earthquake
These three things, I understand,
Betoken the great vengeance and retribution
That should fall on us for our sins,
As this clerk is able to make clear.
Now may we choose to ignore or heed,
This warning we have to beware.

Around 1388 the preacher Thomas Wimbledon delivered a ser-mon at St. Paul's Cross, London, in which he proclaimed that the end of the world would come in the year 1400. The sermon, whose printed version subsequently received wide distribution, argued that the Antichrist, the enemy of all good Christians, would arrive in twelve years' time, for did not Jesus in the Book of Matthew tell his disciples to look for signs of the Apocalypse in wars, pestilence, and "erthe schakynges"? One Englishman in particular, the prolific theologian John Wycliffe, was so obsessed with the Antichrist that he devoted a great many of his sermons to it, and especially in his later writings, the figure of God's enemy seems everywhere. For Wycliffe, the Antichrist already walked the earth in the shape of the pope and his Church, a pro-foundly heretical notion that Wycliffe justified by pointing to the worldly behavior of the papacy, which, he argued, was in every way contrary to Christ's original teaching.

Wycliffe's apocalyptic ideas found a more subdued echo in the prose and poetry of John Gower and William Langland, likewise dating to the last decades of the fourteenth century. In his prose work *Vox Clamantis* (Voice of One Crying), Gower detects signs of the Antichrist in the Roman curia, where gold is more wel-come than true Christian feeling, while in the poem *Piers Plowman*, Langland dreams that the doleful state of society, including the Church, will be replaced by a better one after a final reckoning. In the last chapter of the poem, Antichrist appears to reign over the earth and does battle with Conscience, who calls upon "Kynde," or nature, to kill "fol many" of the unbelievers with all kinds of "pokkes and pestilences." Visions of the Apocalypse, therefore, were common to late medieval English writers, who related their visions to the crises they and their fellow men faced.

Nevertheless, it is not just our fascination with millennial, or apocalyptic, movements that draws us to the later Middle Ages. Such movements have a continuous history in the annals of Christianity, dating to the original Apocalypse of St. John, probably written toward the end of the first century A.D. but owing much to even older Jewish traditions. What made the late medieval era unusual was a confluence of crises that threatened to make these visions of the Apocalypse become real. At no other time in history did so much variegated misery—famine, war, plague, and death—descend all at once as upon England and Europe during the fourteenth and fifteenth centuries. But, as we all know, the world did not end in 1400, or even a hundred years later. Men and women survived, and not only did they endure, but they laid the foundations for that cultural revival we have christened the Renaissance.

The pages that follow reveal how a Western society was confronted with a series of epic disasters, yet somehow managed to cope in a world that seemed to be collapsing around them. Although I focus here on apocalyptic events rather than apocalyptic thoughts, I will borrow a theme from the visions of millenarians through the ages. That theme is twofold: In a time of darkness, suffering, and death, comes the promise of redemption, renewal, and resurrection. The end of the world may be at hand, for reasons only God in his inscrutable design knows, but then a new and better world will take its place. The men and women of the later Middle Ages, in their approach to their accumulating crises, undoubtedly acted within the framework of such beliefs. If we can understand how they acted out this paradox of despair and hope, perhaps we can understand how they found the courage to face the Four Horsemen of the Apocalypse and, in so doing, made the transition from the medieval to the modern.

For these reasons, I believe that the later Middle Ages comprise one of the most significant and inspiring epochs of English, as well as European, history. The story of how late medieval Englishmen survived and eventually overcame the crises of the Apocalypse is worth the telling simply for the drama in it. Yet it is also a story that is changing the way we look at the late medieval and early modern periods. Recently, scholars have been steadily rejecting the dark view of the later Middle Ages as representing a decline, or "waning," of intellect and culture. In its place, a more subtle and far more interesting picture has taken hold, one that sees a transition rather than a decline from the medieval to the modern eras.

There is much that this age can teach us. As we enter a new millennium, apocalyptic studies again have become fashionable. The century just closed has seen its share of famines, wars, and plagues. Nonetheless, some of us like to think that we can conquer death, and our age seems obsessed with cheating the Fourth Rider on his pale horse. While we in the modern West seek the holy grail of longer and healthier lives and literally run from death, our ancestors embraced it, confident that it was the gateway to higher things. This, then, is the story of men and women who faced a daunting and fearful series of crises but faced them squarely, carrying on with their lives and proving remarkably resilient in the process. It is the story of a people who gazed into the abyss of the Apocalypse and then pulled back from the brink.

FAMINE

When God saw that the world was so over proud,
He sent a dearth on earth, and made it full hard.
A bushel of wheat was at four shillings or more,
Of which men might have had a quarter before. . . .
And then they turned pale who had laughed so loud,
And they became all docile who before were so proud.
A man's heart might bleed for to hear the cry
Of poor men who called out, "Alas! For hunger I die . . . !"

—*Poem on the Evil Times of Edward II*, c. 1327

$\mathfrak{F}$amine, our first apocalyptic horseman, connives to wreak its misery repeatedly upon mankind while its victims stand by, seemingly powerless to act. Usually the disaster is attributed to the weather: Cold, wet downpours or dry, hot droughts destroy crops and kill off livestock. Thomas Malthus also is to blame. In 1798 that great English economist condemned man to perpetual bouts of starvation with his theory that population inevitably outgrows food supply at regular intervals throughout human history.

Yet our modern experience with famine has taught us that hunger is not always preordained. Man himself can make famines. No matter how much aid comes to Africa from the West, civil war there ensures that people will starve and die. An earlier part of this century saw what the historian Robert Conquest called "the only case in history of a purely man-made famine," as up to ten million Russian peasants starved during Stalin's collectivization of state farms. During the potato famine of 1845–49, Ireland lost over two million persons—representing a quarter of the population—through a combination of starvation, disease, and emigration. The English government, 150 years later, has apologized for this catastrophe because English policy under the Union was held by many to be responsible. In this respect, Malthus really may have been to blame, for his fatalistic approach to disasters convinced nineteenth-century civil servants such as Sir Charles Trevelyan, assistant secretary to the English treasury, that nothing could or should be done to relieve the "Great Hunger."

The people of the Middle Ages, on the other hand, are believed to have been more at the mercy of nature than modern man. Nevertheless, for them too, human agency played a part in natural disaster, and the horseman of War sometimes rode side by side with the horseman of Famine during the late medieval period. In particular, the Great Famine between 1315 and 1322 coincided with some of the worst years of an ongoing war between England and Scotland, a war that spilled over into Ireland, threatened Wales, and was to provide a model for the coming Hundred Years War with France. Moreover, the dearth resulted not just from the policies of the enemy: Native armies, through their purveyance, or requisitioning, of foodstuffs and services also sorely oppressed the peasantry. Thus, as we will see, even medieval man was able to create famine.

HOW MANY HUNGRY DEATHS?

The Great Famine was the most severe subsistence crisis to hit northern Europe in the later Middle Ages. During its worst years, between 1315 and 1317, mortality significantly increased among the populations of the British Isles, northern France, the Low Countries, Scandinavia, Germany, Poland, and the Baltic States. Stories of cannibalism became rife, the price of grain soared, and some people were reduced to eating moldy or uncooked food that only added to their misery. The suffering and hardships caused by the famine were to haunt the Western consciousness for generations to come.

Chronicles of the period, and other literary sources, provide anecdotal evidence of the widespread suffering. Famine came early to Scotland, "in the year 1310," according to John of Fordun's *Chronicle of the Scottish Nation*. So great was the Scots' hunger that they fed "on the flesh of horses and other unclean cattle." Seven years later the Irish went further, according to their annalists. In 1317, at the height of the Great Famine, the Irish apparently "were so destroyed by hunger that they extracted bodies of the dead from cemeteries and dug out the flesh from their skulls and ate it; and women ate their children out of hunger." Whatever the truth of these accounts, more sober testimony is perhaps more convincing. In Dublin, food became so expensive in 1317 that "many heads of families, and those who sustained many men, became beggars, and many perished from famine." The annals of the regions of Loch Cé and of Connacht record high numbers of deaths, partly due to famine, in 1315.

In England as well, it was reported in 1316 that "poor people stole children and ate them" and ate as well horses, dogs, and cats. In addition, John de Trokelowe, a chronicler from St. Albans Abbey, who provides one of the most detailed descriptions of the famine, claimed that in the same year "men and women furtively ate their children and even strangers in many places . . . also incarcerated thieves recently coming among each other devoured themselves at the moment when they were half alive." Scholars may discount such stories of cannibalism as exaggerated, but they testify to people's desperate attempts to fend off starvation.

Several English authors relate that so many men died that "the living are not sufficient to bury the dead" or that "it was useless for men to bury them," stock phrases that were to reappear during the Black Death. At least two accounts boast that so great a dearth and mortality of men occurred in one year, 1316, as had not been seen for the previous century. John de Trokelowe testifies that people died of food-related disorders, which suggests starvation. According to Trokelowe:

> A dysentery-type illness, contracted on account of spoiled
> food, emasculated nearly everyone, from which followed
> acute fever or a throat ailment. And so men, poisoned
> from spoiled food, succumbed, as did beasts and cattle,
> [who] fell down dead from a poisonous rottenness of the
> grass. Nor does anyone remember so much dearth and
> famine to have prevailed in the past, nor so much mortality
> to have attended it.

The deaths Trokelowe describes may have been due to ergotism, caused by eating moldy grain, and known in the Middle Ages as St. Anthony's Fire. The ergot fungus, once ingested, attacks the muscular system and induces painful spasms. Eventually the contracting muscles cut off circulation of blood to the extremities, which become gangrenous and fall off, and death quickly ensues. If it was any consolation to the victims, the disease also induced mind-bending hallucinations similar to those from LSD, an ergot derivative.

As in Ireland, the famine in England is alleged to have cut across social lines. Echoing the Dublin chronicler, Henry Knighton, canon of Leicester, says that during the famine, "many who had been wealthy men in the kingdom and had an abundance of riches and many goods became beggars on account of a great and irrecoverable scarcity." Trokelowe, as always, is more descriptive:

> There is no doubt but that poor men wasted away from famine and starvation, if the rich continually pined after their splendid repasts. Therefore while this famine prevailed, great lords as well as religious [houses] cut back their courts, withdrew their accustomed alms, and reduced their households. Whence those thus removed from the courts, accustomed to lead a delicate life, did not know how to work by the sweat of their brow [and] were too ashamed to beg, but nevertheless, overcome by want for food and drink, they thirsted for the goods of others, intent on murder and rapine.

Under such conditions, people thought twice about going into the cities, where the streets were clogged with poor beggars and the bodies of the dead.

How did the famine's victims meet their ends? Only in rare cases was there absolutely nothing to eat, but even when starving souls fill their bellies, bad food can cause diarrhea and other intestinal disorders, and historians quite rightly categorize resulting deaths as also caused by famine. Vitamin deficiencies can trigger a host of other potentially fatal complaints. The potato famine in Ireland witnessed scurvy, a disease attacking the gums (caused by a lack of vitamin C); xerophthalmia, resulting in blindness (lack of vitamin A); and pellagra, a disease causing dementia (lack of niacin). These maladies struck even when people found something to eat; they just did not get the right things to eat. In cases of starvation, famine victims drastically lose height and weight, appear shrunken and old, acquire blackish, papery skin and unnatural hair growth, and psychologically become lethargic, depressed, and, understandably, obsessed with food. Eventually the bodily organs simply cease to function.

Nonetheless, most historians attribute deaths during famine years to disease rather than to hunger. Of the one million deaths from the potato famine, for example, only 10 percent, or 100,000, are thought to have been caused directly by starvation, the rest resulting mostly from typhus fever. The problem is that nutritionists and other medical experts these days have destroyed the link once thought to have existed between hunger and disease. Historically speaking, there are two main reasons why this link cannot be sustained. In the first place, populations that were better fed, such as the secular and ecclesiastical upper classes, should have escaped more lightly from epidemics if these are dependent on nutrition. Such, however, was not the case for Englishmen and Europeans during the later Middle Ages. At Christ Church Priory in Canterbury, the monks of the fifteenth century enjoyed what have been called "gargantuan quantities of nutritious food and drink" that included white bread, a variety of fish, beef, pork, poultry, milk, cheese, eggs, fruit, spices, and other delicacies. Indeed, if the Christ Church monks suffered in their diet, it was a result of overeating rather than undernourishment. Yet these monks experienced during the course of the fifteenth century at least twenty-seven major outbreaks of disease that included plague; tuberculosis; the sweat, or flu; dropsy, a neurological disease; and strangury, an affliction of the urinary tract. On average, the monks of Christ Church could expect to live fewer than twenty-three years from birth, one of the lowest life expectancies ever recorded. An analysis of the life spans of another group that lived well, the secular peerage in England between 1350 and 1500, yields life expectancies that are little better than those for the Canterbury monks. At age twenty, for example, a secular peer could expect to live on average another ten years, as opposed to eight for a denizen of Christ Church. In fact, the British upper crust were not to substantially improve their life expectancy relative to the general population until the mid-eighteenth century.

A second, and related, objection to the interdependence between dearth and disease is that epidemics, particularly plague, have proven their virulence even in times of plenty. Grain yields in England were slightly above average in 1348 on the eve of the Black Death, and prices remained low during the plague, despite a sharp drop in productivity, indicating that the population did not suffer from want as it was being roughly halved by the disease. Any attempt to establish that children growing up during the famine would have been more vulnerable to the plague thirty years later is likewise inconclusive. Those in their infancy during the famine, and thus in their late twenties and early thirties during the Black Death, seem to have been no more susceptible, indeed usually less so, than other age groups. Nor did the rising living standards supposedly enjoyed by the peasantry in the aftermath of the first plague keep them from dying in subsequent epidemics. As a matter of fact, a little hunger is thought to help ward off disease, since invading microorganisms need nutrients to survive and reproduce just as much as host cells do.

If famine and plague acted independently of each other, the effects of hunger nevertheless took their own devastating toll, though it is hard to get a handle on just how many deaths occurred during the years of the Great Famine. The most reliable and abundant records come from England. While the previous four decades record no net change in population, the famine years were to see marked declines in community numbers. One study of tithing lists in Essex, which record the names of all males over the age of twelve for the purpose of their appearance before the local "leet" courts, points to a mortality rate of 15 percent between 1315 and 1317. Similar evidence from Taunton in Somerset suggests that more than 9 percent of residents lost their lives during the famine, while the record of heriots, or death taxes, paid on other manors owned by the bishop of Winchester indicate that his serfs were dying at a rate of 10 percent. Court rolls from the manor of Halesowen in Worcestershire record a 15 percent mortality during the second and third decades of the fourteenth century. Finally, a 25 percent increase in mortality during the first five years of the famine is recorded in inquisitions post mortem, which enrolled the deaths of major landowners upon the succession of their heirs.

One type of evidence that might yield greater clues with regard to the Great Famine is the English episcopal registers. It might be argued that these documents, which record every time a parish church lost a priest, are unlikely to include famine deaths, since most clergymen undoubtedly were better fed than their parishioners. Nevertheless, the registers hold some surprises. In the diocese of Hereford, deaths of clergy more than doubled in 1316 compared to the previous year, while twelve vacancies occurred in the space of one month in December 1320, which was as much as or more than was posted in a whole year in 1319 and 1323–26. At Winchester, the six months between December 1317 and May 1318 recorded twenty-nine deaths, besting most figures posted in an entire year. Exeter, on the other hand, shows no significant mortality patterns; the largest number of deaths during the famine occurred in 1318, but this was no higher, and sometimes considerably lower, than in years preceding the famine (see table 1, page 264).

On the Continent, the most exact figures regarding famine mortality come from Flanders, where the towns of Bruges and Ypres kept a week-by-week account of the number of cadavers they were paying to have cleared from the streets. Between the beginning of May and the end of October of the year 1316, Bruges and Ypres lost 5 and 10 percent, respectively, of their total populations. A mortality rate of 10 percent also is argued for Tournai based on testamentary evidence. These percentages are extrapolated to the whole of the Low Countries and northern Germany, which had similar patterns of urban development.

Even with these percentages, it is impossible to know how many of those who died between 1315 and 1322 were starving. One thing we can be rather certain of, however, is the diet that English peasants subsisted on in normal years. This information is derived from maintenance agreements that elderly tenants entered into with their nonhereditary heirs in order to secure their livelihood in their "retirement years." The overwhelmingly favorite food of the average peasant was bread, made from wheat or more usually a mixture of grains that included (or substituted) barley, oats, rye, peas, or beans. Porridge was also made, typically with oats, barley, or pulses. This was washed down with well water or ale if available. Better-off peasants supplemented their meals with milk, cheese, fruits and vegetables, and meat, such as mutton, beef, and, most often, pork. But during the first half of the fourteenth century at least, most people, both in England and on the Continent, lived on a grain-based diet.

Famine ("Fames") points to her hungry mouth as she looks up to a figure of Death astride a winged beast of the Apocalypse. An illumination made at Erfurt, Germany, during the fourteenth century. (Courtesy Stiftung Weimarer Klassik, Herzogin Anna Amalia Bibliothek.)

Significant evidence of dearth, therefore, is any sign of a short-age of bread grains. This was most likely to occur in the spring, after winter reserves had been used up and before a new crop could be planted. It is certainly no accident that the religious observance of Lent is associated with fasting. The unusually high number of deaths that occurred among the Winchester clergy in the year 1318 came predominately in the spring. Likewise, inquisitions post mortem for the year 1316 record the greatest proportion of their deaths—22 percent—in the month of April.

Manorial records for estates in the normally prosperous southern region of England do indicate a dramatic drop-off in grain production, particularly of wheat, the staple of the peasant diet. The wheat harvest, expressed in yield per seed, on the manors of the bishop of Winchester and of the abbey of Westminster was just over 40 percent below normal in 1316, the lowest on record between 1271 and 1410. Hardly better were harvests for 1315 and 1321, at more than a third below normal. Barley and oats also fared poorly in 1316, yielding harvests that were also about a third below normal. The low production of grain was reflected in the price it fetched on the market. During the second decade of the century, the Winchester and Westminster estates sold wheat for an average of 8 shillings a quarter (equivalent to eight bushels), while other grains including barley, oats, rye, and peas fetched an average of 5 shillings per quarter. These prices were about 44 percent above those for the previous decade. At the very start of the famine in 1315, wheat fetched its highest price ever recorded, at 16 shillings a quarter, while barley and rye cost nearly as much, at 11 and 13 shillings respectively. Moreover, a "shopping basket" of consumables, including barley, peas, beef, mutton, bacon, cheese, wool, and salt, rose by over 100 percent in 1315 and remained nearly as high the following year. No figures comparable to England's are available for the Continent during the famine, but the behavior of grain prices in both England and Germany from the late fourteenth to the early sixteenth centuries suggests that there would have been a close correlation between the two.

The English chronicles provide some insight here as well. The price of wheat quoted by the English chroniclers range from about 20 shillings to 40 shillings a quarter during the famine years 1315 and 1316, with 30 shillings seeming to be the average price. This was twice the price posted by the estates of Winchester and Westminster during these years. The discrepancy may be accounted for by price fluctuations depending on the place and even the time grain was sold. Henry Knighton says that wheat sold for as much as 43 shillings a quarter on a Saturday in the marketplace in Leicester, but only 14 shillings on Wednesdays. Probably the chroniclers' prices are the highest for grain sold anywhere and at any time. The duration of the crisis also could vary: Despite evidence of a dramatic fall in prices on the Winchester and Westminster estates between 1317 and 1319, a chronicler from Bridlington Priory in Yorkshire claims that "a sterility of the land and a rarity or deficiency of all grain" kept prices high throughout.

That meat was just as dear as grain during the famine is likewise attested by contemporaries. In January 1315 Parliament, evidently in an attempt to keep the price of food low during scarcity, passed an ordinance fixing the price of, among other animals, a hay-fed ox at 16 shillings, a cow at 12 shillings, and a pig at a little over 3 shillings. (Grain prices were not regulated because the first bad harvest did not emerge until the summer of that year.) These prices are almost exactly in line with those recorded on the Winchester estates during the same decade. Yet Winchester's prices were about 16 percent higher, on average, than those at the beginning of the century, and butchers' prices on the open market must have been higher than this, for a year later, in January 1316, Parliament repealed the ordinance. Indeed, meat sellers seem to have preferred to close shop or simply defy the ordinance rather than submit to its low prices. According to the *Anonimalle Chronicle*, "many of the butchers and poulterers of London were imprisoned and impoverished and the common people experienced a great shortage of such commodities and complained a great deal." The chroniclers are universally agreed that this legislation did more harm than good, for in the words of one, "it is better to buy dear than to find in case of need that there is nothing to be had." Price-fixing was "against reason," explained the Bridlington chronicler, because "the price of everything will be in accordance with the fruitfulness of the harvest, not the will of men." Nevertheless, in 1317 Parliament was to try again, regulating the price of a product perhaps dearer to the heart of its citizens: beer.

Animal murrains, outbreaks of disease that fatally affected sheep and cattle, undoubtedly account for the high price of meat during the famine. This is reflected in the manorial accounts of several large estates. For sheep, the worst years seem to have been 1313 to 1317, when flocks were reduced by anywhere from 20 to 70 percent. Wool exports also suffered, declining from the country overall by about 30 percent, but in some ports, such as Newcastle-on-Tyne, Hartlepool, and Ipswich, by over 60 percent. For cattle, the years of disaster were 1319–21, when losses were similar to those for sheep. It was during these years, according to Trokelowe, that people saw a wondrous sight, namely that the dogs and ravens who fed on such carrion swelled up there and then and died. As a consequence, no one dared to eat fresh meat, let alone flesh from a rotting animal, lest they too be poisoned. However, the Bridlington chronicler claims that people did indeed eat the bodies of dead animals, but only up until lunchtime (midday), after which the meat began to stink and had to be buried.

The *Poem on the Evil Times of Edward II* once again bears witness to the high price wheat fetched during the famine, and, like the chronicles, emphasizes that the miseries of the famine extended over a long period. Just as the first hardships were over, there came a murrain of cattle and a second shortage of grain:

And tho that qualm was astin[t] of beste that bar horn,
Tho sente God on eorthe another derthe of corn,
That spradde over al Engelond bothe north and south,
And made seli pore men afingred in here mouth

And though that mortality was stopped of beasts that
  bear horns,
Then God sent on earth another dearth of corn,
That spread over all England both north and south,
And made simple poor men hungry in their mouth

Nor were famine's effects limited to the first part of the fourteenth century. Starvation struck, according to the English poet William Langland, whenever the peasantry shirked their assigned task of cultivating the soil. Writing at the time of the second greatest famine of the century, in 1370, Langland, in his great poem *Piers Plowman*, punishes "Waster," an allegorical symbol of those who refuse to work, with the effects of famine, appearing, appropriately enough, in the guise of "Hunger":

Then Hunger caught Waster in haste by the maw,
And wrung so his belly, that both his eyes watered;
That Breton he buffeted on both cheeks about,
That he looked like a lantern his lifetime thereafter!
He beat so their bodies, he burst half their ribs.
Had not Piers, with a pease-loaf, prayed Hunger to cease,
They soon had been buried, believe thou naught else!

Piers and the other peasants subsequently appease Hunger with a diet of bread made with peas and beans, "grene cheses," curds, oat cakes, onions, cabbages, and maybe some beef if they are lucky, forgoing their former delicacies of bacon, poultry, eggs, and white bread. Langland's poem testifies to the growing plenty peasants enjoyed by the later Middle Ages but also to the fact that the fearful specter of famine had not disappeared, particularly if the peasants took their plenty for granted. Indeed, Englishmen were to be "buffeted" by hunger yet again during the 1430s, culminating in a general famine throughout northern Europe in 1437–38. Nevertheless, Langland's pious solution, that the peasants merely had to work harder to avoid hunger, would not have succeeded during the Great Famine when the vagaries of war and weather could not be laid at the door of the third estate.

On the Continent, some chroniclers of the Great Famine sound much like their counterparts in England and Ireland. In Poland and the Baltic States, for example, it was reported that parents out of hunger "devoured" their own children and vice versa, that many ate the flesh of cadavers suspended from gibbets, and that the starving crawled into tombs simply to wait to die. Gilles li Muisis, abbot of St. Giles in Tournai, claimed that "so many poor beggars were dying one after the other" that the city paid men to carry their bodies into the surrounding countryside and bury them there; this is the more believable when one remembers that other Flemish towns such as Bruges and Ypres actually recorded the number of dead so disposed. Another Flemish chronicler recalled how "the common and poor people were oppressed by so great a famine that the hungry, wandering through villages, expired [after] falling supine on the ground." In nearby Holland, John de Beka noted with evident distaste that paupers "gnawed on the raw carcasses of cattle like dogs, and ate the uncooked grass of meadows like cows; also this famine and pestilence was so bitter, that beggars without number camped out in fields, woods, or scrub, and their bodies were consigned to burial in these country places without the usual last rites." A fellow Dutchman testified to the economies that had to be made even by the relatively well-off, when in the famine year 1316 "all

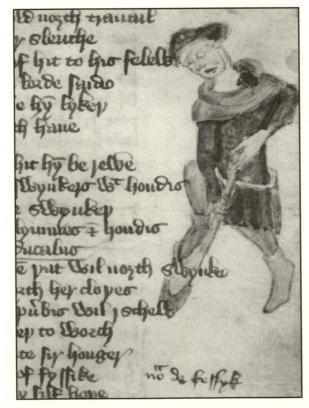

A marginal illustration of a peasant digging against hunger, from a fifteenth-century manuscript of William Langland's Piers Plowman. *(Courtesy Bodleian Library, Oxford.)*

piety and all charity is neglected, very few alms are distributed." This policy affected not only poor strangers, but even family members: "Parents do not wish to assist their children, nor children their parents, in their great need, even though they have an abundance of the necessities for life." Finally, high grain prices were universally reported for northern Europe in 1315 and 1316. As a consequence, according to Gilles li Muisis, "people began to eat little bread in many places because they had none. And as many as were able mixed beans, barley, vetches, and other grains in whatever quantity they could get, making and eating bread from this." The bakers of Paris, according to the chronicler Jean de Saint-Victor, tried to profit from this situation by extending their bread with "many disgusting ingredients—the dregs of wine, pig droppings, and several other things," a testament both to human greed and human desperation.

Historians of the Great Famine generally conclude that it had little lasting impact on pre-plague population. Nevertheless, the chronicles, both English and European, agree on several points. First, the price of grain was high and remained so for several years in succession. This fell especially hard on the peasantry, whose diet revolved around wheat and other cereals. Second, the poor in particular, but others as well, were reduced to begging and more desperate measures to keep from starving. Inevitably, some of them died. And third, even the very rich were forced to sacrifice and cut back their food consumption.

So many of the chroniclers mention famine and disease in the same breath that it is to be wondered whether they made any distinction between the two. But in the end, it does not really matter exactly how many people died solely by starvation during the Great Famine. Their sufferings, it is clear, were real enough.

FAMINE AND THE "AGRARIAN CRISIS"

Historians like to find great causes for great events. The Great Famine is no exception, and its roots are sought deep in the economic trends of the previous century. Like all subsistence crises, the Great Famine traditionally has been thought to have been the result of a race between population and its food supply. As first articulated by Thomas Malthus in his famous essay *On the Principle of Population*, published in 1798, the race goes like this:

> Population, when unchecked, increases in a geometrical ratio. Subsistence increases only in an arithmetical ratio. A slight acquaintance with numbers will show the immensity of the first power in comparison of the second.
>
> By that law of our nature which makes food necessary to the life of man, the effects of these two unequal powers must be kept equal.
>
> This implies a strong and constantly operating check on population from the difficulty of subsistence. This difficulty must fall somewhere; and must necessarily be severely felt by a large portion of mankind.

Famines do—indeed they *must*—occur because populations, short of placing artificial restraints on their reproduction, periodically outgrow their capacity to feed themselves.

As reconstituted and applied to the Middle Ages, Malthus's theory transmuted into the Postan thesis, named after the Cambridge historian M. M. Postan, who began publishing his ideas in the decades after the Second World War. In Postan's thesis, the population of medieval Europe had a limited capacity to expand—one that obviously was much lower than was possible after the agricultural revolution of Malthus's day. In fact, the more medieval farmers tried to increase their agricultural output, according to Postan, the more certain they were to be less productive. This is because their efforts to increase cultivation actually exhausted the productivity of the soil. They grew crops, for example, at the expense of grazing their livestock, resulting in less and less of the land being fertilized, or manured, by animals. Another attempt to increase production, by cultivating marginal or waste land beyond the traditional demesne, known as assarting, was destined for failure because the soil was of poor quality and was quickly exhausted. The grim turning point came around

1300; up until then the land had continued to support population growth, although far less robustly as the thirteenth century
came to a close. After that, Malthusian checks, such as famine,
were ready to take effect.

In recent years there has been much reevaluation of Postan's
thesis. Medieval agriculture, we now are learning, was not nearly
as static as once was thought. Traditionally, agricultural progress
in the Middle Ages has been associated with the development of
open or common field systems, in which individual peasant holdings were consolidated into large, efficient units and subdivided
into two and eventually three large fields that allowed for the
rotation of crops with fallow. These developments, once thought
to have come rather late to England as opposed to the Continent,
are now believed to have predated the Norman Conquest of
1066 in at least some parts of the country. However, it is not clear
that even without fully developed open fields, England was any
less agriculturally advanced. Small, independent holdings may
have given more scope for individual innovation and initiative;
two fields may have been just as efficient as three and allowed for
just as many crop rotations; the heavier, more effective moldboard plow may have developed independently of the field systems; and considerable local variation with regard to agricultural
techniques seems to have existed in late medieval England, with
the southern and eastern parts of the country usually more pro-
gressive than the northern and western regions.

One innovation that we can more confidently trace in England
concerns the type of animal pulling the plow. Up through the
thirteenth century, oxen predominated as the plow beast. This
was because oxen, although slow, were strong and could be eaten
once they got too old to work. By the fourteenth century, perhaps as a result of widespread murrains among oxen during the
Great Famine, horses began to be mixed into plow teams and
eventually took over altogether. Horses already had been widely
used in the previous century for harrowing, or the drawing of an
iron-toothed implement over the ground in preparation for
planting. The horses that were so used generally were not the
same as those for riding; workhorses tended to be of a smaller

variety, known as stots or affers. Even though horses were expensive to feed, requiring oats as well as hay, and though medieval people were reluctant to convert that investment into meat (except of course during famine), the plow horse had two great advantages over the ox. It was fast, allegedly 50 percent faster than the ox, and it had greater stamina, meaning that fewer animals were required for an effective team, typically six horses in place of eight oxen. The use of horses took hold especially in East Anglia. That region's denizens had introduced them into mixed plow teams even as early as the twelfth century; by the middle of the fourteenth, horses made up half the draft animals in these counties, 100 percent by the following century. No doubt this was partly due to the fact that East Anglia's light, loamy soils and flat terrain were ideally suited to a faster beast. And it should not be imagined that peasants lagged behind their lords in this new technology. If anything, peasants were ahead of the curve on using horses, owning a greater proportion of them on account of their versatility. Workhorses had many other uses beside plowing, including hauling, carting, and, in a pinch, transport. A peasant did not have to buy as many horses to plow: Teams of as few as two were common. Finally, horses had great resale value. A horse trader typically would sell his young stock for a high price and buy older animals for personal use, much like used car dealers today.

But the advances in agricultural technology from the fourteenth century onwards that proved most productive were in fertilization. Late medieval farmers did not simply leave fallow land to go to waste. They nurtured and exploited it in a number of ways. Animal manure was the most commonly available and highly prized fertilizer, so much so that piles of it, called "mukke-hillocks" or "muck hills," were hoarded in the courtyards of manor houses and just outside the doorways of more modest homes. As anyone who has passed by a slurry pit knows, the smell of ripe dung can be overpowering, and the job of spreading it was unpleasant enough, even for peasants who cannot have smelled too sweetly themselves, that on some manors it was considered an extra detail that necessitated rewarding workers with quit time or

The old and new technologies of late medieval farming. Opposite, cumbersome oxen pull a moldboard plow. Above, the faster, more efficient horse pulls a harrow. From the Luttrell Psalter, c. 1340. (Courtesy British Library.)

a special meal. Alternatively, animals could spread the dung naturally by being "folded," or temporarily penned in, on fallow land,
a procedure that was highly valued since lords penalized their
peasants for removing beasts from the fold. Other fertilizers used
included marl, a clay-and-sand combination high in calcium car-
bonate, night soil, lime, ashes, and, in the coastal areas, seaweed.

Another method used to regenerate the soil was to plant
nitrogen-enriching legumes, such as peas, beans, and vetches (a
member of the pea family but whose seed is similar to the bean).
How aware medieval farmers were of legumes' benefits is hard to
tell, since they were also grown as cheap fodder. Nevertheless,
legumes did make possible continuous cultivation of the land
without rotating a fallow field, a practice known in some localities as inhoking. Other techniques included heavy sowing of seed
in order to choke out weeds, and stall-feeding of livestock, allowing a more efficient collection and distribution of manure.

The evidence indicates that for most manors, fertilization, if
practiced, occupied a small percentage of the total estate, but
some regions of the country were more advanced than others.
Norfolk in East Anglia led the way. Already in the thirteenth century it had adopted continuous rotation of crops, cultivation of
legumes, and other techniques that were to anticipate its agricultural revolution several centuries later. Ironically, this may have
been because the county had a high population density, bad in
Malthusian terms but good in the sense that it made for a cheap
labor supply that lords may have used to good advantage on their
land. In addition there may have been some cross fertilization of
farming ideas between East Anglia and the Low Countries, which
were developing similar innovations in agriculture at this time.
Battle Abbey in Sussex and Christ Church Priory in Kent also
seem to have been especially receptive to the new techniques, but
manuring in particular was being practiced, to a greater or lesser
degree, all over the country and in Wales.

Better farming practices should have spelled better yields, and
this is indeed the case in Norfolk. Yields of wheat per acre from
various manors throughout the county averaged around 15
bushels between the late thirteenth and the first half of the four-

teenth centuries. This was anywhere from 20 to nearly 50 percent higher than the most common wheat yields per acre from the manors of the bishop of Winchester in southern England over a longer time period, which included the supposedly more productive earlier part of the thirteenth century. The highest wheat yields per acre at Norfolk, around 30 bushels, also exceeded those at Winchester by more than 16 bushels, or, in other words, they were more than 50 percent higher. Moreover, the wheat yield per seed of a Norfolk manor like Martham, owned by Norwich Cathedral Priory, could outproduce the average at Winchester or in the Low Countries by more than one measure of seed, or by more than 23 percent. Norfolk's agricultural output is all the more impressive in that it was practicing intensive, continuous cultivation at this time, which according to Postan should have quickly led to soil exhaustion.

High wheat yields, comparable to those at Norfolk, were obtained during the first half of the fourteenth century at the manor of Ottery, Devon, owned by Tavistock Abbey; at Adisham, Kent, owned by Christ Church Priory; at Cuxham, Oxfordshire, owned by Merton College, Oxford; at Bonshill, Herefordshire, owned by Aconbury Priory; at Oakington, Cambridgeshire, owned by Crowland Abbey; at Bovecumbe and Penne on the Isle of Wight, owned by the countess of Aumale; and on several manors in Monmouthshire, Wales, owned by the bishop of St. David's. All these estates probably practiced similar farming techniques to those in Norfolk. Even on the estates of the bishop of Winchester, which were used by Postan to demonstrate agricultural decline over the course of the late thirteenth and early fourteenth centuries, there were some improvements. After the first two and a half decades of the fourteenth century, which included the disastrous years of the Great Famine, seven manors out of thirty-eight increased their yields by over 5 percent, eight by over 10 percent, three by over 20 percent, and one by over 30 percent. The most marked improvements in the yields of wheat and barley, the main crops, occurred in Wiltshire and Somerset. Nevertheless, the Winchester estates were among the more conservative in the country in terms of their farming practices.

The Postan thesis can no longer be sustained as a long-term cause of the Great Famine. Even the growth of marginal or uncultivatable land, one of the mainstays of Postan's theory, is no longer assured. Evidence of the spread of marginal relative to arable land perhaps can be found in southern England or the Midlands, but not so in East Anglia. In the Southwest, the North, and in Wales, marginal land always had been part of the economy, being put to productive use as pasture. Moreover, the very concept of marginal land recently has been challenged, for its definition depends on a variety of other factors beside soil productivity, such as distance from the market, the number of laborers available to work it, and so on. But if Malthus is no longer to blame for the Great Famine, who or what is? The answer, as always in farming, seems to be the weather.

WATER, WATER EVERYWHERE

Weather patterns, as everyone knows, are notoriously hard to predict. Nor is it easier for historians to tell us what was happening in the skies of the past, particularly as long ago as the Middle Ages. One method of gauging weather historically is to use crop yields and prices, on the assumption that agricultural production naturally reflects the weather. A poor harvest of spring crops, such as barley or oats, may indicate a drought, whereas a poor harvest of winter grains, such as wheat or rye, points to a flood. Unfortunately, so many other factors aside from the weather affect farming that relating the two quickly becomes a circular argument: Low yields are used as evidence of bad weather, and bad weather is used to explain low yields. At best, the evidence of manorial accounts can only corroborate testimony about the weather from more reliable sources.

Probably the most trustworthy testimony about the medieval climate can be found in the chronicles. It may be objected that these accounts largely concern themselves with political events and that their statements about the weather thus tend to mirror the political fortunes of the rulers: A sunny reign produces literally glorious days, while a stormy rule will induce the author to write about cloudy skies. But if enough chronicles from different localities agree on the same weather patterns, the risk of bias in their accounts is much reduced. One recent study of medieval climate uses hundreds of accounts to establish a weather pattern that spans the years 1000 to 1425 and ranges over France, Germany, and northern Italy (but not England). The general trend that emerges is of western Europe entering a period of severely cold winters and exceptionally rainy summers during the first half of the fourteenth century. This may have been the beginning of a "Little Ice Age" in Europe that was to last until the eighteenth century and was in marked contrast to the thirteenth century, which generally knew mild winters and dry summers. The decades of 1310–30 saw some of the coldest winters and those of 1310–20 and 1340–50 some of the rainiest summers on record.

A more scientific, though still experimental, approach to mapping historical weather patterns involves various kinds of analyses of earth and plant remains. One of the best-known, and more accurate, of such techniques is the measurement of tree rings, called in scientific parlance dendrochronology. The remains of ancient oak trees, which not only live long lives but also grow in close correlation to the amount of rainfall, have been uncovered from the bogs of Ireland and testify to some strange weather in the second and third decades of the fourteenth century. Based on this evidence, rainfalls were 7 to 10 percent wetter than normal between 1315 and 1318 (indicated by wide rings), followed by seasons that were 10 to 22 percent drier during the 1320s (narrow rings). Thus, between 1318 and 1324, the medieval Irish farmer had to cope with a climate that swung by as much as 30 percent from one extreme to the other. Tree rings from Germany confirm that the period from 1312 to 1319 was an extremely wet one and was succeeded by a dry period. Pollen, fossil, and soil chemistry analyses of peat bog from Carlisle in the northwest of England indicate that this area of the country was entering its wettest climate stage in seven hundred years at the start of the fourteenth century and that the earth was not to become any drier until the close of the fifteenth.

For more descriptive evidence of the English climate during the Great Famine, we must turn again to the chronicles. One account claims that there was "a very great deluge of rain for nearly the whole year" in 1315, another that "a copious flood of rain" fell continually from May of that year until the following April, and a third that the rains came in the summer and autumn of 1316. Too much rain, of course, was bad for crops. According to one record, so much rain fell that "in one year there could not be found seven days of good weather"; the result was that in 1316, "little grain grew that year, nearly all of it having perished." Rain killed the crop the previous year as well, when another account reports that because of the wet weather, hardly any wheat could be harvested or stored in barns. Seeds rotted in the ground, and "in many places the hay lay so long under water that it could neither be mown nor gathered." Trokelowe confirms that the summer rains of 1315 were so abundant "that the grain could not ripen." The wetness remained until September 8, during which time grain "could not be harvested for baking bread, unless it was placed first in ovens to dry it out." Nor did the grain have its usual nutritious value, according to Trokelowe, since "it did not have the nourishment from the heat of the summer sun." No sooner did this first crisis pass, according to the *Poem on the Evil Times of Edward II*, than:

> *Tho com ther another sorwe that spradde over al the lond;*
> *A thusent winter ther bifore com nevere non so strong.*
> *To binde alle the mene men in mourning and in care,*
> *The orf deiede al bidene, and maden the lond al bare,*
>   *so faste,*
> *Com nevere wrecche into Engelond that made men*
>   *more agaste.*

> Came there another sorrow that spread over all the land;
> A winter that was stronger than a thousand that came
>   before
> To bind all the many men in mourning and in care,
> The cattle died all forthwith, and made the land all bare,
>   so fast,
> Came never a wretch into England that made men
>   more agast.

Extreme cold was generally reported in England for 1317, while John of Fordun of Scotland corroborates that freezing weather was known late in the famine. He assigns to the year 1321 "a very hard winter, which distressed men, and killed nearly all animals." In addition, the eastern coast of England (along with Holland) was blasted throughout the first half of the fourteenth century by storms and floods that, according to local inquests, washed hundreds of acres of land and scores of houses out to sea.

If the weather was so bad, what could the medieval farmer do? In practical terms, perhaps not very much, but this does not mean he believed he was helpless. Medieval men assumed they could change weather patterns by appealing to the mercy of God, the author of their downpours. After all, had not Theodosius the Great, Roman emperor in the East, defeated his rivals in the West, Eugenius and Arbogast, at the battle of the Frigid River in A.D. 394 by calling down the Bora, a strong north wind, to turn back the javelins of his enemies? In 1416 Henry Chichele, archbishop of Canterbury, used this example to try to inspire his parishioners' "tepid devotion" during one round of processions for the "serenity of the air." By Chichele's time, prayers for fine weather had become fairly commonplace and were lumped together, as in 1416, with heavenward appeals for the king's success in war and unity of the schismatic Church. Yet early in the fourteenth century, such withdrawals from the Treasury of Merits for the sake of a better climate were rare enough that they may have been saved up for a special disaster like the Great Famine.

As early as 1296, Oliver Sutton, bishop of Lincoln, exhorted his parishioners to pray that God reverse their low crop yields, a murrain of cattle, an invasion of the Scots, and finally, "a scourge of rain falling steadily from above for so long a time, still inundating us more and more." The era of the Great Famine was to see further mandates for processions for fine weather. On July 8, 1316, Walter Giffard, archbishop of Canterbury, ordered processions throughout the province every Wednesday and Friday of the week in order to pray for, among other things, "a suitable serenity of the air." The usual indulgence of forty days' remission of penance was offered to encourage people to take part. Giffard opened his letter with the standard explanation that miseries such as pestilence and famines were sent down by a God "provoked to anger on account of [man's] wickedness and sin." Such self-castigation was indulged in the same year by King Edward II in a letter to Richard de Kellawe, bishop of Durham, and by a chronicler from Malmesbury Abbey, Wiltshire. The latter, however, added astrological explanations centering on the planets Saturn and Jupiter, which were to anticipate explanations of the plague.

The result of so much bad behavior, according to Archbishop Giffard, was an intemperate climate producing a famine so miserable that the people, formerly used to abundance, "are compelled to wretchedly beg, being in want of sustenance and lacking food, and no small part of the populace is crucified by the affliction of famine to the point that, O woe! they have died." Nevertheless, despite their unworthiness, the faithful could expect that the Lord, moved by their tearful prayers, and "who is known to be the consoler of the melancholy . . . may mercifully bestow upon his afflicted people a welcome remedy causing the famine and other miseries that have lasted so long to utterly cease." The Malmesbury chronicler asserts that "I firmly believe that unless the English Church had interceded for us, we should have perished long ago." Living in a more secular time, it may be hard for us to believe that many would have derived comfort from this promise of help from on high. But that such processions were actually carried out is attested by a London chronicler, who in an entry for the year 1315 wrote that the city's churchmen, in order to avert the famine, processed in bare feet every Friday and carried on display the host and other relics.

Contemporaries clearly believed that the weather was the main cause of the dearth, as their willingness to perform these rites testifies. But there is something unsatisfactory about the weather as the sole explanation of the Great Famine. If people were to truly starve, then even the seed corn lying safe from the elements in their granaries would have had to have been destroyed. That something else beside the weather did indeed threaten their livelihood, especially of border dwellers in the north of the country, is testified by another object of their averting prayers: the Scots.

THE RAVAGES OF FOES

Despite the primacy of the weather as the source of suffering, war, no less than in our own times, disrupted food consumption during the Middle Ages. During the Great Famine, war invaded the border regions of England and Scotland, as well as Ireland and, for a brief time, Wales, where it compounded the hardships and deaths wrought by hunger.

The counties of England most affected by this dual onslaught of famine and war were the northern ones of Cumbria, Northumberland, Durham, and Yorkshire. Between 1311 and 1327, Scottish armies crossed the border numerous times to spread havoc and destruction on the hapless populations of these regions. These attacks had a strategic purpose: to force the English king, Edward II, to officially recognize his would-be Scottish counterpart, Robert the Bruce. As we'll see, the means of accomplishing this task anticipates England's own great chevauchées, or raiding marches, during the Hundred Years War in France. These combined economic devastation that lessened a country's ability to wage war with a political challenge to the reigning monarch as the protector of his people. Moreover, the Scots may have deliberately timed their raids to coincide with the famine. The first raids took place in August and September 1311, just as harvest time was approaching and the grain would have been ripe enough to burn. Thereafter, a Scottish raid coincided with nearly every year of the famine, sometimes occurring late in the autumn after the grain had been stored in barns and could be easily destroyed. The political purposes to which famine may have been put in the fourteenth century anticipate the use of starvation as state policy in the Ukraine and Biafra during the twentieth century, when the death of millions was the result.

By the Treaty of Edinburgh/Northampton of 1328, the Bruce finally became Robert I of Scotland. However, a change in English government after the death of Edward II in 1327 may have been just as responsible for this royal recognition as any scorched-earth strategy. What is without a doubt is that between 1306 and 1326 the north of England was transformed into a place where the laws and customs of the rest of the country no longer applied. The chronicle accounts serve as some of our best sources for how the people living on the border at this time were affected. As with the French and English chronicles of the Hundred Years War, a national bias can be detected on both sides of the struggle. The Scotsman John of Fordun, for example, portrays the "havoc with fire and sword" unleashed by "King Robert" on the North as "God's righteous judgement" upon "the faithless English nation." An anonymous chronicler from Lanercost Priory in Cumbria, by contrast, says the Scots burned and looted even when they had hostages for their tribute, and he characterizes their raids as attacks on defenseless men and women, who were forced to hide themselves in the woods, much like the French peasants were to do in the face of marauding English soldiers during the Hundred Years War.

It soon becomes clear from reading these accounts that, despite their thirst for tribute money, the Scots were intent on destroying the very livelihood of their enemies, which must have been hard to bear during the famine. In 1316, according to the Malmesbury chronicler, the people of Northumberland were eating dogs, horses, "and other unclean things" because "the accursed Scots despoil the people daily of their food." An author from Meaux Abbey in Yorkshire, after recounting raids throughout the North in that year in which villages were burned and resisters put to the sword, claims that Northumberland was to remain a wasteland for fifteen years, "deserted by men and wild and domestic beasts" and where no one dared stay "except in some castle or walled village." In Cumbria as well, the Lanercost chronicler confirms that during raids in 1314 and 1319 the Scots pursued a policy of manufactured starvation, either by "trampling down the crops by themselves and their beasts as much as they could" or by burning the harvest "when the crop had been stored in barns . . . both the corn upon which the people depended for sustenance during that year and the houses wherein they had been able to take refuge." The Bridlington chronicler, reflecting in 1322 on the Scottish invasions, draws an explicit connection between the raids and famine. He says that when the enemy invades the north of England, they bring with them "a true famine, so that many villeins of those parts, who possessed a very full abundance of sheep and cattle on their farms and among their goods, now are compelled to go through the countryside, begging." Nor were the Scots the only ones scorching English earth. Natives of Northumberland joined in the orgy of destruction, according to Thomas Walsingham's *Historia Anglicana,* which he bases on an earlier source:

> In the same year [1317] certain men, seeing the frequent
> invasions, depredations, depopulations, and burnings
> of the Scots in nearly the whole of the countryside of
> Northumbria, and that no one wished to remedy so great
> an evil, took up arms, as it were in default of the king and
> his nobles, and were ready to resist the Scots. But after
> they had done this well for some time, in the end, on
> account of a lack of food and money, they became tyrants
> over their soldiers, destroyers of our defenders, and trai-
> tors to our champions. Moreover, gathering many about
> them, vowed to each other as equals, they robbed rustics
> in their homes and their neighbors in the fields, releasing
> their oxen from wagons or plows and killing them for
> their food. Indeed they left nothing behind in the villages
> that seemed suitable as food, for bread, grain, cows,
> sheep, pigs, and other kinds of meat, capons and chick-
> ens, cheese and oats, they plundered for themselves. And
> not only did they perpetrate such evils, but they robbed
> the common people to the point of carrying off gold, sil-
> ver, breeches and other clothing, and utensils. And thus
> so great a number of them did these things, that hardly
> anyone feared them, and they continued the said madness
> for nearly four years.

These were the activities of the *schavaldores,* literally "robbers," who roamed the border in the wake of the chaos introduced by the Scots. They were to be the forerunners of the Free Companies that did the same in France during the Hundred Years War. There is some evidence to back up Walsingham's descrip-tion, for in 1333 King Edward III granted an earlier petition from the inhabitants of Cumbria and Westmoreland that they be allowed to flee the scene of the Scottish wars, not because of the Scots but because the keepers of castles in those parts "exact such outrageous sums from them that they would prefer to evacuate the land for the time being rather than seek such security."

Before we leave the chronicle evidence, it is important to mention two other lands to which the Scottish wars spilled over and undoubtedly contributed to famine conditions. In 1315, Edward the Bruce, Robert's brother, invaded Ireland, landing in Ulster in the northeast. The purpose of this invasion was probably to give Robert's ambitious brother some role as putative king of Ireland and to open another front in the war with England. Nearly all the Irish annals agree that once he landed, Edward the Bruce pursued the same policy as his brother in the north of England: burning and looting the countryside on his march south toward the English pale around Dublin. Taking their cue from the Scots, local chieftains also joined in the devastation, especially in the provinces of Leinster and Connacht. In fact, Edward's death in battle in October 1318 was widely celebrated in Ireland, for his three-year sojourn there was synonymous with the famine that allegedly drove the Irish to eat each other (but which also did not spare the Scots themselves). The other incident of unrest during the famine, perhaps indirectly inspired by the Scots, was a revolt in Wales in 1316 under the leadership of a local nobleman, Llewelyn Bren. Here again we have the familiar story of people killed and villages burned, especially in those areas loyal to the English.

Recently, scholars have been trying to assess for the border country what has long been gauged for France during the Hundred Years War: to measure as quantitatively as possible the damage that was done by wartime raiding. One of the most important of these border studies is that of the estates of Bolton Priory in the West Riding of Yorkshire. Bolton suffered from at least two raids, one in 1318 during the spring, when loss of grain storehouses would have been catastrophic, and again in 1319 at the end of September, when the newly harvested grain had just been stored in barns. Total output of oats, by far the most important crop, was 27 percent lower in 1317 than in the previous year, a reflection not of poor production but of the Scots' destruction in the following spring, before the harvest had been tallied. No grain output was recorded in 1319, because even the account roll for that year was lost to the Scots. From 1320 to 1324, oat production averaged about a third of what it had been before the famine, and the total output of all grain was more than 60 percent lower, on average, than during the fourteen years prior to 1315. It was during these years that the Bolton canons were forced to disperse to the hospitality of other houses, and we know that during part of this time some canons were forced to take refuge in Skipton Castle. But equal, perhaps even greater, contributors as the Scots to Bolton's misfortunes were the waterlogged harvests and animal murrains so familiar to the rest of the country.

If it was any comfort to the canons of Bolton, their priory's ruin due to the devastating combination of famine and war was shared by several other houses near the Scottish border. Perhaps the agricultural setbacks suffered by Bolton at the hands of the Scots, where these can be disentangled from the effects of famine, are to be expected on an estate whose large-scale farms would have presented a natural target for raiding parties. But did the common people suffer in proportionate measure to Bolton? Other records available to us suggest that they did. The best window we have onto what happened to the peasantry living along the border during the Scottish raids are taxation reassessments ordered by the archbishop of York. These reviews of parish valuations were conducted precisely in order to assess the damage wrought by the Scots. The first revaluation was completed in July 1317 at the behest of Archbishop William Melton in order to gauge the effects of a Scottish raid in the summer of 1316 that had come down the eastern part of the archdiocese through Durham and back up in the west along the coast of Cumbria. By far the most severe damage had been done in the west, where twenty-five parishes had their original valuations reduced by 50 percent or more.

Successive raids were to prove even more destructive. In the spring of 1318 the Scots conducted a deeper raid into the heart of Yorkshire. In that county alone, a second reassessment conducted the same year reveals that no fewer than 77 parishes had their tax valuations cut by more than half. In the diocese of Carlisle, all parishes were devastated, as were all the parishes in the deanery of Copeland in Cumbria (part of the diocese of York). In 1319 the Scots raided deep into Yorkshire yet again. Although this time no taxation reassessment survives, the lay subsidy of an eighteenth part of movable goods that Edward II attempted to collect in that year had to be waived for forty-nine villages in the North Riding of Yorkshire and for forty-six villages in the West Riding. In 1322 it was the turn of the East Riding to experience widespread damage from the Scots: A taxation reassessment conducted there five years later in 1327 revealed that fifty-five parishes were worth less than half their value in more peaceful times.

Other evidence that the common people suffered a greatly reduced ability to pay their taxes in the aftermath of raids can be found in tithing and rental incomes. Between 1316 and 1320 grain tithes from twenty-four towns along the border whose churches were owned by Durham Priory amounted to nearly nothing, when between 1300 and 1315 these had realized more than £200 per year. Burning by the Scots, either of standing grain or of storehouses, was the cause of these shortfalls according to both the priory's bursar and its chronicler. Wool and lamb tithes from Durham's border parishes suffered a similar fate: These are virtually nonexistent between 1317 and 1328, even though the parishes had rendered five to six sacks of wool annually until at least 1314. The Honour of Penrith in Cumbria, which returned rents into the royal exchequer, suffered catastrophic dips between 1314 and 1327: At the manors of Carlatton and Scotby, incomes were once again reduced to almost nothing, while at Penrith, Langwathby, and Castle Sowerby, they fell by as much as 30 to 35 percent. But perhaps the most dramatic testimony to the devastating effect the Scottish raids had on the peasantry of northern England comes from the town of Easingwold, nestled in the forest of Galtres near York. Raided in 1319 and 1322, the tenants of Easingwold were the subjects of a royal inquest of 1326 into their ability to pay rents that had been confiscated from their usual lord, the earl of Lancaster. At least thirty-one tenants were reported to have been killed outright by the Scots, one of whom burned to death in his own house; seventeen had their homes and lands "burnt and destroyed"; and seven more were driven into exile by the poverty that the raids had imposed. If only more of such detailed investigations had been conducted or survived, no doubt many more Easingwolds would come to light.

One final point needs to be stressed with regard to raiding by the Scots. Just as French kings would be held partly to blame for failing to stop or at least curb English incursions into their territory during the Hundred Years War, so Edward II has been accorded, by both contemporary and modern historians alike, some of the responsibility for the ruinous state of the border that held true for most of his reign. For much of the Scottish War, Edward was content to abandon the defense of the northern part of his realm to "superior captains," known as *chevetaignes*. Along with castle garrisons, the followers of the *chevetaignes* all too easily evolved into *schavaldores* whose depredations upon local communities were just as bad, if not worse, than those of the Scots. As the Malmesbury chronicler puts it, "the Scots used to spare the inhabitants of Northumbria for a time in return for a moderate tribute, but those who were supposed to be set over them for their protection were constantly at leisure to oppress them every day." But when Edward did lead armies north, he seemed no more effective. In June of 1314, for example, he was decisively defeated at Bannockburn. Such futile outcomes must have been particularly galling to the northern populace since, as the army marched their way, its belly had to be fed. Confiscations of money and food for the sake of one's defenders only compounded the other miseries of famine and war.

THE RAVAGES OF FRIENDS

Whenever medieval English kings raised an army to supposedly succor their subjects, they also needed to raise a tax to pay for it. Taxes always have been, and always will be, unpopular, and never more so than during the Middle Ages. The Great Famine was sandwiched by two periods of particularly intense taxation: during the 1290s, when Edward I was engaged in war on three fronts—in Scotland, Wales, and Gascony—and during the 1330s, when Edward III fought the Scots and opened the Hundred Years War with France. In comparison, taxation during the reign of Edward II may be said to have been light; however, of the seven levies assessed during the reign, four fell within the years of the famine between 1315 and 1322. Moreover, the rate of taxation was heavier during those eight years than during the previous eight, amounting at its highest to one-sixth of all movable goods. Thus, of the £307,200 that was actually collected from both the clergy and laity throughout the reign, £187,200, or roughly 61 percent, was raised during the famine. Edward taxed his subjects most when they were least able to pay.

There is some evidence that northern communities, buffeted as they were by both the Scots and the weather, were unable or simply refused to pay their taxes. Lancashire contributed nothing to the lay subsidies of 1315 and 1319, probably because of Scottish raids in those years. In 1315, Richard de Kellawe, bishop of Durham, wrote to Edward saying that he could not even collect the arrears of the half owed from his father's reign because the goods of delinquent churchmen in his diocese had been "completely carried away and consumed by the Scots." Although the clergy of the diocese of Carlisle had been granted a new tax assessment in 1318 to take into account devastation by the Scots, John de Halton, their bishop, informed the king in the following year that no tax collectors had been appointed because there was nothing to collect. "Robert the Bruce has twice in that year [1317] invaded our diocese of Carlisle with his army," Halton bemoaned to Edward, "burning and laying waste almost the whole of it." A similar excuse was offered in 1322. From 1321 the king's subjects in Cumbria, Westmoreland, and Northumberland, who described themselves as "devastated by war and a sudden murrain of beasts so that they have no means of sustenance nor of tillage," were granted a moratorium on payments to the royal exchequer, to last indefinitely. In 1330, the clergy of these counties and of Durham were granted a new tax assessment on the grounds that for the past thirty-four years, "the Scottish war . . . has devastated their goods, their churches and manors are burnt, their books, chalices and church ornaments looted and carried off, and they are so impoverished that they can scarcely maintain their functions."

But just because taxpayers resisted royal revenues does not mean that they got off scot free. Money, if not collected by the king, was collected by the Scots as tribute so that they would not raid in the future (although often they did both). The historian R. A. Lomas has called this "a state-run protection racket," essentially blackmail on a large scale. Between 1311 and 1327, thirteen truces were purchased by the counties of Cumbria, Northumberland, and Durham, amounting in all to probably £16,000. If other, more local truces are factored in, the total may come to £20,000, which would not include additional expenses such as payments for hostages, to *schavaldores*, and to go-betweens traveling to Scotland. The money for such tributes was collected just like a tax for the king, but with no exemptions. If actually viewed as taxes, these truces, considering the small area in which they were collected, would comprise a far heavier rate of assessment than any under the English crown.

Whether and by how much taxation affected agricultural investment is another matter. A big farm such as one run by a lord or a monastery presumably could absorb the extra expense of a tax without too much hardship. Peasants, on the other hand, had far less margin to work with. Admittedly, the poorest were exempt, since one had to own at least 10 shillings' worth of movable goods to be taxed, and even if one owned more than this, his possessions were assessed at well below their true value. Yet court rolls reveal that much extortion by tax collectors occurred, and, in the case of arrears, collection could occur at most inconvenient times, such as in the spring when food resources were low. That too much tax could be absolutely devastating to peasants' livelihood is proved by the inquisitions of 1341 into the assessment of a ninth part of possessions. Tenants in Cambridgeshire and Herefordshire were found to be reduced to poverty and their land gone to waste on account of this exceptionally heavy rate of taxation assessed during the previous decade.

A more eloquent and descriptive tale of the debilitating effect of taxation is to be found in several poems dating perhaps to the second and third decades of the fourteenth century. Although surely not written by peasants, who usually were illiterate, the poems may have been composed by clergymen who had firsthand knowledge of the poor. In one, the *Poem on the Evil Times of Edward II*, the author complains of the disproportionate burden that the king's taxes place on those least able to pay:

And if the king in his lond maketh a taxacioun
And everi man is i-set to a certein raunczoun,
Hit shal be so for-pinched, to-toilled, and to-twiht,
That halvendel shal gon in the fendes fliht off helle;
Ther beth so manye parteners may no tunge telle.

A man of xl. Poundes-worth god is leid to xii. pans rounde;
And also much paieth another that poverte hath broult to grounde,
And hath an hep of girles sittende aboute the flet.
Godes curs moten hii have! But that be wel set and sworn,
That the pore is thus i-piled, and the riche forborn.

And if the king levies a tax in his land,
And every man is assessed at a certain rate,
They shall be so pinched to pieces, labored and twitted
    away,
That one-half shall pay for the fiend's flight from hell;
There be so many partners that no tongue may tell.

A man worth £40 in goods is assessed at around 12 pence;
And also much pays another whom poverty has brought
    low,
And who has a heap of daughters sitting upon the floor.
God's curse may they have! Let it be well set down and
    sworn
That the poor are thus robbed, and the rich forborn.

Two anonymous authors are more specific in their indictment of how taxation affects the peasantry. In the *Song of the Husbandman*, written in English, the poet testifies that taxes could only be paid at the expense of a farmer's seed grain: "To seek silver for the king I sold my seed / Wherefore my land lies fallow and learns to sleep." *The Song against the King's Taxes*, composed in French (which apparently some English peasants could understand), protests a specific tax, a fifteenth part of movable goods, that forces the common folk to "sell their cows, their utensils, and even clothing." It also bears witness to the corruptions of tax collectors, and, like the *Poem on the Evil Times of Edward II*, it bemoans the heavier burden often borne by the poor.

Unlike taxation, "purveyance" may be an unfamiliar word to many nowadays because few of us have felt its effects. Except during the First and Second World Wars, when scrap metal drives and food rations were imposed in order to feed and supply the armies, modern Western militaries make few direct demands on the populations they are assigned to protect. The victualing, clothing, and arming of latter-day troops is usually done by private contractors. In the Middle Ages, armies had to live off the land; if they were in enemy territory, they simply took what they needed. When they were supplied at home, the necessary items had to be "purveyed." Often there was little difference between the two practices.

Purveyance was far more devastating to peasant agriculture than taxation because it directly appropriated grain and livestock from farms in order to feed the army. Technically speaking, purveyors were supposed to pay for the food they took and account for it all at the exchequer. Because some of their records survive, we can reconstruct pretty well how they went about their business. Typically, the king would order his sheriffs, or men specially appointed for the purpose, to "provide and buy" so many quantities of grain, meat, cheese, and salt from their localities and deliver them to a specified place at a specified time. They were to do all this "at the least inconvenience on the part of the people," namely by paying for what they took out of the tax receipts, rents, and other income owed to the king. The purveyors then rendered their accounts directly to the exchequer or to a receiver of victuals, who accounted for them (after making an indenture with each purveyor confirming delivery of goods). These accounts specified the quantity of goods purveyed, at what price, and from where they had been taken. At the local level, purveyors made an indenture with each individual or village representative who had "sold" him goods; again, these memoranda recorded how much changed hands at what price. No fewer than forty-four such indentures survive in a file compiled in 1338 and 1339, when Gilbert de Ledred, sheriff of Lincoln, and two purveyors, Nicholas de Stanford and Herbert de Gresseby, provided victuals for the king's campaign in Scotland. In not one instance were the contributors paid up front; rather, "because the sheriff does not have at present money from the issues of his bailiwick," those from whom goods had been purveyed had to go in person to the exchequer, either at Westminster or York, in order to collect their due. There can be little doubt that payment by such IOUs was an all too frequent occurrence, and the cashing in of them equally rare.

Nevertheless, purveyance was limited in its scope to certain times and places. The counties of England most affected by it tended to be the grain-producing regions within easy land or sea access of the border: Yorkshire, Lincolnshire, Nottinghamshire, Norfolk and Suffolk, Cambridgeshire, and Huntingdonshire. Even though most purveyance thus took place farther south, northern communities still may have had to support armies passing through on their way to Scotland. During the 1330s, for example, the clergy of the diocese of Carlisle petitioned their bishop, John Kirkby, for a reassessment of the tax of a tenth because "revenues of benefices in the march of England were destroyed by invading armies and by English people often coming to defend them." Moreover, northerners may have been indirectly affected by purveyance if they relied, like the king's army, on grain supplied to them from the outside. A city like Carlisle, surrounded more by pasture than by arable land, and during the Scottish raids by simply wasteland, had to import its food, but from 1315 onwards its normal suppliers in Ireland to the west had been cut off by the invasion of Edward the Bruce. Consequently, it depended greatly on markets in the southwest of the country, whose goods were brought up along the Irish Sea.

Purveyors had to commandeer southern markets and shipping services, and inevitably this would mean less available for other customers.

Although purveyance, like taxation, seems to have been heaviest during the 1290s and 1330s, when it supported concentrated campaigns in Scotland, it undoubtedly occurred during the Great Famine, when it would have sorely afflicted everyone, north and south. Edward II led armies north in 1319 and 1322, the latter an especially large force of 20,000 men. He also made preparations to campaign in 1316, 1317, and 1318, during which purveyance may have occurred. The army of at least 15,000 men Edward took with him to Bannockburn in 1314 was supplied with almost 7,000 quarters of wheat and nearly 4,000 quarters of oats. The army of 20,000 in 1322 was provided with almost 4,000 quarters of wheat and more than 3,000 quarters of oats. Nor would this have been all of the grain purveyed. Sheriffs and other purveyors are known to have taken foodstuffs without issuing any kind of "tally" for future payment and then sold them, often back to the original owners, for substantial profit. This kind of abuse was alleged to have been committed by purveyors assigned to provision the English garrison at Berwick-on-Tweed on the Scottish border in 1316. It was an especially tempting extortion racket in time of famine, when food prices were astronomically high.

Rampant corruption among the king's officers, especially purveyors, was exposed in 1341 by a series of investigations ordered by Edward III. The heights to which purveyors' graft could reach can be reconstructed. To take the most extortionate year, 1338, in Lincolnshire, a county that was one of the largest and most frequent suppliers of the army's victuals, 2,488 quarters of grain and 884 animals were alleged to have been taken illegally, along with £127 in coin (see table 2, page 265). Either the purveyors never tallied and paid for what they took, or the victuals never reached their intended destination in Scotland, the purveyors selling foodstuffs for their own profit. Money was extorted either for the release of grain and animals back to their owners or so that communities would be spared the burden of purveyance. The main culprits were the sheriff, Gilbert de Ledred; the king's receiver of victuals in that year, William de Dunstapel; his deputy, Thomas de Dunstapel; and various specially appointed purveyors, including Sir William Frank, Sir John de Podenhale, Nicholas de Stanford, Herbert de Gresseby, and his deputy, Robert de Severby. Some of the extortions were on a very large scale indeed: Sir William Frank was said to have taken up to 2,000 marks (roughly £1,300) from the county on the pretext of purchasing victuals in 1337. In 1338 and 1339, Herbert de Gresseby and Robert de Severby supposedly purveyed up to 1,000 quarters of grain that they mostly resold to the original owners. In these same two years, Sir John de Podenhale was said to have taken 200 large oxen and cows worth a total of £100. By the time these investigations were wrapped up, in the spring and autumn of 1341, all of these men had either paid fines on cognizance of their guilt or been outlawed for nonappearance in the court at Lincoln, except for Sir William Frank, who was pardoned. The fruit of their extortion in 1338 was, in the case of grain, 25 percent greater than what had been officially tallied and received in that year, and in the case of animals, 88 percent greater.

A similar story can be told for Nottinghamshire (see table 3, page 266). There, the primary offenders were, once again, the sheriff, in this instance John de Oxford, along with his deputies, Hugh de Normanton and his son, William, and the purveyor, William de Walingford and his deputies, Robert Rolle and William de la March. Their worst offenses, if not quite on the scale as those of their Lincolnshire colleagues, are still impressive. In 1337 Oxford and his deputy, William de Normanton, were said to have taken a total of 550 quarters of wheat, barley malt, and oats that did not end up in the hands of the king or of his army. In 1338 John de Oxford took for the king's larder 200 large oxen, which he allegedly sold back to their owners for his own profit. It is certainly suggestive that, according to his own account, Oxford came up short in 1338 by nearly 900 quarters of wheat, malt, and oats that was supposed to have been provided "for castles and towns in Scottish parts." As at Lincoln, all of the accused were either outlawed or fined by the court at Nottingham in July 1341, except for Robert de Lyndeby, Oxford's deputy, and Richard de Herthill, purveyor, who were acquitted of their relatively minor offenses. Their combined extortions of just over 770 quarters of grain in 1338 was 30 percent higher than what was legitimately accounted for at the exchequer. All this malfeasance suggests that the true demand purveyance made upon the country's agricultural productivity was significantly greater than what was actually consumed by the army.

In certain instances the purveyors directly interfered with their victims' farming. In 1338, Sir John de Podenhale seized thirty-two oxen at Sutton-in-Holland, Lincolnshire, which put sixteen plows out of action for half a year and more. John de Oxford took twelve oxen out of their plows and eight lactating cows, worth a total of over £8, from the villagers of Bole, Nottinghamshire, in 1336 and did not return them until he was paid 6 shillings and 8 pence. Walter Golyas, an associate of Oxford's deputy, William de Normanton, seized a plow horse from John Golightly of Sturton-in-the-Clay, Nottinghamshire, in 1338 and was reported to still have had it in 1341. Another horse, taken this time by Henry atte Halle, bailiff of Ness in Lincolnshire, for the purpose of transporting victuals, prevented Robert Russell of Stamford from harrowing his field for four days running, as a result of which he allegedly lost the potential cropping of one acre of wheat, worth 40 pence. The straits to which men living at the margins of subsistence could be reduced by such confiscations is illustrated by a case that was said to have occurred in 1338, when John de Oxford took twenty oxen from four men described as "powerless." This "destroyed and disturbed their plows"; moreover, the sheriff forced them "to hand over their winter seed, on account of which they sold their land and are utterly reduced to nothing." One of these unfortunates, John Asseball, who had four oxen worth over £2 taken, traveled to York twice and several times to Nottingham in a vain attempt to be paid for his beasts. Finally, in 1338 and 1339, certain men had beef, bacon, and salted mutton "set aside for their sustenance" taken from them by Sir John de Podenhale, not to be returned until they paid him £40.

We may round off this discussion of purveyance with the literary evidence as to its detrimental effects. One poem, a *Song on the Times* dating perhaps to 1308, complains how armies, and particularly the hobelars, or lightly armed horsemen, feed at the expense of the peasantry. For such men the poem demands a harsh punishment:

> *And thos hoblurs, namelich,*
> *That husbond benimeth eri of grund;*
> *Men ne schold ham biri in non chirch,*
> *Bot cast ham ute as a hund.*

> And those hobelars, especially,
> Who take from the husbandman the fruit of his ground,
> Men should not bury them in any church
> But cast them out like a hound.

A *Song against the King's Taxes* dating almost two decades later, in Anglo-Norman French, declares that the king ought to pay for his victuals with hard silver rather than with the wood tallies given to those divested of their food:

> If the king would take my advice, I would praise him then,
> For it would be better to eat out of wood, and to give
>   money for victuals,
> Than to serve the body out of silver and to pay with
>   wood.
> It is a sign of vice to pay for victuals with wood.

But by far the most passionately indignant protest against purveyance is the *Speculum Regis Edwardi Tertii* (Mirror of King Edward III), thought to have been penned by William of Pagula, a parish priest of Winkfield, Berkshire. The *Speculum Regis* was written as an open letter (in Latin) to Edward III and concerned itself almost entirely with abuses arising out of the necessity to victual the king. It is valuable as a reflection of the mind-set of the king's subjects, with whom the author undoubtedly had frequent contact in his capacity as their pastor. Like other complaints about purveyance, the *Speculum* is limited in time and place: to Windsor Castle around 1331, where resided the king, queen, and his son, each attended by a substantial household. But its outcry against the injustice of royalty living off commoners seems to ring true of any time and any place great numbers of men had to be fed.

Two things should be noted about the complaints in the *Speculum*. For one, they are most eloquent in defense of the poor, or those peasants least able to support a loss of their food-stuffs and a disruption in their agricultural activities. While the rich can obtain letters of protection, the poor are compelled to leave their homes, bringing with them their horses and carts, and carry wood or other goods for up to ten miles, keeping them away from their farms for many days without being paid for their labor. On account of these unwanted tasks their land is not culti-vated or sown, nor do they have any spare supplies to fall back on, and so they cry out to God like the enslaved Israelites in the Old Testament. Nothing seems to be safe from seizure, neither horses, oxen, cows, sheep, pigs, or chickens, nor wheat, barley, oats, beans, peas, or beer. None of this is ever paid for, or, if it is, at well below its true value. Not even widows, orphans, and poor women down to their last chicken are spared.

The other remarkable aspect of the *Speculum* is the severity with which it treats purveyance as a crime. Indeed, it threatens the young King Edward with loss of his kingdom as well as his soul, "so many are the men these days, in this land, who have grievances against you before the high God." This was an extremely audacious boast, considering that the king's father, Edward II, had been murdered only a few years before. His death the *Speculum* lays at the door of abusive purveyance, which he allegedly had practiced for "the whole term of his life." As a mat-ter of fact, Edward II faced a rebellion in 1321–22 brought on partly because of the "prise," the explosive possibilities of which the king had been duly warned by the Ordinances of 1311. The Ordinances had asked the king to cease all purveyance that was in violation of the Statute of 1297, "forasmuch as it is to be feared that the people of the land will rise, for the prises and divers oppressions made in these times." Nevertheless, Edward formally renounced the Ordinances in 1322.

Edward III, at this stage, seemed little better than his father, for wherever the present king goes, his arrival is dreaded, except for London, where "you do not buy anything for a lower price than the seller is willing to give for it." So much was purveyance to be avoided, says the author, that "I would rather that you take away from your realm that diabolical prerogative than that you obtain for me the whole kingdom of England, France, and Scotland." Finally, the *Speculum* ends on an apocalyptic note. Purveyors, the "precursors of the Antichrist," may allow the king and his entourage to eat, drink, and be merry, but soon enough they will be neighbors in hell.

If nothing else, a study of purveyance in England during the early fourteenth century is worthwhile for the light it sheds on the plight of Frenchmen, who must have faced similar demands throughout the later Middle Ages as a consequence of the Hundred Years War. The French employed a system similar to the English, assigning the *prise* to a *panetier du roi*, who was assisted by *baillis* and captains in the actual collection from the provinces. And like the English purveyance, the French *prise* was blighted by abuses: Victuals were supposed to be paid for, but payments were slow and insufficient. The French poet Eustache Deschamps mocks the impossible dream of a country where the evils of purveyance are unknown:

> There is no marching over the fields there,
> No heavy-handed extortions:
> There, no one takes horses, nor work animals,
> Linen, cloth, and other such booty, nor securities,
> Chickens, or sheep. Violence
> Is not done. There no dog barks;
> The cock does not crow; the common good
> Reigns there in great authority:
> There, lives no Sarracen or pagan.
> Everyone says it is a great pity.

The same devastating combination of circumstances that plagued English northerners during the Great Famine—bad weather, enemy raids, and heavy purveyance in support of the army marching in its defense—are likely to have applied to the inhabitants of northern France during the 1340s. Death from starvation must have been the fate of many, and depopulation can be shown to have occurred, whether it be in Northumberland or Normandy.

There was therefore more to the making of medieval famines than the arbitrary whims of the weather or the inexorable logic of Thomas Malthus. At the same time, medieval man was not helpless before the onslaught of hunger. Psychologically speaking, formulaic and regular appeals heavenward to the Almighty for deliverance seem to have given victims some confidence that their sufferings at some point would end. In more practical terms, Edward II and his Parliament attempted a number of measures to alleviate the dearth: In addition to price-fixing, the government exhorted against grain hoarding and offered incentives to grain merchants to import their surplus wares into the island. Yet despite claims by the king's apologists to the contrary, these efforts proved woefully inadequate. It is probably unfair, though, to expect medieval governments to have been able to do much in the way of what we now call "disaster relief"; after all, the very idea that governments *should* do something during a famine did not invade the Western consciousness until relatively recently.

By the 1340s and 1350s, the English crown seemed to be more responsive to complaints about purveyance, and it began to arrange for this task to be carried out by merchant middlemen, who perhaps were more accountable and less open to corruption than purveyors. As we will see in the next chapter, toward the close of the century, the court of Richard II began to recognize that peace had its benefits and war its dire consequences. Medieval kings, should they wish to halt the horseman of Famine riding among their subjects, had to halt the horseman of War that they had unleashed upon their enemies.

WAR

What a joyous thing is war. . . . When one sees that one's quarrel is just and one's blood is fighting well, a tear comes to the eye. There comes to the heart a sweet feeling of loyalty and pity to see one's friend, who so valiantly exposes his body in order to do and accomplish the command of our Creator. And then one is disposed to go and live or die with him, and for love not at all abandon him. From that comes such a delectation, that he who has not tried it is a man who cannot say what a delight is. Do you think that a man who does that fears death? Not at all; for he is so comforted, he is so elated that he does not know where he is. Truly he fears nothing.

—Jean de Bueil, *Le Jouvencel*, c. 1466

Both the refinement of chivalry and the frenzied bloodlust in the heat of battle characterize war during the later Middle Ages. In his epic poem *Le Jouvencel* (The Youth), Jean de Bueil's sacrificial warriors fight with a mystical, almost erotic gusto, and one can imagine that armored soldiers during the fifteenth century did just that since they were encased in metal plates that gave them the feeling, if not the reality, of impenetrable protection. How different is war for modern man, who for the past fifty years or more has witnessed the proliferation of weapons of mass destruction capable of the complete annihilation of our civilization. Our medieval forebears seem to have enjoyed the luxury of waging war without the specter of an apocalyptic outcome. As a consequence, medieval men are rarely associated with dovish pursuits.

This is, of course, too simplistic a picture of how most people viewed war during the Middle Ages. The vast majority of the population—namely the peasants—can have been little enamored of an activity that on occasion threatened their livelihood and even their lives, with few opportunities of fighting back. An English *Song on the Times*, dating to the early decades of the fourteenth century, seems to give vent to an authentic cry of the people, who implore: "May peace be in the land, through thee, God, bountiful power! / Prevent war, may want not afflict us!" The Church, too, suffered from war's depredations and tried to limit its scope during the Peace and Truce of God movements of the tenth and eleventh centuries. Manuals for princely behavior hold up the pursuit of peace rather than of war as a model for their royal readers. Even Bueil himself, a battle-hardened veteran, speaks of the desolation and destruction wrought by war on a nation and its people. But it is *Les Voeux du Héron* (The Vows of the Heron), a fourteenth-century French poem, that most effectively satirizes the kind of bravado bruited about by Bueil:

> When we are in taverns, drinking strong wine, and ladies
> with white throats and tight bodices pass and look at us,
> their sparkling eyes resplendent with smiling beauty,
> nature makes our hearts desire to fight, looking for mercy
> from them as a result. Then we could defeat Yaumont and

Aguilant, and others Oliver and Roland. But when we are
in the field, on our trotting warhorses, shields hung
'round our necks and lances lowered, a great frost numb-
ing us, limbs crushed before and behind, and our enemies
advancing on us, then we would like to be in a great cel-
lar, and never make a vow again.

This, it seems, was the reality of war, which even a well-armored
knight secretly dreaded.

Nonetheless, however warlike we may think the Middle Ages
to be, the later period of that era was to see an unprecedented
amount of bloodshed. This was not only because there were
more battles fought, but because the nature of war was rapidly
and dramatically changing. Most of these changes came about
during the Hundred Years War between 1337 and 1453 in which
England and France fought an intermittent series of engage-
ments. During the fourteenth century, battle was joined between,
on the one side, the English king Edward III and his eldest son,
Edward the Black Prince, and, on the other, the French kings
Philip VI and John II; the war's causes mainly had to do with the
status of English territories in Aquitaine in southwestern France,
which Edward wanted free from the homage, or a feudal oath of
loyalty, to be performed for it to his French overlord. This conflict can be considered the prelude to the more nationalistic, and
modern, struggle during the fifteenth century, when King Henry
V of England claimed to be the rightful ruler over the whole of
France—to the detriment of the Valois heir, the dauphin
Charles—basing this claim on a genealogical link between the
royal houses of the two countries that made these respective
princes first cousins.

It was during this time that a "military revolution" emerged,
in which infantry demonstrated its ability to defeat cavalry, and
missile technology, such as the longbow and later the gun, played
a decisive factor in battle. Both of these developments did not
always respect the knight's armor nor the rich ransoms to be had
upon his capture, which previously had kept casualties low. But
there was another movement developing at this time, what I call
a revolution in the language of war. The propaganda that was

being churned out on both the English and French sides, particularly during the 1340s and 1350s, which saw a concentrated
period of fighting, was helping to develop, for the first time, a
growing sense of nationalism that looked upon the enemy as out
to destroy one's way of life and, consequently, itself had to be
destroyed. In addition, this propaganda involved the noncom-
batant—the average peasant—more directly in war than ever
before, and in turn he became the target of war in a more systematic and deliberate way than he had yet known. A modern
consciousness toward war had begun.

If war, from a historical perspective, thus became more brutal,
contemporaries were not entirely unaware of the fact. By the late
fourteenth century, Frenchmen had long known and complained
of the devastating raids made by the English and others on their
soil, while on the other side, some Englishmen were becoming
distinctly disenchanted with an increasingly expensive and seemingly fruitless struggle. Peacemongers pinned their hopes on the
English king, Richard II (his French counterpart, Charles VI, suffered periodic bouts of insanity), and in 1396, Richard concluded
a twenty-eight-year truce with France, sealed by his marriage to
the French princess, Isabella. This truce was not to last, for in
1399 Richard was forced to abdicate in favor of his cousin, Henry
Bolingbroke, duke of Lancaster, and sixteen years later, in 1415,
the English were to reopen the war with victorious results at
Agincourt. The flowering of peace toward the close of the century therefore may have been brief, but it is still worthy of study.
But before peace, there is war.

THE DAWN OF MODERN WARFARE

Europe's rise to supremacy as a world power during the modern
era, commanding far-flung colonial empires, is usually attributed,
at least in part, to a military revolution that gave its armies an
overwhelming advantage over their enemies in battle. Exactly
what this revolution was depends on when it is supposed to have
occurred, and its origins can probably be pushed back into the

past indefinitely. But recently some historians have argued, with I believe considerable conviction, that if the revolution had any beginning at all, it is to be found in the later Middle Ages. It was then that the whole character of war changed, with armies evincing a new desire and determination to exterminate the enemy, not just capture them for their rich ransoms or drive them from the field. This was a revolution more of the mind than of any new weapon, tactic, or strategy. It was a war of words rather than of arms. How did Europe, and England especially, come to such a pass? Before we can explain this new mentality, we must explain how it was carried out.

Shortly before the beginning of the Hundred Years War with France two revolutionary methods of fighting emerged in England that were to win it every pitched battle during the conflict. Both had important implications for modern warfare. They also made waging war far more bloody than had ever before been known. One of these methods was to emphasize infantry over cavalry in the tactical order of battle. Infantry, of course, had been a part of medieval armies all along. But prior to the fourteenth century they had occupied a secondary role, acting as the "shield to the sword" of the cavalry: That is, foot soldiers provided protection for knights while they mounted their warhorses and formed up for battle. Now infantry became the main weapon of the army. Provided they stood their ground, were armed with long pikes or halberds, and the enemy was willing to hurl itself against such an immovable object, armies composed almost entirely of infantry proved they could defeat cavalry charges.

More infantry meant more violence for a number of reasons. Infantry were far cheaper to pay and equip, largely because they did not bring with them the added expense of a warhorse, which cost on average anywhere from £7 to £16 to buy and nearly 7 pence per day to maintain, more than the daily wages of an archer. Even when mounted to improve their mobility on the march, English men-at-arms and archers still fought on foot during the battle, thus necessitating a less expensive horse and one far less likely to need replacing. Therefore, a greater proportion of infantry in an army meant that more men could be brought to battle; the more men brought to battle, the more the potential victims. Socially speaking, the common foot soldier was less inclined than his superiors to respect the international law of arms or code of chivalry that had made war a gentleman's game among knights. Besides, an infantryman facing the thundering charge of a heavily armored cavalryman was not about to pull any punches. Likewise, knights had little reason to spare commoners, who could offer little or no ransom for their capture.

The other military revolution in England during the later Middle Ages was the use and development of the missile technology of the longbow, which anticipated artillery in its destructive capacities. Arrows traveling at speeds of over 200 feet per second were not about to pay knights the courtesy of enquiring whether they wished to surrender. But while knights could safely ensconce themselves in plate armor, which was to gradually encase the entire body and replace chain mail as the Hundred Years War progressed, the knights' horses were by no means so well protected. A horse with several barbed arrows in its body quickly became unridable. And a knight wearing approximately seventy pounds of metal would have been stunned, at the very least, after a fall from such a height. "The medieval tank," once deprived of his horse and lance, would have quickly lost his most deadly "firepower." Yet even on foot and in his armor, the knight was still vulnerable to penetration from the arrow, which could bear down with, on average, 100 pounds of force behind it, and as much as 180 pounds when released from a six-foot bow drawn back to the ear. Armor was designed to stop missiles not so much by its thickness but by the deflecting angle of the plates. But the possibilities of penetration were greatly increased when arrows were approaching such surfaces in the hundreds and even thousands. It is estimated that the English archers unleashed half a million arrows against the French at the battle of Crécy in 1346.

It was actually the skillful interaction between these two units—dismounted men-at-arms and archers—that proved so successful for the English and so devastating for the French. Archery, a distinctly English pastime, as the Robin Hood ballads

The battle of Crécy, 1346, from a fifteenth-century manuscript of Froissart's Chronicles. The English longbowmen, at right, demonstrate their effectiveness against enemy crossbowmen, who are about to be cut down by their own cavalry. (Courtesy Bibliothèque Nationale de France.)

can attest, is no longer seen as the secret weapon that alone won battles. Rather, the longbowman, even if he did not kill his target outright, harassed and channeled him into killing fields where the more heavily armed soldiers fighting on foot could do their worst. This combination, missile power teamed up with a flexible yet disciplined infantry, would continue to be the essential ingredient that won battles for Cromwell in the 1640s, for Napoleon in the first decade of the nineteenth century, and for Rommel and Patton during the Second World War.

The bloody effectiveness of the new warfare was amply demonstrated in the three main battles of the Hundred Years War—Crécy in 1346, Poitiers in 1356, and Agincourt in 1415. All three were resounding English victories achieved by the lethal

The battle of Poitiers, 1356, where the English once again defeated the French using the longbow, incapacitating both horse and rider. From a fifteenth-century manuscript of Froissart's Chronicles. *(Courtesy Bibliothèque Nationale de France.)*

combination of dismounted men-at-arms and archers. The destructive power of this reinforcing arrangement impressed itself most forcefully upon contemporaries with the first great English victory at Crécy. Jean Froissart, a native of the county of Hainault on the French-Flemish border, says in his famous account of the battle that the murderous fire of the archers "fell like snow" upon the enemy and that their arrows "impaled or wounded horses and riders, who fell to the ground in great distress, unable to get up again without the help of several men." His countryman, Jean le Bel, who had fought with the English on the Weardale campaign in Scotland in 1327, commented that at Crécy:

> the [English] archers shot so well that horse and rider,
> feeling their flesh pierced, behaved strangely: one did
> not want to go further, another sallied forward as
> arranged; one defied [the arrows] courageously, the
> other turned its back to the enemy in spite of its master
> on account of the arrows that it felt, and the others let
> themselves fall, for they could not do any better; and the
> English men-at-arms advanced on foot and struck out
> among those men, who could not help themselves nor
> their horses.

English chroniclers, of course, were not at a loss to document their victory. Geoffrey le Baker almost pitied the enemy when he noted that "a great cry went up . . . from the horses wounded by arrows, while the French line of battle was badly disordered by stumbling horses. When they attacked the well-armed English, they were cut down with swords and spears, and many were crushed to death, without a mark on them, in the middle of the French army, because the press was so great." Other authors, following an official report of the battle by Richard Wynkeley, King Edward III's confessor, remarked how the king of France, Philip VI, was himself wounded in the face by an arrow and was twice unhorsed. Even French chroniclers admitted the superiority of English tactics. A Norman author noted that "the horses of the French, when they felt the points of the arrows, began to break ranks, and many fell down dead."

Another writer commented that the English archers "distressed many of [our] horses and did much other harm to the point that it is a pity and a sorrow to record." Jean de Venette, normally a patriotic defender of the French cause, says that "the enemy . . . bravely attacked our ill-ordered French lines, wounding the French soldiers with bows and arrows and swords, until they could not stand against them in conflict." The pattern established at Crécy was one that was to be repeated, with slight variations, throughout the war.

Another aspect of these battles upon which nearly all the chroniclers agree is that their casualties were immense. Horror was expressed not only at the quantity of men who fell, but their quality: For the first time, it seemed, nobles were seriously in danger of losing their lives. Perhaps getting their information from Bishop Michael Northburgh reporting back from the front, several English chroniclers boast that 2,000 French knights died at Crécy; Geoffrey le Baker, however, claims more than 4,000. The lowest estimate listed no fewer than 1,200 knights killed. According to Wynkeley's report, among the enemy slain were two kings (of Bohemia and Majorca), a duke, twelve counts, and two archbishops, "the flower of the whole knighthood of France." In addition, anywhere between 15,000 and 32,000 other French soldiers were claimed to have been killed; more often, the chroniclers profess themselves unable to count up this mass of men. The English, rather implausibly, were said to have lost only two knights and a squire. Although the higher numbers of French dead are probably not reliable either, they nevertheless testify to the shock the fatalities caused: Jean de Venette exclaimed that his countrymen "fell in battle in numbers that cannot be believed." Poitiers and Agincourt were no less bloody. A list drawn up of the French dead from the former battle counted 2,000 men-at-arms and 300 to 800 others. Included among them were two dukes, the constable and a marshal of France, three viscounts, a bishop, and sixteen bannerets. At Agincourt, the death roll on the French side tallied up three dukes, five counts, over ninety barons and bannerets, 1,500 knights, and 4–5,000 gentlemen, casualties not unrealistic out of an army estimated to be around

25,000 strong. As at Crécy, the English allegedly missed very few: a duke, an earl, two knights, and a score of others.

One wonders why the French, in the face of these mounting death tolls, continued to go like lambs to the slaughter and did not alter their tactics. It must be remembered that the English themselves learned the hard lesson of infantry warfare at the hands of the Scots, most famously at the battles of Stirling in 1297 and Bannockburn in 1314, where their taskmasters were none other than William Wallace and Robert the Bruce. The production of longbowmen, the best of whom could fire off twenty arrows in the time it took to load and fire one bolt of the crossbow, required years of training. By 1363 the English crown was compelled to urge its citizens to take up the bow and desist from "dishonest games" such as handball, football, cricket, hockey, and cockfighting. Nor did the French spurn English methods of fighting. They used artillery, in the form of Genoese crossbowmen, at Crécy, but the French knights ended up killing their own archers in the mistaken belief that they were fleeing the battle, in such evident contrast to the coordinated efforts of the English. At Poitiers, French knights dismounted on the advice of a Scotsman, William Douglas, but they still were defeated by the English men-at-arms and archers, whose "shooting was so heavy and accurate that the French did not know where to turn to avoid their arrows."

In addition to the greater number of casualties that the new war technologies afforded, a more ruthless and realpolitik approach to battle than ever before emerged in the Hundred Years War. At Crécy the English "took no prisoners and asked no ransoms, acting as they had decided among themselves in the morning when they were aware of the huge numbers of the enemy." Apparently, "Welsh and Cornishmen armed with long knives" were allowed by the army to wander among the injured, and "when they found any in difficulty, whether they were counts, barons, knights or squires, they killed them without mercy." John of Luxemburg, king of Bohemia, although blind and clearly not much of a threat to his enemies, nevertheless was found dead on the battlefield along with all his companions, who had tied their horses' bridles together in order to lead him to the fray. Before the battle of Poitiers, the French king, John II, ordered that no Englishman be left alive except the Black Prince. The Black Prince, in turn, sent the body of Sir Robert de Duras as his calling card to the dead man's uncle, Cardinal Talleyrand de Périgord, who the day before had attempted to arrange a truce between the two sides. According to a contemporary poem, Henry V made a speech before the battle of Agincourt to his men in which he announced that "for me this day schalle never Inglond rawnsome pay," sentiments that found an echo in Shakespeare's play.

But the clearest sign of things to come was a far more ruthless act that Henry committed at Agincourt: his order to kill all French prisoners in anticipation of an attack (that never came) from the enemy's third line of battle. It could be argued that this was just as much a violation of the law of arms as the French massacre of the "baggage boys" that so incensed Fluellen, the Welsh officer, in Shakespeare's play *Henry V*. Yet the previous scene, in which Henry gives "the word through" that "every soldier kill his prisoners" is rarely performed in its entirety, with Pistol's rallying cry to slaughter—"coup' la gorge!" ("slit the throat!")—as he proceeds to execute his prisoner in obedience to Henry's order. As one critic suggests, in the disbelieving face of the falling French prisoner was to be read the dawn of modern war.

THE LANGUAGE OF WAR

What made Englishmen and Frenchmen more willing to kill each other during the Hundred Years War was the propaganda being churned out and disseminated on both sides. This propaganda worked on several levels, but had essentially the same effect: to glorify one's own cause by imbuing it with an almost religious aura, and at the same time demonize one's enemies by depicting them as motivated almost entirely by malice and evil. This was the essence of the new nationalism: to suffer and deal out death in the name of a country or sovereign who can do no wrong, against a dehumanized enemy who is never in the right. The patriotic fer-

vor that led more than eight million men to their deaths in
Europe during World War I was already bestirring itself in the
later Middle Ages.

At its highest level, propaganda assumed the genteel form of
an appeal to chivalry. This was subtle propaganda, perhaps, but
words with a purpose nonetheless. For most Englishmen and
many Europeans, then and now, chivalry is synonymous with
King Arthur. Of the real, historical Arthur, possibly a fifth- or
sixth-century ruler who led British resistance against the Anglo-
Saxons, not much is known. What is far more interesting is how
the Arthurian legend was manipulated for political purposes by
various medieval monarchs. By far the most skillful in this regard
were Edward I and his grandson, Edward III. In 1278, Edward
I and his queen, Eleanor, presided over the translation of what
were claimed to be the bones of Arthur and Guinevere to the
high altar of Glastonbury Abbey. Edward III tried to go one better in 1344: At a tournament held in February at Windsor Castle,
he announced before a glittering array of lords and ladies that
"when the opportunity should be favorable to him, he would set
up a round table, in the same manner and condition in which
Lord Arthur, formerly king of England, left it, namely to the
number of 300 knights, and that he would cherish and maintain
it on behalf of [all] men, always increasing its number." The
round table may never have been realized, but shortly thereafter,
Edward founded the Order of the Garter, an international chivalric society that survives to this day. It was a propaganda coup that
any modern politician would envy.

Clearly, the cachet of limited membership that such a society
conferred greatly appealed to an upper-crust audience. This was
particularly important to Edward III, who sorely needed to
improve his standing among the aristocratic community after the
disastrous reign of his father, Edward II. Chivalry therefore was
not the dead letter many think it had become by the end of the
Middle Ages. Witness, for example, the continued popularity of
the Arthurian legend in works such as the anonymous poems
Morte Arthure and *Le Morte Arthur*, and Sir Thomas Malory's
prose masterpiece *Le Morte d'Arthur*, all dating to the late fourteenth and fifteenth centuries. As the titles imply, these works cli-

max in an "Arthurian Apocalypse" in which Arthur is betrayed
and mortally wounded by Mordred but then immediately departs
for Avalon to be healed with a promise to return. Arthur, in most
of these works, seems to symbolize the sacrifice and promised second coming of Christ at the Apocalypse. By successfully compar-
ing himself to Arthur, the English monarch undoubtedly imbibed
some of chivalry's quasi-religious overtones. Divine right, the
cornerstone of the coming absolutism, was taking shape.

The next level of propaganda disseminated during the Hundred Years War catered to the educated middle class: the country
squires and town burgesses who paid a lion's share of the taxes
and helped finance the war, and whose support and enthusiasm it
was therefore vital to sustain. This propaganda was much more
virulently anti-French than that served up to the nobility, whose
chivalric camaraderie retained an international flair. It usually
took the form of doggerel verse written perhaps by one of the
king's clerks or minstrels who accompanied him on campaign.

A typical example of this sort of patriotic poetry is *An Invective against France*, written by an anonymous author shortly after
the English victory at Crécy in 1346. An extremely long poem of
no fewer than 391 lines in Latin rhyming couplets, the *Invective*
does not foster national identity so much as a hatred of the Valois
monarchy. Much of the poem, in fact, is devoted to persuading
the French to adopt as their rightful ruler Edward III, who had a
legitimate claim to the throne through his mother, Isabella, and
who had formally assumed the title of king of France in 1340.
Whereas "Philip Valois" is compared to sly and cruel animals such
as the lynx, the viper, the fox, or the wolf, Edward is represented
by the noble boar and leopard. Philip's historical models are
Xerxes and Darius, the Persian tyrants defeated by the ancient
Greeks, while Edward's are David, Judas Maccabaeus, and, of
course, Arthur, who are among the "nine worthies" of chivalric
literature. Perhaps the most pointed lines of the poem employ a
clever pun on Philip's Latinized name, *Philippus*: "*Phy* [a fish]
stinks, *lippus* [a blind man] does harm with his eyes, / Therefore
Duke Philip does harm and stinks; he will reap a sordid fate."

As propaganda, the *Invective* takes rather astonishing liberties
with the truth. Its description of Edward's mother as "a bright

star of virtue" is laughable in light of the fact that her son in 1330 engineered a coup against her regency that resulted in the execution of her lover, Roger Mortimer, and her comfortable retirement to Castle Rising in Norfolk. Yet this flattering characterization was essential if Edward was to make a convincing claim to the French throne. At another point in the poem, Philip Valois is described as a man "cruel, piratical, of rare faith," who has "captured, destroyed, raped many" by means of his navy. This undoubtedly refers to the French raids upon the southern English coast in 1338, which terrified Englishmen into believing that a full-scale invasion was imminent. In addition, Philip is the "accursed of Christ" who is out to conquer England and divide up the spoils. Should this happen, "honor and love will be driven underground, true faith will die, the law, merit, peace will not be found." Edward, by contrast, is the "English angel," the "friend of justice . . . peaceful, patient, pious and modest, just, generous, merciful, moderate, even-tempered, truthful, distinguished, affable." He also is "devoted to Christ, pleasing to his people"; he rides through France "in Christ's name," disdaining "filthy lucre" and false truces. All this hyperbole is rather hard to swallow when for two months prior to the battle of Crécy, the English army, according to its own diary of the campaign, pillaged and burned its way through Normandy "until the sky itself glowed with a fiery colour."

Truly, national stereotypes begin to emerge with *The Dispute between the Englishman and the Frenchman*, another anonymous Latin poem also dating probably to the 1340s. Though written by an Englishman, the poem is remarkable for presenting a candid French view of the English, although the Englishman is allowed the last laugh. The Frenchman caricatures the English as unkempt, uncouth, and insatiable. Nothing but filth comes out of their mouths, they commit all sorts of crimes, and, worst of all, their hair is uncombed. "Their belly is their God" to which they offer sacrifices until they resemble beasts more than humans. They prefer "vats of corn" (beer) rather than the "liquor of the vine" (wine), and even if they drink the latter it is only the dregs. When the Englishman is allowed to speak, he mocks the French as cowardly and feminine (a characterization also applied to Philip

Valois). Hence the hen, a female chicken, rather than the more virile rooster, is an appropriate symbol of the French nation. The Englishman's hair may be uncombed, but the Frenchman combs his locks in a mirror by turning his head this way and that "until it does not wish to be yours." If the Englishman drinks the dregs, he at least has something, while the Frenchman is left with nothing. Since the Frenchman prefers to hear his own language spoken rather than English, the Englishman will make him suffer so that he cries out in French words of pain. The epithets "frog" and "*le rosbif*" (roast beef) still in use today have a very long history.

Another way that the English monarchy communicated national prejudices to its more learned subjects was through the official chronicles, or histories, of the period. History as propaganda was an old technique in England, dating back to at least the reign of Alfred the Great during the ninth century. Toward the end of the thirteenth, there was perhaps the first systematic use of an official history when Edward I distributed "proofs" of his overlordship of Scotland to various monasteries, along with instructions to copy the evidence into their chronicles. By the early fourteenth century, even before the Hundred Years War, the concept of nationalism was already emerging in English annals. The histories of Robert of Gloucester and Robert Manning, for example, consciously foster a sense of nationhood by telling the entire story of the island in its native language. Given these precedents, it is no surprise to find that information from the despatches Edward III and his ministers regularly sent back from the front during the Crécy campaign found their way, sometimes verbatim, into the histories. By far the most incendiary piece of propaganda sent back to England was a copy of an alleged invasion plan drawn up by Philip VI in March 1339, which was said to have been discovered in the muniments of the town of Caen, taken by Edward's forces toward the end of July 1346. The plan reportedly called for a second Norman Conquest of the island by means of the mustering of a large army in Normandy to be led by its duke, none other than the dauphin, John (the future John II). Should England be conquered, the realm was to be divided up among John and his Norman nobles, to be held as a fief of the French king. This "find" was read out to the English populace by

Archbishop John Stratford at St. Paul's churchyard in London, which is perhaps how the chroniclers learned of it. It also conveniently justified Edward's chevauchée, or armed raiding march, through Normandy, which he claimed was being conducted for the better security of the realm. Although the invasion plot is treated as genuine by most modern historians, there is no way of confirming it outside of its appearance in English documents and chronicles. If the French really did have a secret plan to conquer England, there is no evidence that they attempted to carry it out.

Patriotic propaganda was no less indulged in across the Channel. The French monarchy had its own chivalric society, the Order of the Star, but its most sublime expression of patriotic royalism came from the mouth of a young girl from Domrémy, Joan of Arc. As the Maid led Charles VII to his coronation at Rheims on July 17, 1429, she began the process of restoring the sacred character of the royalist cause at a time of its lowest ebb, when it had been in real danger of being supplanted by the English house. For in Joan, the French found their equivalent of England's King Arthur: a figure who lent a divine stamp of approval to the crown. It should be remembered, however, that Joan's contribution to French nationalism only emerged years later at her rehabilitation and was by no means accepted by all of her countrymen.

Earlier in the war, anonymous French poems such as *Le Dit de la Rébellion d'Angleterre et de Flandre* (The Tale of the Rebellion of England and Flanders), *Les Voeux du Héron*, *Poème sur la Bataille de Crécy* (Poem on the Battle of Crécy), and *Complainte sur la Bataille de Poitiers* (Complaint on the Battle of Poitiers) mirrored their English counterparts both in the extreme bias of their points of view and in the poor quality of their verse. It was perhaps from one such poem that a most effective piece of French propaganda wormed its way into the chronicles: the story of the rape of the countess of Salisbury by Edward III, alleged to have taken place in 1342. The rape story was a particularly damaging slur on Edward's reputation, as legend holds that it was by his picking up the countess's fallen garter belt that the Order of the Garter, founded in 1348, received its emblem. Thus, in the French mind, Edward's chivalrous act was transmuted into a crime. Yet it is highly unlikely that, if the rape truly occurred, the victim's garter belt would have been adopted as a symbol of an order of chivalry. Highly suspicious is that the rape story is not backed by authorities outside of French sources and that it follows a standard scenario dating back to Livy: King falls in love with another's wife, king ravishes wife, wife confesses to her husband, husband and wife are separated forever. Nevertheless, the story was disseminated by Jean le Bel, a chronicler normally well disposed to the English, and more recently was cited by the historian Barbara Tuchman to demonstrate the hollowness of Edward's chivalry.

By far, the type of propaganda that influenced the most Englishmen the most often was that propounded by the clergy on the crown's behalf to their congregations during church services. The machinery that accomplished this task was impressive: Usually the crown issued a writ out of chancery directed to the prelates asking that certain religious ceremonies be performed— which could include prayers, processions, masses, litanies, psalms, vigils, fasts, and even bell ringing—whose purpose was to anticipate or give thanks for a victorious battle or diplomatic enterprise; the archbishops and bishops then forwarded the royal request for execution to their archdeacons or officials; and from there the message was relayed to every priest in every parish of every diocese. Sometimes sermons, or even a proclamation in English giving news from the front (provided that this was favorable), also were ordered. The people themselves were encouraged to take part in the ceremonies by the promise of forty days' indulgence against their assigned penances. Theoretically, if this whole process worked according to plan, an awareness of and support for the king's exploits would have been demanded of every churchgoer in the country, which would have included just about everyone except Jews, heretics, and foreigners. Six hundred years before the age of television and radio, a more effective means of "broadcasting" to the nation cannot be imagined.

How often and to what effect did the crown employ this extraordinary propaganda tool? If we restrict ourselves to the first phase of the Hundred Years War, between the opening of the conflict in 1337 and the death of Edward III in 1377, we can see how well it worked. Royal propaganda was issued by the clergy for twenty-five of the forty-one years during this period, sometimes more than once a year, and in as many as thirteen out of the seventeen dioceses throughout the country (see table 4, page 267). By following the propaganda, one can gain a complete blow-by-blow narrative of the king's progress in his struggle with France, often involving sideshows in Scotland, Spain, or Prussia. When victories occurred, such as at Sluys (1340), Crécy (1346), Poitiers (1356), and Nájera (1367), news of them, so vital to maintaining enthusiasm for the war, was communicated to at least a substantial portion of the population. Medieval Englishmen and Englishwomen, flocking to their parish churches to hear the word of God, also harkened to the voice of their king.

Despite being disseminated by the Church, such propaganda twisted the truth no less than other forms. Even when undertaking offensive campaigns, the English army was described as facing an enemy out to "devastate," "destroy," "subvert," "submerge," "overthrow," and "exterminate" the king and his realm, his people, his Church, even the English language itself. In reality, England was rarely in danger of being invaded by the French. Likewise, when Englishmen were exhorted to pray for peace, often they were really sanctioning war: It is hard to imagine the Black Prince in 1356 going to France "for the purpose of acquiring peace," when in fact he led a chevauchée through the country that culminated in the battle at Poitiers.

How exactly were the people's prayers supposed to help the king and his army, and how important were they to the war effort? It is clear that prayers were considered an essential part of the preparations for a campaign, so much so that they were ordered to be said on a regular basis. In a typical turn of phrase, the king commanded prayers "because the outcomes of wars are in doubt and a triumph comes not from man but from God, in that every victory and every triumph [resides] not in the arms of a nation, in an abundant virtue of the army, or in the strength of the human arm, but in the dues paid to God." Alarms were raised when the people seemed "sluggish" or "tepid" in their devotions on these occasions, as was reported by English prelates in 1359, 1370, 1377, 1382, 1386, 1388, and 1416–18. Historical and biblical examples were invoked to demonstrate how the power of prayer could turn the tide of battle. Perhaps the one most often cited was that of Moses from the Book of Exodus in the Old Testament, who defeated Pharaoh's armies in Egypt by calling down a pillar of fire and parting the Red Sea. Indeed, prayers were thought of in almost the same terms as the material weapons of an army. In the words of John Trillek, bishop of Hereford, who ordered prayers for the Crécy campaign in 1346:

> We believe that nothing in this life more immediately renders succor than the humble instance of prayer, judging it to be, if well and suitably done, like our soldiers gathered for the defense of our public weal, for the repulsion of our injuries, for the well-being of our persons and goods, for the peace and quiet of our bodies and the ministration of our hearts . . . and we take comfort in the labors of the people left behind in our care, whose arms are reckoned to be their prayers and tears.

The aid of ordinary citizens, including women and children, was being enlisted in the English war effort as never before, and this undoubtedly affected how noncombatants on the opposite side of the Channel were treated when encountered by the English army.

Although clerical propaganda during the Hundred Years War focused on benediction of one's own side rather than malediction of the other, the actual language employed makes it clear how hated was the adversary. It is rather disturbing to see members of the Church giving thanks for the deaths of other Christians, as Simon Langham, archbishop of Canterbury, did in 1367 when he ordered prayers of thanksgiving for "the great slaughter of the enemy . . . namely to the number of 6,000 or thereabouts" in the course of the Black Prince's victory over Henry of Trastamara at Nájera in Spain. It could certainly be argued that this went against the spirit, if not the letter, of Christ's command to "love your enemies . . . and pray for them that persecute and calumniate you" or to "love your neighbor as yourself" (Matthew 5:44–45 and 22:39–40). As a matter of fact, Richard Fitzralph, archbishop of Armagh in Ireland, did so object to prayers in support of the king's wars on these very grounds in a sermon preached in London in 1346. Yet Fitzralph's "conscientious objection" was exceptional and even his was qualified by the assurance that Edward III and his army were still deserving of prayers since their war was a just one.

Some priests not only prayed against their enemies, but fought and shed their blood as well. The great theologian St. Thomas Aquinas wrote that "warlike pursuits are altogether incompatible with the duties of a bishop and a cleric," while a fourteenth-century arbiter of the laws of war, Honoré Bouvet, declared that a priest could shed blood in self-defense, but not in attack. Yet during the later Middle Ages, English clerics were being called upon more and more not merely to pray, but to fight. In 1369 Edward III issued the first writ of array for the clergy, who were to act as a kind of home defense in case of invasion, and further calls to arms were issued to the first estate no fewer than ten times during the rest of the fourteenth and early fifteenth centuries. The weaponry that was required of these fighting fathers—lances, swords, knives, axes, and, if suitably trained, bows and arrows—was not exactly designed to maim rather than shed blood, which was permitted for a cleric under a narrow interpretation of canon law.

Even though Edward's 1369 order established an official precedent for clerical violence, it was by no means the first time that the clergy were armed and arrayed on a wide scale. On April 22, 1338, a month after a devastating French raid upon Portsmouth that burned nearly the entire town, Edward III ordered an array on the Isle of Wight in anticipation of a similar attack there. All ecclesiastical personnel on the island were "to find men-at-arms, archers, and others . . . in proportion to the quantity of their lands and goods." This was followed up with similar orders directed to the clergy of the Isle and of the whole diocese of Winchester on February 16 and 28, 1339. When the French assault on Wight finally came in 1340, one of the men commissioned to supervise the array, Sir John de Langford, warden of Carisbrooke Castle, wrote an indignant letter (in French) to the bishop of Winchester, Adam Orleton. Langford accused the Isle's clergy, led by one Thomas de Lisle, parson of Shentling, of refusing to cooperate in the island's defense, resulting in the death of the commander of the local militia, Sir Theobald Russell. Bishop Orelton wrote a sharp letter (again in French) back to Langford on September 12, 1340. In it, he reminded the knight that he had no business arraying the clergy, since this more properly belonged to their ordinary, or ecclesiastical superior, namely himself. Yet on the very same day, Orleton ordered the Isle's dean and Father de Lisle to "warn and induce all and several rectors and vicars of the Isle" to find "suitable arms" in order "to resist the enemy wishing to invade the same Isle" (which in any case was too late since the invasion had already occurred on August 1). At the same time, Orleton, perhaps hoping to avoid the necessity to use arms, ordered that nearly all the spiritual weapons at the Church's command—including prayers, processions, masses, litanies, psalms, and bell ringing—be brought to bear for the sake of peace. Other fighting clerics included John Furneux, rector of Bokesworth in the diocese of Ely, who fell overboard and drowned in June 1340 at the naval battle of Sluys, and priests from the northern dioceses who invaded Scotland in 1346 armed with "swords and arrows at their waists and bows under their arms."

The fourteenth century was by no means the first time the English priesthood took up arms. But by 1369 the English clergy seem to have become almost an extension of the royal army, so thoroughly entwined were they in the war effort. It was not always thus. During the tenth and eleventh centuries the Church proclaimed the Peace and Truce of God that tried, if not to eliminate fighting, at least to limit its destructive scope. When the Church became more involved in war during the crusading movement of the subsequent two centuries, its propaganda was geared toward fighting for a religious cause rather than a national one. There probably was nothing late medieval English clerics could have done but acquiesce in the inexorable onslaught of nationalism. Nevertheless, the Church as an institution was practically the only one capable of halting the Second Rider of the

Apocalypse; yet it surrendered the reins when it placed its services at the disposal of the state.

The Church in France was equally caught up in the propaganda machine of the monarchs. Although no episcopal registers survive in France from the Middle Ages, we know from other records that prayers were on occasion ordered to be said for the well-being of the king and his realm. The chronicler Jean Froissart testifies that on both sides of the Channel the kings sought to explain to their subjects their reasons for going to war, an effort that would imply the medium of parish priests. In addition, we possess a sermon in support of the Valois cause delivered in February 1338, at the very start of the Hundred Years War. In it, Pierre Roger, archbishop of Rouen, trusted adviser and diplomat to King Philip VI, and future Pope Clement VI, harnessed the theory of "just war" to the Valois bandwagon. According to medieval theologians, a just war was one waged by a legitimate authority, for a "just cause," and motivated by a "right intention." The French monarchy was about to face a serious challenge to its legitimacy from its English rival, and Roger chose to ignore the whole question of Edward III's claim to the French throne, focusing instead on Edward's rebelliousness as Philip's vassal for the duchy of Aquitaine. This enabled Roger to portray the French as possessing the all-important just cause that destined them for victory.

On the other hand, the English no less vehemently claimed that *they* were waging a just war. A sermon preached in support of Edward III's Scottish campaign by the archbishop of Canterbury, John Stratford, sometime during the 1330s declared that a just war was one fought "for country" and compared the young king to Christ because he sacrificed his body in battle. Edward himself, in his writs requesting prayers, regularly referred to the "truth and justice of our cause" in his prosecution of the war with France. Both sides thus claimed a monopoly on just wars. There seemed little prospect for peace when neither side was willing to admit that its waging of war was anything less than divinely inspired.

THE FAILURE OF PAPAL DIPLOMACY

In 1309 Pope Clement V moved the headquarters of the Holy See from Rome to Avignon, just outside the southeastern border of France. For the next seventy years, this so-called Babylonian Captivity, evoking the bondage of the Jews to the Babylonians in the Old Testament, fatally undermined the power and prestige of these popes. As long as they resided in Avignon, it seemed to the rest of Europe, and especially to the English, as if they and their conclaves of predominantly French cardinals were mere puppets of the French crown. By the time the Captivity ended with the return of the Apostolic See to Rome in 1378, a even graver crisis erupted when the College of Cardinals split apart and a French contingent elected a pope in Avignon to rival the one in the Eternal City. Antipopes had existed before in papal history, but none before the Great Schism threatened to divide all of Europe along with the pontifical throne.

Unfortunately, the papacy attempted to mediate in the war between England and France at the very time that the Babylonian Captivity compromised any reputation for impartiality that previously it may have had. All three of the French popes who reigned successively from 1334 to 1362—Benedict XII, Clement VI, and Innocent VI—made valiant efforts to make peace during this first and very bloody phase of the Hundred Years War. All three failed miserably. A large part of the reason for this must be that these men were unable to shed their national prejudices along with their French names when they ascended the throne of St. Peter. More important, the English were convinced that French popes could never be fair arbitrators, despite protestations such as the one by Clement upon his accession in 1342 that he wished "to minister to the good of peace, which is our highest aspiration."

At every opportunity, Edward III and his Parliament expressed their distrust of papal intentions and of French churchmen in general. They sought to limit papal influence by a range of restrictions, including the forbidding of appointments of foreigners to English Church offices, forbidding Church appeals outside English courts, suppressing alien priories, stopping papal bulls from entering the realm, and appropriating or forbidding the collection of papal revenues, including even those to pay for cardinals coming to discuss peace terms. In October 1346, two months after Crécy, Archbishop Stratford had to issue what was in effect a countermeasure against royal propaganda in defense of the international crusading order, the Knights of the Hospital of St. John. Due to their association with the French, the Knights, or their representatives, were not even allowed inside parish churches to collect alms, since Stratford had to admonish parishioners to readmit them. After the battle of Poitiers in 1356, taunting graffiti appeared on walls all over Europe: "Now is the pope a Frenchman born, and Christ an Englishman / And the world shall see what the pope can do, more than his Saviour can." An indication of how little faith the English placed in papal diplomacy can be seen when in 1348 Edward believed that a papal-arranged truce was providing cover for the French to make preparations for a massive invasion of his realm. Nor, it must be admitted, did the papacy give the English much reason to be less conspiratorial about its motives. From the very start of the war Benedict XII authorized King Philip to tax the French Church in order to repulse his secular enemies, while Clement VI went even further and allowed taxes collected ostensibly for a crusade to be used by Philip in his private war with England (a concession that Benedict, to his credit, refused to countenance).

Despite its good intentions, the Avignon and subsequently schismatic papacy was an ineffectual mediator throughout the Hundred Years War. It surrendered its international character to the new spirit of nationalism the moment it moved to its "Babylon." The implications of the move were already evident in 1311, when Clement V condemned the international crusading order of the Knights Templar, on charges that included sodomy, idolatry, denial of Jesus Christ, and desecration of the crucifix. Suppression of the order had been initiated four years earlier, when King Philip IV of France, who coveted the order's wealth, arrested all Templars in his realm without consulting the pope. Clement's condemnation was all the more remarkable in that none of the confessions elicited from the Templars in France were repeated in other countries, including England, which forbade the use of torture in judicial procedure. When Clement, under

French pressure, allowed the order of the Templars to die, the appearance, if not the reality, of his successors' impartiality died with it.

WAR AND THE NONCOMBATANT

The implications of the new propaganda—that all citizens, even noncombatants, were participants in, and therefore legitimate targets of, war—were fully realized by the chevauchées, or raids, conducted by English soldiers marching through France, especially during the middle decades of the fourteenth century. It is often pondered how knights, supposedly bound by the code of chivalry, could have perpetrated such ungracious deeds. The answer usually found is that warriors did not consider themselves bound by chivalry's rules when engaging their inferiors, or that armies—in particular the lower class of soldiers—disregarded chivalry altogether during the day-to-day operations of a campaign. If we look at the question from another angle, however, the atrocities appear slightly more justifiable. A victim's actions may, in the eyes of an invading army, bring him lawfully within the purview of war. Especially if the French populace was assumed to be supporting the war effort just as much as in England, there may have been no "innocents" in wartime. Honoré Bouvet, the author of *L'Arbe des Batailles* (The Tree of Battles), a famous fourteenth-century treatise on the laws of war, deplores that "in these days all wars are directed against the poor labouring people and against their goods and chattels. I do not call that war, but it seems to be pillage and robbery." Nonetheless, elsewhere Bouvet declares that ordinary citizens are immune only if they "are unwilling to aid their King in war," which was extremely unlikely. The far more probable scenario, as was the case in the Hundred Years War, was that "if on both sides war is decided upon and begun by the Councils of the two kings, the soldiery may take spoil from the kingdom at will, and make war freely; and if sometimes the humble and innocent suffer harm and lose their goods, it cannot be otherwise." Peasants, like the clergy, were no longer assigned one task in society, namely their work in the fields, but were being drafted into the integrated organism of the state, sharing in all its benefits and misfortunes.

What was the purpose behind these incredibly destructive raids? An obvious motive was the profit and plunder to be had from ransoming prisoners and looting houses and churches, especially if the king was short of cash to pay his troops. But it does not explain some of the seemingly wanton destruction caused by English armies, such as the burning of whole villages that might range ten to forty miles outside their line of march and thus allow little time to seek out valuables. Perhaps this can be explained as part of a general "scorched-earth" policy to sap enemy morale, challenge the legitimacy of the local authority (whose primary function was to protect his subjects), reduce the physical resources with which the enemy could fight, and induce him to accept unfavorable peace terms. Recently, however, a more specifically strategic reason has been offered for the chevauchées: The English were trying to bring the French to battle, despite being outnumbered and seemingly on the run, because they *knew* they could win, having learned a bitter lesson from the Scots (who had employed exactly the same strategy against them). This was not a new tactic, of course. William the Conqueror seems to have employed it in order to induce Harold, his Anglo-Saxon rival, to meet him at Hastings in 1066. The difference is that during the fourteenth century these raids were conducted more often and on a much larger and more systematic scale than ever before. According to one estimate, a two-week chevauchée led by Edward III in 1339 through northeastern France caused as much as £5 million worth of damage, while a campaign led by the Black Prince in 1355 in the southwest of the country inflicted devastation on a total of 18,000 square miles in a little over two months. Nor do these raids made by the regular army represent the ultimate devastation. In addition, there were the depredations of the "Free Companies," or *routiers*, bands of soldiers who had nothing better to do once a campaign was over than continue to prey at leisure on local populations, and who established strongholds for a considerable length of time and over a considerable area of the French countryside. Although not in the pay or under the supervision of the English crown, the Free Companies neverthe-less aided the overall English strategy of undermining the Valois monarchy. As the military historian Clifford Rogers has remarked, France "probably suffered no comparably destructive invasions" as those between 1346 and 1356 until the twentieth century.

There is no shortage of contemporary descriptions of the debilitating effect of the English chevauchées. Perhaps the most famous and often-quoted account is that of the Italian poet Petrarch, who wrote in February 1361 to a French friend:

> As I recently passed through your kingdom on an official
> mission, I could scarcely recognize it as the same one I
> had previously visited. Everywhere were dismal devasta-
> tion, grief, and desolation, everywhere wild and unculti-
> vated fields, everywhere ruined and deserted homes
> except for those spared by being within the walls of a
> fortress or a city, in short, everywhere remained the sad
> vestiges of the Angli [English] and the recent, loathsome
> scars of defeat.

The poet Eustache Deschamps, directing his countrymen's atten-tion to the horrors of war in a 1380 ballad, mourns his home-town, Virtus, burned to the ground by enemy soldiers:

> If you would see great poverty,
> The countryside destroyed and the village deserted,
> Walls ruined where the shield had been,
> Poor abodes and the people discomfited,
> Go straight to Virtus; that's the thing.

The most indignant Frenchman was probably Jean de Venette, prior of the French province of the Carmelite order, who had come from humble beginnings and therefore sympathized with the plight of the poor. In a journal entry for the year 1359, he describes the state of his hometown, Venette near Compiegne in northeastern France, after the passing of some English soldiers:

Soldiers looting and destroying a house: in the fourteenth century (opposite) and in 1066 (pages 88 and 89). (Courtesy British Library and Centre des Monuments Nationaux, Paris.)

The vines in this region, which supply the most pleasant
and desirable liquor which maketh glad the heart of man,
were not pruned or kept from rotting by the labors of
men's hands. The fields were not sown or ploughed.
There were no cattle or fowl in the fields. No cock
crowed in the depths of the night to tell the hours. No
hen called to her chicks. It was of no use for the kite to
lie in wait for chickens in March of this year nor for children to hunt for eggs in secret hiding places. No lambs or
calves bleated after their mothers in this region. The wolf
might seek its prey elsewhere and here fill his capacious
gullet with green grass instead of rams. At this time rab-
bits and hares played freely about in the deserted fields
with no fear of hunting dogs, for no one dared go cours-
ing through the pleasant woods and fields. Larks soared
safely through the air and lifted their unending songs with
no thought of the whistling attacks of eyas or falcon. No
wayfarers went along the roads, carrying their best cheese
and dairy produce to market. Throughout the parishes
and villages, alas! went no mendicants to hear confessions
and to preach in Lent but rather robbers and thieves to
carry off openly whatever they could find. Houses and
churches no longer presented a smiling appearance with
newly repaired roofs but rather the lamentable spectacle

of scattered, smoking ruins to which they had been
reduced by devouring flames. The eye of man was no
longer rejoiced by the accustomed sight of green pastures
and fields charmingly colored by the growing grain, but
rather saddened by the looks of the nettles and thistles
springing up on every side. The pleasant sound of bells
was heard indeed, not as a summons to divine worship,
but as a warning of hostile incursions, in order that men
might seek out hiding places while the enemy were yet on
the way.

Not everyone, of course, was able to successfully hide from the
English raiders. One unfortunate victim, Hugh de Montgeron,
prior of Saint-Thibault of Brailet in the Gâtinais region in east-
central France, pitifully describes the fate of those who were
unable or unwilling to pay the ransoms demanded by the English:

Some they shut up in very dark dungeons, threatening
them daily with death, and continually punishing them
with whippings, wounds, hunger, and want beyond belief.
But others had nothing with which to pay ransom or they

were unwilling to submit to the power of the English. To escape from their hands these made themselves huts in the woods and there ate their bread with fear, sorrow, and great anguish. But the English learned of this and they resolutely sought out these hiding places, searching numerous woods and putting many men to death there. Some they killed, others they captured, still others escaped.

Although Hugh was one of those able to escape for a time by hiding in his hut or fleeing to the swamps, "shivering and shaking with the cold," eventually he was captured twice and deprived of his wine, oats, pigeons, clothes, and all other movable goods. Writing on the inside cover of his prayer book while hiding out from the English behind his barn on November 11, 1359, he ends by addressing his countrymen, "Do you who live in cities and castles ever see trouble equal to my trouble? Farewell."

On the opposite side of the Channel, Englishmen such as Thomas Walsingham gloried in the booty brought back from campaigns. Writing in 1348, Walsingham crowed, "there was not a woman of good name who did not possess something out of the

hands [of former owners] in Caen, Calais, and other towns across the sea: cloth, furs, quilts and utensils, table cloths and necklaces, wooden bowls and silver goblets, linen thread and cloth, were to be seen here and there in every home throughout England." Official campaign letters from the front in 1346 and 1355–56, some by the king and the Black Prince, take evident pride in all the towns and countryside "burnt and destroyed" or "laid waste" by both land and sea. Finally, from Froissart we get an intimate portrait of a freebooter, Squire Bascot de Mauléon, who, somewhat perversely, regales the chronicler with his tale of a career of extortion and general mayhem one night while the two are staying in the same tavern. Perhaps the most entertaining story the old campaigner tells is of how he and five companions dressed up and disguised their voices in order to pass themselves off as women, so that they could approach a town gate unrecognized and give the signal to their band to take it by storm.

To this day, national perspectives are still apparent among historians when discussing the fate of noncombatants during the Hundred Years War. As the French historian Jean Favier has remarked, the chevauchée may be described as a "pleasant jaunt for some, a catastrophe for others." One hundred years ago, Henri Denifle chronicled for his countrymen the "desolation" of French churches and their lands at the hands of English soldiers and freebooters. Basing his study primarily on records in the Vatican archives, he summed up the fourteenth-century evidence thus: "I do not believe that there was in France, in the fourteenth century, a church, a monastery, a hospital that was, if not destroyed, at least untested by the general misery, and that had no cause to deplore, either the devastation of its goods, or the theft of its movables, or the reduction of its revenues, or the diminution of its alms, or a general disorder." Writing shortly after the Second World War, Robert Boutruche chose to find hope in the reconstruction and regeneration of French society in the aftermath of its devastation by France's erstwhile enemies lately turned allies. Most recently, regional studies, such as that by Guy Bois of eastern Normandy, have found evidence of significant demographic decline during the course of the Hundred Years War. Of the 50 percent drop in population in the region between 1347 and 1374, Bois estimates that perhaps 20 percent was due to the ravages of war beginning in the 1350s. As is usual with such studies, however, it is extremely difficult to disentangle the disparate deaths to be accorded to each of the apocalyptic horsemen: Famine, War, and Plague.

If French historians have been preoccupied with counting up their dead, some English scholars have seemed almost willfully ignorant of them. For some decades, the leading medieval historians in England preferred to debate the contributions made to their country's economy by the booty taken from raids in France, to the virtual exclusion of the human factor. A. R. Bridbury, in fact, cavalierly dismissed the damage done by English chevauchées as limited "because there was so little to destroy that could not be quickly and easily rebuilt or made good." The latest attempt by an Englishman to assess the effects of the war on French noncombatants has concluded that their sufferings have been exaggerated by both medieval and modern historians. Instead, Nicholas Wright argues, the French peasant was far from helpless because he had the options of armed resistance or refuge in communal defenses, such as a fortified parish church. One imagines that the men, women, and children who actually suffered through the agonies of war would have seen things quite differently.

THE DISILLUSIONMENT OF DEFEAT

In the long run, England was bound to lose a war in which it was trying to occupy a country and a population many times its size. The strategy of occupation, however, did not fully emerge until the fifteenth century under Henry V. Yet even the limited objectives of Edward III—to acquire the duchy of Aquitaine in full sovereignty, which he nominally achieved by the terms of the Treaty of Brétigny of 1360—proved too much for the administrative abilities of his son, the Black Prince. By the 1370s, under Charles V, "the Wise," the French were turning the tide of war firmly in their favor. Charles achieved this end by actually avoiding open battle and resorting to tactics that slowly whittled the English gains of 1360 to practically nothing. This was a strategy that, as we have seen, was wholly alien to the English. Nonetheless, it worked for two reasons: The political consequences of a major defeat, such as had occurred earlier for France at Crécy and Poitiers, were thereby avoided, and unpopular taxation required to finance a major expedition could be put to better use or dispensed with altogether. By the time of Edward's death in 1377, when England mourned the passing of its heroic warrior king, whose "like," according to Froissart, "had not been seen since the days of King Arthur," the strategy of forgoing full-scale war had become no less attractive on the northern side of the Channel.

What probably determined Edward's grandson and successor, Richard II, to at last put an end to the conflict and pursue a policy of peace was the Peasants' Revolt of 1381. This mass rebellion of commoners, which occurred when the king was just fourteen years of age, was unprecedented in England's history and undoubtedly impressed itself upon the young king's mind. One of the immediate causes of the revolt was the spectacular failure of English campaigns in France in the years leading up to 1381. It has been estimated that the English spent nearly £500,000 on maintaining a military presence abroad in the four years from Richard's accession to the outbreak of the revolt. These expenditures had to be paid for by heavy taxation, culminating in the hated poll tax, or a tax per head, that was the immediate spark of the rebellion. Moreover, not only had English armies failed to make any headway in France, but, since the defeat of the English navy at La Rochelle in 1372, Britain was once again exposed, as at the start of the war, to raids on the southern coast by French and Spanish pirates. The situation was remarkably similar to that in France in 1358, when it faced the extremely bloodthirsty revolt of the Jacquerie, who were rumored to have roasted the bodies of their lords and then forced their wives and children to eat them. As was to be the case in England, the French crisis was provoked by a military defeat, in this instance the capture of King John at Poitiers two years earlier, which in turn had necessitated the imposition of taxes to pay the huge ransom of 3 million écus, or approximately £500,000, for John's release. The eighteen-year-old dauphin Charles (the future Charles V), roundly criticized for fleeing the battle, was left to face an attempted usurpation of the government in Paris at the same time as the Jacques rose in the countryside.

There also might be said to have been a "grass-roots" campaign for peace at this time. Perhaps the most outspoken critic, not only of the Hundred Years War but of war in general, was the Oxford theologian and sermonist John Wycliffe. By equating war with sin, especially anger, and adopting a literal approach to biblical admonitions against killing, Wycliffe was led to reject wars altogether, even just ones. Moreover, he accused the Church, headed by the pope, of bearing the primary responsibility for war's proliferation, going so far as to call clergymen the "enemies of peace" whose "prayers are cursed." Yet Wycliffe and his later Lollard followers went too far in rejecting any type of killing, even in self defense, to be considered a part of the cultural mainstream. At the same time, entirely orthodox preachers like Thomas Brinton, bishop of Rochester, and the Dominican John Bromyard took up the cause of encouraging their audience to pray for peace rather than war, viewing the latter as a scourge from God brought upon man by his sin, much like famine and plague.

If Wycliffe was too radical for most Englishmen's blood, an author more representative of the educated gentry class, John Gower, nevertheless echoes some of the fiery sentiments against war. For Gower, a just war can become unjust through the greed, pride, lust, and other unworthy motives of those who wage it. Gower likewise rounds on the clergy for supporting and engaging in war, which in his view both goes against the example of Christ and is unnatural. Just as "it is not the function of a knight to offer sacrifice at the altar," so it is not "that of a priest to carry on wars of state." He fears that if the Church continues to engage in war "then war will last forever," for "if those who ought to restore peace practice war, I do not know how one can safely enter upon the path of peace." Even when he abandons his political support of Richard II in favor of his usurper, Henry IV, Gower continues to extol the benefits of peace as a more natural state of man than war in his address to the new king.

Gower's more famous contemporary, Chaucer, despite having had actual experience of war, is more circumspect in his pacifist leanings, perhaps becaues of his greater prominence and patronage at court. Even so, Chaucer's knights are typically fainthearted warriors, and significantly, the only story in *The Canterbury Tales* narrated by the author himself, the "Tale of Melibeus," is adapted from a political work of the thirteenth century that explicitly counsels against war. Prudence's persistent advice to her husband, Melibeus, that he avoid war at any cost may have been a thinly veiled message to the young Richard II.

Yet another fin de siècle poet, William Langland, in his allegorical poem *Piers Plowman*, has Peace complain to the King of all the wrongs committed against him in war:

Then came Peace into parliament, and put forth a plea,
How Wrong 'gainst his will, had abducted his wife,
Had borne away Rose, Sir Reginald's love,
And Malkin the maiden, with merciless force—
"My geese and my swine his serving-men steal,
I dare not, for fear of him, fight or complain.
My bay horse he borrowed, and brought him home never,
For pence, in repayment, I pleaded in vain.
His men he maintaineth, to murder my hinds,
Forestalleth my fairs, and fights in my market,
Breaks up my barn-doors, and bears away wheat,
Tenders a tally for ten quarters of oats,
Mauls me with bruises, maltreats my maid;
I scarce have the boldness his presence to bear."

Rape, theft, unpaid requisitions, or purveyance, disruption of trade, assaults: All were part of the horrors of war and potent arguments for peace. Nevertheless, Langland, writing the B-text of his poem in the late 1370s, disillusioned by the end of one reign and before evidence of promise in another, predicted that lasting peace would only come with the Second Coming of Christ at the Apocalypse.

Even when a work such as the *Morte Arthure,* an alliterative poem that can be considered typical of many other late medieval

English romances, treats of a theme that would have been dear to the heart of Richard's grandfather, it does so in a way that seems very critical of the warmaking policies of the previous reign. Dating perhaps to the last decade of the fourteenth century, the *Morte Arthure* contains many of the usual elements of the Arthur story—the round table, Arthur's betrayal by "Mordrede," and the king's final departure for Avalon—yet its realistic depiction of Arthur's war against the Roman emperor, Lucius, on the Continent bears some striking similarities to Edward III's campaigns of the 1340s and 1350s. Rather than indulge in the usual glorification of the Arthurian regime, the anonymous poet portrays Arthur as motivated by overweening pride and ambition, which leads to the sacking and pillaging of towns, the death of his knights, and the neglect of his island kingdom. By stripping Arthur—a figure so closely identified with Edward III—of much of his heroic and supernatural qualities, and by depicting war in so graphic and violent a manner, the *Morte Arthure* strikes a powerful blow at the warrior ethos of the mid-fourteenth century.

Across the Channel in France, the most outspoken advocate of peace was Philippe de Mézières, close friend and adviser to Charles V and tutor to his son and successor, Charles VI. A writer who, like Chaucer, had direct knowledge of war, Mézières made his most urgent appeal for concord between England and France in his *Epistre au Roi Richart* (Letter to King Richard II). Although obviously addressed to the English monarch, the letter urges both kings (Richard II and Charles VI) to stay the course of peace negotiations and warns of the terrible consequences of a resumption of war. In his famous parable of the "Garden of Horror and Perils," Mézières conjures up a nightmarish world ruled by war, where armies are like leeches and locusts, who "suck the blood of the poor" and devour "all the green things of the garden, right down to the roots." Elsewhere, he is even more explicit about the evils attendant upon war:

O evil, perilous and mortal wound, by whose poison so
many kings, dukes, counts, and barons, and the ancient
and valiant chivalry, both of France and England, and
elsewhere, have been brought so tragically to destruction

of body and soul: Alas, alas, how many churches by the venom of the said wound have been destroyed! How many widows and orphans created, to die of hunger and ill-treatment!

Mézières was joined in his abhorrence of war by the court poet Eustache Deschamps. In one ballad, the poet, exasperated by forty years of praying for peace while waiting for negotiators to come to an agreement, suggests that men fight for no better reason than that "if we cannot have peace, let us have war! War!" In another poem, he warns two friends about to go off on a "war of adventure" of the coming dangers and hardships they will face and urges them to "come back home" if war persists too long.

The pacifist sentiments expressed by all these men were no passing fancies. They were taken up in the next century by the Englishmen Thomas Hoccleve, John Lydgate, and George Ashby and by the French authors Christine de Pisan, Georges Chastellain, Jean Meschinot, and Pierre de Nesson. Lydate especially in his *Praise of Peace*, written between 1422 and 1443, expressed a new desire to condemn war without exception: "All war is dreadful," as the author says emphatically toward the end of the poem. Yet foreign policy was a royal prerogative that paid little heed to the fanciful whims of writers. Arguably the only attempt to find a peaceful settlement without resort to war during more than a hundred years of conflict began and ended with the reign of one man: Richard II.

A BRIEF FLOWERING OF PEACE

It may have been easy for pacifists to condemn war, but negotiating the diplomatics of peace was another matter. In 1396 Richard II and Charles VI concluded a twenty-eight-year truce between their kingdoms, which had been at war for over half a century. Hopes were entertained of arranging a final, permanent peace between the two sides, but these were dashed by irreconcilable differences over the English duchy of Aquitaine and its relationship to the French crown. Nevertheless, by the terms of the truce, fighting was to cease for at least a generation.

Simply to get to this point had required over a decade of subtle diplomacy. From at least 1383, the English had been negotiating for an end to the war, and from 1389, a series of short-term truces had preceded the settlement of 1396. Along the way, abundant obstacles had to be overcome. In 1388, five Appellants temporarily took charge of the English government, purging ministers key to the king's peacemaking policies in the so-called Merciless Parliament, and reviving a warlike stance toward France. In 1393 a peace treaty that was to be hammered out during a meeting between Richard and Charles had to be abandoned because the latter went mad. Another factor that scuttled negotiations that year was a rising of pro-war gentry in Cheshire that forced the recall of the English delegation. The next year, 1394, saw a second revolt against peace, this time among the commons of Gascony in southwestern France, who protested their proposed separation from the English crown. It may have been England's failure to adequately suppress the uprising in this diplomatically crucial duchy that convinced the French that they could never make an enduring peace with their enemy.

That a truce lasting as long as twenty-eight years was made at all was a personal triumph for Richard II. To a large degree, it was his individual initiative that brought about this brief flowering of peace. Apparently, his search for a new wife after the death of his beloved queen, Anne of Bohemia, in 1394 prompted the French into offering the hand of their six-year-old princess, Isabella, rather than see him married off to a rival. Although the truce was to remain in force even should the marriage be annulled, Richard's union with Isabella, accompanied by a dowry of 800,000 francs, was looked upon by contemporaries as the lynchpin that would hold the two countries together in an embrace of love rather than discord. In his open letter to Richard, Philippe de Mézières devotes a whole chapter to the much-anticipated nuptials; Mézières sternly warns the king to marry for the right reasons, that is, for the sake of peace and the good qualities of his

future consort, rather than for the more mundane objects of producing heirs or making strategic alliances. Eustache Deschamps,
more confidently upbeat about the union, celebrates it as the end
to the war and its attendant sufferings, for, "Every peace comes
by a holy marriage." Deschamps's optimism was to find an echo
in that of Hoccleve upon yet another union between an English
king and a daughter of Charles VI, the marriage of Henry V and
Catherine as arranged by the Treaty of Troyes of 1420. The second marriage, however, could be said to have been predicated on
dynastic usurpation and conquest rather than, as Hoccleve naively
believed, a truly amicable peace.

The ceremonial delivery of Isabella by her father, Charles, at
Ardres near Calais in October 1396 gave Richard ample scope to
display his particular talents. At this first and last conference
between the two monarchs, Richard indulged in the visual display
that he so loved and relied upon to define his kingship. According
to an eyewitness account, the English king came splendidly
attired in a long gown of red velvet emblazoned over the chest
with his badge, the white hart, and sporting on his head "a full
bonnet [encrusted] with precious stones." This last article of
clothing had been a gift from Charles and ironically was used by
Richard to outshine his French counterpart. That he succeeded
admirably in this is attested by the space devoted to describing his
dress, a rarity in medieval annals. The two kings advanced from
their respective pavilions over an equidistant field and then
greeted each other as their kneeling attendants looked on. Such
a public forum was a perfect setting for Richard to flaunt his sar-
torial prowess. To make peace, he waged a fashion war.

Needless to say, not everyone was so enchanted with what was
regarded in some circles as a foppish and lily-livered foreign policy. This was particularly true of a rapidly aging generation of
English nobility and gentry who had participated in, and fondly
remembered, the "glory days" of English victories in France.
Their archetype and spokesman was Thomas of Woodstock, duke
of Gloucester, the youngest of the king's uncles. Ironically, his
own military career had been less than stellar. In 1380 he led a
chevauchée of more than 5,000 men across northern France that
achieved little and necessitated the imposition of the third poll tax

that directly led to the Peasants' Revolt. In 1388, as leader of the Appellants who reversed the king's pacific policies, he reopened the war with France only to see a naval expedition to Brittany founder and, what was worse, the North invaded by the Scots, who defeated an English army at Otterburn. To cap it all, these failures had to be paid for by yet more taxes.

By 1396, in what must have been for him a bitter twist of fate, Gloucester took part in the lavish peacefest at Ardres, though he never seems to have lost his battle-hardened bravado. In this setting, Froissart attributes to him words that, if not actually spoken, capture just the right tone of an unrepentantly belligerent duke:

> I am the youngest of King Edward's sons, but if I was listened to I would be the first to renew the wars and put a stop to the encroachments we have suffered and are still suffering every day, thanks to our simplicity and slackness. I mean particularly the slackness of our leader the king, who has just allied himself by marriage with his principal enemy. That's hardly a sign that he wants to fight him. No, he's too fat in the arse and only interested in eating and drinking. That's no life for a fighting man, who ought to be hard and lean and bent on glory. I still remember my last campaign in France. I suppose I had two thousand lances and eight thousand archers with me. [Actually, the duke had half this number during his chevauchée of 1380.] We sliced right through the kingdom of France, moving out and across from Calais, and we never found anyone who dared come out and fight us.

Undoubtedly, many close to the king considered this to be an extremely reactionary attitude, one best ignored. Despite Gloucester's confident assertion that "the people of this country want war," it is hard to believe that many would not have welcomed the relief from taxation that peace would bring.

While Gloucester and his jingoism may have been regarded by Richard's courtiers as somewhat ridiculous, the king himself did not seem to be laughing. By 1397, Richard felt threatened enough by his uncle to have him summarily arrested and eventually murdered in his prison at Calais. The main cause of Richard's grievance with the duke was the humiliation and possibly a brief usurpation he had suffered at the latter's hands during the days of the Appellants' triumph in 1388. But Gloucester's known opposition to the 1396 truce, with its undertones of rebellion and which Richard seems to have been secretly monitoring, may have revived in the king a decade-long grudge harbored against his nemesis.

A less drastic but no less imperative response required of the king, if the truce was to remain in force, was to reverse the war culture that had been in place for two generations or more since 1337. This was going to be far harder to dislodge, since, as we have seen, a very effective propaganda machine had been devoted to its cause. Moreover, the celebrated victories of the 1340s and 1350s had created their own momentum and conviction that more were on the way if only the war was continued.

Nevertheless, there are indications that Richard began taking steps in this regard even before the peace was sealed. In 1383, he had prefaced his commission to his uncle, John of Gaunt, duke of Lancaster, to treat for peace with France by denouncing war in the strongest terms. War, the king had said, resulted in "a shedding of Christian blood, a great destruction and sacrilegious desolation of churches and monasteries and other pious places, the deflowering of virgins, the violation of wives and a most heinous dishonoring of other women, a most impious oppression of innocent people, and other detestable evils which are more than can be easily described by word or speech."

From this time onwards, in fact, the king was to regularly employ in his diplomatic correspondence some formulaic phrase that expressed his preference for peace over war. When the king ordered prayers to be said in support of Gaunt's peace mission of 1384, he declared, in a reversal of previous wartime propaganda, that "always we have especially desired in our prayers that our subjects . . . may repose in a firm peace under our rule," and that "we wish nothing more than to try to our utmost to have the said peace." In 1389 Richard ordered all the sheriffs to proclaim to the people that the latest taxes of a tenth and a fifteenth of movable goods would be waived provided he concluded a truce with France, a promise that, in this instance, he was able to make good. In 1396 another round of prayers was offered in support of the "perpetual peace" to be sealed at Ardres. At the parliament held in January 1397, the king "with his own mouth" defended before the assembled commons his recently enacted twenty-eight-year truce with France. The truce came under fire (led, pre-dictably, by Gloucester) when Richard proposed aiding a French expedition against Milan in order to help end the Great Schism and fulfill one of the peace terms. The king's first and primary justification for upholding the truce, he said, was

> to bring peace and stop the wars of his realm, and
> to avoid the misfortunes that came from war to his realm
> and to his people, and also in order that the very great
> benefits and promises [produced] by reason of a lengthy
> state of peace, quiet, and safety will endure in his realm
> and for his subjects of England, and to arouse in his said
> father-in-law [the king] of France a greater love toward
> himself and his realm and his people in times to come.

Nor was this all. Richard privately communicated to many his peaceful intentions, which were passed down the grapevine to end up in chronicles and other works, no doubt exactly as the king had planned. Thus, Froissart reports the gossip, probably dating to 1395, of Sir Jean de Grailly, bastard son of a French nobleman, that Richard was prepared to make peace by marrying Isabella no matter what the cost in terms of bad publicity:

> He is attracted to the daughter of the king of France and
> to no one else, and it has caused some dismay in this
> country that he should wish to marry his adversary's
> daughter. It does him no good with his people, but he
> takes no notice. He makes it clear, as he has always done,
> that he would rather make war elsewhere than on France,
> desiring—as we already know of him by past experience—
> that there should be a lasting peace between him and the

king of France and their two countries. He says that the
war has gone on too long between him and his ancestors
and the French, that too many brave men have been
killed in it, too many evil deeds perpetrated, and too
many Christian people destroyed or ruined, to the detriment of the Christian faith.

Eight years before, in 1387, the *Westminster Chronicle* had put
it about that the king wished to avoid war because otherwise "he
would inevitably be compelled to be for ever burdening his people with new imposts, with damaging results for himself." But
perhaps the most enthusiastic peace propagandist on Richard's
behalf was Philippe de Mézières. In his *Songe de Vieil Pèlerin*
(Song of the Old Pilgrim), written perhaps in 1389, shortly after
the Merciless Parliament, Mézières urges both kings to "pay no
heed to the advice of certain generals, who have been reared in
war and enriched by it." In an allegorical passage (conveying a
similar message perhaps to that in Chaucer's "Tale of Melibeus"),
Mézières describes Richard as the "white boar" who wishes to
"sheathe the sword and make a good peace with the king of
France" but is impeded by the "black boars," namely his warlike
uncles. Mézières pursues a similar allegorical conceit in his *Epistre*
of 1395, in which he praises Richard's departure from the warmaking heritage of his father and grandfather (respectively, the
Black Prince and Edward III):

> The very gracious and loving King Richard, following the
> vocation to which he had been called and predestined by
> Jesus, the gentle Author of peace, was, so to say, trans-
> muted from the nature of the Black Boars from whom he
> sprang, into the precious lodestone, with its miraculous
> power of attraction, as we have explained earlier, and
> afterwards into the rich diamond. And he was transported
> by fraternal love towards his brother, King Charles, and
> the transport was so strong and great that, by the good-
> ness of God, in a brief moment the glowing carbuncle
> was also transmuted figuratively speaking by the virtue

and love of the diamond, and carried into the heart and
soul of our diamond in such a way that the love of the
two precious stones, by the grace of God, became merged
into one whole, to the satisfaction of this Old Solitary and
all good men.

By astutely appealing to Richard's love of the visually beautiful,
Mézières hoped to persuade his royal correspondent, as well as
others, to stay the course of peace.

Whether and by how much all this peaceful propaganda
changed people's attitudes toward war is difficult to say.
According to Ben Lowe, an expert on late medieval English pacifism, "opposition to war . . . had permeated all layers of society
by the end of the fourteenth century." Lowe's contention, however, that widespread opposition in England to war continued
even during the victorious and popular reign of Henry V is hard
to accept. Disillusionment with war probably did not set in again
until the 1430s, with the decisive reversal of English fortunes,
despite the execution of Joan of Arc. And of course, the end of
the Hundred Years War in 1453 was followed almost immediately
by the War of the Roses, in which Englishmen discovered an
appetite to wage war on each other. Perhaps if Richard had
reigned longer, a "peace cluture" would have emerged to tame
late medieval Englishmen's warlike ways. By the end of
September 1399 Richard was deposed by his exiled cousin,
Henry Bolingbroke, who took advantage of widespread disaffec-
tion with Richard's tyranny and the king's absence on campaign
in Ireland to return home to be crowned Henry IV. By February
1400 Richard was dead, probably starved to death by his jailers at
Henry's castle at Pontefract, Yorkshire. In 1401 Isabella,
Richard's former queen, was sent back to France, and well could
Deschamps wonder, "What will become of the grieving widow?"
The very personal foundation of the truce between the two countries was therefore at an end.

We are told by one historian of the Hundred Years War, A. R.
Bridbury, that "peacetime, when it did not serve some profes-
sional or political purpose, was merely a wearisome break, a

demoralizing interlude which had to be got through somehow without loss of spirit or skill, self respect or honour." Likewise, the fourteenth-century expert on war Honoré Bouvet pessimistically declared that just as "it is impossible for the sky to be at rest," so is it for the world to be at peace, although if God wished it so, it could certainly happen. This fatalistic approach to the possibilities of peace was fairly typical of the time and can be traced all the way back to St. Augustine's concept of just war in the early Christian era, which declared war to be the unavoidable lot of fallen man, with peace reserved for the heavenly realm. Yet it could be argued that Richard II had demonstrated peace to be possible, and therefore his efforts represent an ideological seachange: As Lowe points out, late medieval pacifism laid the foundations for a "peace ethic" that emerged during the early modern period, when English humanists no longer viewed peace as an unattainable ideal but as a practical objective of foreign policy. Indeed, if Richard's reign had continued, we might now be talking of a war of fifty rather than a hundred years. Relations between Richard and the French court remained amicable right up until his deposition, and chroniclers across the Channel loudly lamented his demise. In England itself, none of the thiry-three "objections" presented before the Parliament of October 6, 1399, in order to justify the deposition mention the truce, except insofar that Richard did not use it to alleviate the tax burden on his subjects, as he had originally promised. Richard's reign ended for reasons of domestic political tyranny that began to emerge in 1397 and had little to do with foreign policy.

So many factors went into the making of war and peace, even in the fledgling medieval state, that we probably will never know what tipped the balance in favor of one or the other. Unquestionably, the public mood played a large role in influencing royal policy. Both Edward III and Henry V badly needed to restore confidence in the monarchy after a recent, quasi-legal transition from a hated tyranny. Uniting the country in war was one way of achieving that end. Richard, on the other hand, sought to avoid the political costs that seeking taxes from Parliament in order to pay for war would have necessitated, an absolutist policy that invites comparison with a later king of England who also came to a bad end: Charles I.

In addition there were private and personal factors at work that can only be explained in terms of an individual ruler's psychology. Edward's father, Edward II, was a homosexual, a fact that, according to several chronicles, influenced the horrible manner of his death by a branding iron thrust into his bowels. Thus there is the possibility that once on the throne, the son felt the need to raise the royal testosterone level by plunging into war, hosting tournaments (which had been banned under his father), and siring no fewer than five sons. Henry V likewise seems to have succumbed to the urge to make a clean break with the past, in his case by renouncing a dissolute youth and assuming the stern raiment of war.

Richard had believed differently. According to his own words and the words of others, he had a genuine liking for peace and a sincere abhorrence of war. This was apparently matched by his desire to lower violence within the realm, chiefly by legislating against the giving of liveries—or distinctive clothing and badges—by noblemen and the wearing of them by retainers in order to signify that they enjoyed their patron's protection and thereby were virtually immune from the law. English lords' maintenance of large private armies of ruffians by a system of monetary contract rather than traditional grants of land has been dubbed by historians as "bastard feudalism" and blamed for the endemic bloodshed of the War of the Roses during the latter half of the fifteenth century. Like the evils of war itself, those of bastard feudalism seem to have presented an insoluble problem to the English crown. But that does not mean that solutions were not worth being tried.

Richard's reign represents an important departure from the warmongering that had characterized the foreign policy of his predecessor. It gave both England and France an important breathing space in order to recover from the miseries and pressures that war had inflicted. This does not mean that Richard was an ideal monarch. In domestic terms his rule, especially toward the end, was a disaster. He murdered and exiled enemies, suppressed dissent in the Commons, arbitrarily raised forced loans and taxes, and, perhaps most shortsightedly of all, confiscated private property, whose inviolability was one of the cornerstones of the English constitution. But Richard's commitment to the cause of ending war is surely one of his few qualities worthy of our emulation. In a reversal of previous policy, his propaganda trumpeted the benefits of peace rather than the glories of war, and if only such sentiments had arisen earlier in the century, starving peasants during the Great Famine might have suffered a little less. Richard was the rare king who tried to rein in the horseman of War, but he did not reign long enough or well enough to give peace a fighting chance.

PLAGUE

And in many places in Siena great pits were dug and piled deep with the multitude of dead. And they died by the hundreds, both day and night, and all were thrown in those ditches and covered with earth. And as soon as those ditches were filled, more were dug. And I, Agnolo di Tura, called the Fat, buried my five children with my own hands. And there were also those who were so sparsely covered with earth that the dogs dragged them forth and devoured many bodies throughout the city. There was no one who wept for any death, for all awaited death. And so many died that all believed it was the end of the world.

—Agnolo di Tura, *Cronaca Senese*, 1348

Ever since man began to settle down several millennia ago and live in close quarters with his fellow human beings, along with his newly domesticated animals, he has been plagued by epidemic diseases. Smallpox, cholera, influenza, tuberculosis, typhoid fever, and most recently AIDS are but a few of the many maladies that caused the deaths of untold millions before we had begun to find a cure. Some of these diseases have changed history. During the thirteenth century B.C. a succession of plagues convinced the pharaoh of Egypt to let his Hebrew slaves, led by Moses, return to their "promised land" in Palestine, an event recorded in the Book of Exodus in the Old Testament. Between 430 and 426 B.C. a plague devastated the crowded city of Athens, killing its leading statesman, Pericles, and bringing to the fore political newcomers like Alcibiades who altered the course of the Peloponnesian War. In the early sixteenth century A.D. the Spanish adventurers Hernando Cortés and Francisco Pizarro conquered the Aztec and Inca empires of Central and South America largely with the help of the smallpox virus, to which the Indians had no prior exposure and therefore no immunity. And in 1861 typhoid fever from the sewers of Windsor Castle struck down Prince Albert, consort of Queen Victoria, plunging her and her empire into protracted mourning.

But even compared to these remarkable events, the Black Death of 1348–49 was unique in history. Never before and never since has so much disproportionate death come in such a short period of time. Imagine that, tomorrow or the next day, every other person you see around you may be dead, and you may grasp something of the terror that this disease could inspire. Nor did the Black Death strike just once but many times, although with a virulence that never matched the original outbreak, throughout the second half of the fourteenth and the fifteenth centuries. Little wonder that chroniclers of the plague, such as Gabriele de Mussis, Louis Heyligen, and John Clynn, saw it as a sign that the Apocalypse, the end of the world, was at hand.

CAUSES AND CURES

Today the plague holds little of its former mystery and horror, for we know exactly how it is spread and how it can be cured. The Black Death is caused by a bacterium called *Yersina pestis* or *Pasteurella pestis*, a microscopic, one-celled organism that multiplies rapidly once inside its host and produces three types of symptoms, depending on how it is spread. In the most famous and perhaps the most common type, known as bubonic plague, the deadly bacteria are carried in the stomach of a flea, such as *Xenopsylla cheopsis*, which normally resides in the fur of animals (though it is less discriminating when its usual hosts are dead), or *Pulex irritans*, which feasts on humans. A flea infested with plague bacteria must constantly feed since its stomach is full of perhaps thousands of such organisms, leaving no room for its ordinary food, blood. Consequently, when a "blocked" flea "bites" its victim, it regurgitates a blood and bacterial mixture back into the host, thus transmitting the disease. The resultant swellings, known as buboes (hence bubonic) appear where the lymph glands, part of the body's immune system, are trying to combat the disease, namely in the neck, armpits, and the groin. Other symptoms may include fever, violent headaches, subcutaneous bleeding, and neurological disorders, such as chorea, an uncontrollable movement of the limbs that may have given rise, as we will see, to the tradition of the Danse Macabre. Death occurs in about 60 percent of the cases of bubonic plague, usually within five days of the onset of symptoms. Some victims therefore survived this form of the disease, albeit scarred from where their buboes had burst and released their pus.

With a second type of plague, called pneumonic, the bacteria invade the lungs and are spread by airborne droplets, much like the common cold. Its symptoms include the coughing up of blood, and pneumonic plague is very contagious and quite fatal, causing death in almost 100 percent of its victims within three days. It seems to have waxed during the winter months, unlike bubonic plague, which is associated with the summer when a warm, moist climate favors flea activity.

Lastly, some contemporary accounts describe cases of plague where people die suddenly, on the day of infection, dropping dead in the streets or simply never waking from their slumbers. At Cambridge, a new master of the Hospital of St. John, Robert de Sprouston, having assumed his post on May 2, 1349, died within a day. He was replaced by a new master, Roger de Broom, on the next. Evidence such as this indicates a third type of the disease, known as septicemic plague, that could kill within hours. How exactly it was transmitted remains a mystery, for it acted so quickly as to leave almost no symptoms. A Paduan chronicler described it as a "blood poisoning," suggesting a sudden and overwhelming invasion of the bloodstream by the bacteria.

It has been wondered how plague, especially the bubonic kind, could have traveled throughout Europe "with the speed," to borrow the words from the introduction to Giovanni Boccaccio's *Decameron*, "of a fire racing through dry or oily substances that happened to be placed within its reach." Undoubtedly medieval hygiene was a major factor in the spread of the disease. One can speculate about how rarely the average person of the Middle Ages took a bath: For many peasants, especially those who lived far from a major waterway, baptism was probably the first and last full immersion. Public baths were equated with houses of prostitution, and bathing in general was looked upon with suspicion as leading to immoral acts. King John of England may have indulged in princely extravagance when he took three baths in as many months in 1212, while the monks of the great Benedictine house of Cluny in east-central France were required to bathe but twice a year. Clothes were rarely changed, except perhaps for church. People probably also slept in them for the sake of warmth and protection against the irritation of straw mattresses, while often one bed had to accommodate all members of the family. At the same time, human waste could not simply be flushed out of sight. Urine, excrement, and the blood of slaughtered animals all mingled together in the streets.

By the fourteenth century, most peasant houses in England and northern Europe were made of timber frames set on stone foundations. Even so, their earthen floors and walls and thatch roofs gave ample hospitality to the black rat, or *Rattus rattus*, which is thought to have introduced fleas bearing the plague bacteria into Europe. Houses that were still of the "long" variety housed other animals, such as cows, pigs, sheep, chickens, and, of course, cats and dogs—all of whom carried fleas—together with their masters under one roof. Floors were not swept, but lain with rushes that, as the great humanist Erasmus testifies, sometimes were not changed for twenty years. Not surprisingly, most people hosted a microscopic zoo, including the flea, on their bodies as well as in their clothes and in their bedding. In fact, fleas have been a scourge of human hygiene until relatively recently: Seventeenth-century French fashion introduced puce, a brownish purple dye specifically to hide the unflattering creatures on the body. It was not until fumigation techniques were introduced into the trenches of World War I that the flea was eliminated as a constant companion.

Although other bacterial diseases, such as anthrax or typhus, have been proposed as alternative candidates for what we call the Black Death, none of them fit the mortality patterns any better than the plague. Skeptics of plague virulence note that there may not have been enough rats to spread the disease, that some symptoms described by contemporaries are not indicative of plague, and that some carriers, particularly rats, escaped death themselves. None of these arguments disproves the presence of plague. Rats, for instance, are not essential for transmission of the disease. In addition to airborne contagion, plague bacilli can travel long distances in fleas that burrow in merchandise such as wool packs, and the mild, wet winters reported for 1348–49 may have made it possible for them to do so year round. What is more, the mutating ability of the DNA in the plague bacillus may have drastically increased its virulence (and the variety of its symptoms) during the fourteenth century. The mystery, such as it is, probably will be solved in the near future by increasingly sophisticated forensic techniques on the remains of our unfortunate ancestors.

Though plague is now easily cured by a dose of penicillin, the Middle Ages, of course, lacked our modern medical knowledge, as causes and cures of disease remained, for the most part, elusive. The medieval diagnosis for the Black Death generally fell into one of two categories. The more common explanation was that the plague was God's scourge, his righteous retribution raining down like arrows from the sky upon man in terrible judgment of his abundant wickedness and sin. Some such lament occurs in most chronicles of the plague and in the preambles of letters by which English bishops ordered processions and prayers to ward off the pestilence. Even authors like Gilles li Muisis, abbot of St. Giles in Tournai, who subscribed to a "scientific" explanation of the disease, were careful to emphasize that they did not "put more trust in the sayings and prognostications of astrologers and mathematicians than faith allows." Medical authorities frankly admitted that they could do little or nothing if the plague sprang directly from the will of God. Such references to the plague as the agent of God's vengeance tended to be self-castigating. Perhaps the most scolding of such lectures on how well man deserved this great mortality came from Gabriele de Mussis, a lawyer from Piacenza who died in 1356. In a dialogue between God and Earth with which he opens his *Historia de Morbo* (History of "the Death"), Mussis condemns man to the just hatred of God:

> May this stand as a perpetual reminder to everyone, now living and yet to be born, how almighty God, king of heaven, lord of the living and of the dead, who holds all things in his hand, looked down from heaven and saw the entire human race wallowing in the mire of manifold wickedness, enmeshed in wrongdoing, pursuing numberless vices, drowning in a sea of depravity because of a limitless capacity for evil, bereft of all goodness, not fearing the judgements of God, and chasing after everything evil, regardless of how hateful and loathsome it was. Seeing such things He called out to the earth: "What are you doing, held captive by gangs of worthless men, soiled with the filth of sinners? Are you totally helpless? What are you doing? Why do you not demand human blood in vengeance for this wrongdoing? Why do you tolerate my enemies and adversaries? When confronted by such wantonness you should have swallowed my opponents. Make yourself ready to exercise the vengeance which lies within your power."

Mussis follows this scolding with a long list of ways in which the human race could improve itself, which, as we will see, were rivaled by the Flagellants' own terrible answer to the call for atonement.

Despite the primacy of God's anger as the acknowledged cause of the pestilence, a scientific—primarily astrological—explanation gained wide circulation. The authority of the scholars at the University of Paris undoubtedly counted for much in this regard. In October 1348, in response to a request from King Philip VI of France, the medical faculty pronounced that the plague had been caused by a conjunction of the planets Saturn, Jupiter, and Mars at precisely 1:00 P.M. on March 20, 1345. The essence of this "universal and distant" cause is that when the three planets line up in their respective orbits, Saturn and Mars, both malevolent planets breeding illnesses and wars, outweigh the benign influence of Jupiter. In the words of the medical faculty, "Jupiter, being wet and hot, draws up evil vapors from the earth, and Mars, because it is immoderately hot and dry, then ignites the vapors, and as a result there were lightnings, sparks, noxious vapors and fires throughout the air." Nevertheless, the dons of Paris also admitted of "particular and near" causes of the vile, plague-producing vapors, such as earthquakes and exhalations from swamps and rotting corpses. All these explanations were repeated in various forms by other authorities and chroniclers. If at times their confident assertions—based on the observations of such unimpeachable authorities as Aristotle, Ptolemy, and Albertus Magnus—sound pompous and obscure, one suspects that they are in fact hiding their utter bafflement in the face of a catastrophe such as the Black Death.

However this may be, the idea that the plague traveled in corrupted air conditioned the preventive measures men took to try to ward off the disease. The most common antidote recommended against the poisoned atmosphere were aromatics, such as sweet-smelling herbs, flowers, and perfumes, that were to be sprinkled in the house or carried under the nose. On the other hand, a rival medical opinion advised ingesting foul odors, such as by collecting the contents of privies and sitting over them with a towel over one's head. Under no circumstances should baths be taken, lest they open up the pores of the body to the infected air, or miasma (a prescription no doubt much appreciated by fleas). Violent exercise, especially of the sexual kind, should be avoided as it could overheat the body and make one more susceptible to invasion. Diet had to be carefully regulated. Hot or spicy foods were to be shunned, but wine was beneficial, as Gilles li Muisis testifies when he claims that no one who drank wine in Tournai died. Purging the body with laxatives or by vomiting on an empty stomach once a day also was recommended. Some even bathed in their own urine or drank the pus of lanced buboes in their desperation to find a way to "vaccinate" themselves against the epidemic.

Cures for the plague were even more hard to come by. The standard medieval medical response to serious illness, taking its cue from the ancient Greek physician Hippocrates, was to open the veins with a knife or use leeches in order to let out a certain amount of blood from the body. The purpose of this was to restore the balance of the body's four humors—blood, phlegm, choler or yellow bile, and melancholy or black bile. An excess of one of the humors, it was believed, could produce unhealthy conditions described as sanguine, or excessively passionate (literally "bloody-minded"); phlegmatic, or sluggish; choleric, or bad-tempered and irritable; and melancholic, or sad and depressed. Bloodletting, called in medical terms a phlebotomy, was to prevail as a cure until the late eighteenth century. In the case of plague, doctors mapped out those veins that should be opened depending on where the buboes or swellings appeared. The fact that some observed the letted blood to be thick and black, even containing a thin green scum on the surface, would have confirmed in their minds that they were releasing poison from the system. But a loss of blood from the patient, even to the point of making him unconscious, could not have helped any possible recovery from bubonic plague.

The alternative to bloodletting was to take a theriac or electuary, a substance or mixture of substances that was thought to have the ability to neutralize poison inside the body. Such "miracle cures," taken in the form of treacles or syrups, could be composed of almost anything. Snakeskin was a favorite, but other remedies included the bone from the heart of a stag, Armenian clay, precious metals and gems such as gold, silver, pearls, and emeralds (ground up into powder form), and exotic plant extracts such as aloe, myrrh, and saffron. Gentile da Foligno, a lecturer in medicine at the University of Padua and author of a popular plague tract who himself died in June 1348, swore by the powers of the emerald since it was proven to crack the eyes of a toad. Another authority set store by a recipe containing no fewer than sixty elements aged for at least ten years. Attempts also were made to suppurate the symptomatic boils, either by applying a specially prepared plaster or by actually cutting open or cauterizing the swelled skin.

But in fact there was little anyone could do to stop the onslaught of death. Writing fifteen years after the plague, Guy de Chauliac, physician to Pope Clement VI and master at the leading medical school at Montpellier, complains in his *Grande Chirurgie* (Great Surgery) that in 1348, doctors refused to visit the sick and could not cure them if they did. Chauliac's complaints of medical cowardice and impotence are echoed by others. When doctors admitted to the powerlessness of their own profession, we know that the Black Death had conquered medieval medicine. The only preventive that may have had some effect was to burn aromatic woods or compounds, especially those containing sulfur; Chauliac himself prescribed that the pope sit between two huge fires in his private chamber. Originally designed to ward off what was thought to be infectious air, the fumes actually may have smoked out the fleas bearing the plague. Some cities, such as Pistoia and Tournai, probably adopting the advice of physicians, introduced stringent regulations to improve their hygiene, to include quarantine, street cleaning, and coffins for the dead. And although the twelfth-century Arab chronicler Usāmah chided Western physicians for disdaining the scientific approach of their Middle Eastern counterparts, by the time of the Black Death the two were to be remarkably similar in their diagnoses. By the fourteenth century Europeans had caught up with the Muslim world in their familiarity with such medical authorities as Hippocrates, Galen, and Avicenna.

There is something of the magician, the alchemist, the shaman in these medical "experts" and their desperate remedies for the plague. Although some advice, such as avoiding contact with the sick, makes good sense, the strongest impression that emerges from plague manuals or tracts—some of which were much copied and thus apparently quite popular—is their utter impotence. And yet, we in the modern world are not immune from a little hocus-pocus ourselves: The difference is that we have come to expect, and rightly so, that our potions will work. Ever since the success of penicillin and other "wonder drugs," our attitude toward medicines and the doctors who administer them has changed. But to the men of the Middle Ages, the physicians who went around in their beaklike masks to ward off contagion became known as "quacks."

If all this expert knowledge was unavailing, there is some sense that contemporaries did not expect miracles of their medicine. Although some doctors tailored their advice depending on the social circumstance of their patients, it is hard to see how many outside of major towns could afford or even have access to the elaborate and sometimes peculiar prescriptions for the plague. Fourteenth-century medicine, particularly at the universities, may well have been improving as a result of its encounter with the Black Death, as well as through the growing acceptance of the benefits of dissection and surgery, but it remained deeply suspect among the ordinary population. The late-fourteenth-century English poet William Langland called physicians "leches," making a pun on their peculiar brand of medicine as well as its effect on patients. Their "drynkes," instead of curing the sick, murders them "ar destine it wolde." Likewise, Chaucer in the prologue to the *Canterbury Tales* puns on the "gold" that doctors use in their "cordials" and extract from their patients, especially during time of "pestilence." *The Poem on the Evil Times of Edward II*, dating a couple of decades before the plague, was equally harsh toward physicians, mocking both their manner of diagnosis (to examine the patient's urine) and their bedside manner, in which they prey on soon-to-be widows:

> . . . *thise false fisiciens that helpen men to die;*
> *He wole wagge his urine in a vessel of glaz,*
> *And swereth that he is sekere than evere yit he was,*
>   *and sein,*

"Dame, for faute of helpe, thin housebonde is neih
slain."
Thus he wole afraien al that ther is inne,
And make many a lesing silver for to winne.
Ac afterward he fondeth to comforte the wif,
And seith, "Dame, for of thin I wole holde his lyf,"
a[n]d liye;
Thouh he wite no more than a gos wheither he wole
live or die.

. . . these false physicians that help men to die;
He will wag his urine in a vessel of glass
And swear that he is sicker than ever yet he was,
  and say,
"Madam, but for my help, your husband is neigh
  slain."
Thus he will frighten all who are therein,
And make many a falsehood for silver to win.
And afterward he tries to comfort the wife,
And says, "Madam, for your sake I will save his life,"
  and he lies.
Though he knows no more than a goose whether he
  will live or die.

Instead of "physick," men seemed to place their trust in prayers
and processions. The citizens of Messina, Sicily, for example, petitioned that the holy shrine of St. Agatha at Catania be carried in
procession to their town, believing "that if the relics come to
Messina the city will be saved completely from this disease."
Likewise, the denizens of Hereford in England placed great faith
in the newly translated shrine of St. Thomas Cantilupe, a local
thirteenth-century bishop. Cantilupe's reputation for sanctity and
the miracle-working powers of his shrine, which had led to his
canonization in 1320, made his cult especially attractive to plague
victims. As we will see, religious devotion did not seem to suffer
even when plague persisted in spite of these holy measures.

Although they were unable to explain the causes and cures of
the plague, the contemporary chronicles are practically our only

source as to how the Black Death arrived and then spread in the West. The story of the first infectious contacts between East and West told by Gabriele de Mussis, that Tartars besieged Christians at the Black Sea port of Caffa by lobbing plague-infected bodies into the town, may be apocryphal. But Mussis grasped the general idea that European (primarily Italian) merchants trading in the East brought back home more than one kind of cargo. When three galleys whose crew were infected with the plague arrived in Genoa at the end of 1347, their "ships were driven from the port with burning arrows and other engines of war," so that, seeking refuge from place to place, they eventually communicated the disease to the whole of the Mediterranean. Disasters such as a rain of frogs or of fire that were reported to have taken place in the East indicate that some kind of natural upheavals—floods, earthquakes, drought—brought the squirrel-like Manchurian marmot, continuous carriers of the plague bacillus, into contact with humans amid the steppes of central Asia. From there the Black Death spread along the well-established trade routes of the Mongol empire, explored in the previous century by such intrepid westerners as Marco Polo and John of Monte Corvino. Thus a disease that previously had been endemic—that is, locally contained—became pandemic, as nearly all races of people east of Europe, according to Mussis, became infected. Based on chronicle accounts, the plague, after arriving on the shores of Italy and southeastern France in December 1347, traveled north to Paris and south to Spain by the summer of 1348, reached the southern coasts of England and Wales in the winter of that year, then east to Germany and north to the Midlands of England by June 1349, and finally encompassed Ireland, Scotland, and Scandinavia by late 1349 and 1350. The only large area seemingly untouched was Bohemia and Poland, perhaps because of relatively few trading contacts there.

Contemporaries also were well aware that the plague traveled from person to person—in other words, that it was highly infectious. Boccaccio witnessed how pigs rooted around in the discarded rags of a victim and then suddenly dropped dead. The city of Pistoia even tried to quarantine such "old linen or woollen cloths," without actually realizing that they may have carried fleas that spread bubonic plague. However, some of the theories as to contagion were quite bizarre. In addition to the role of touch and breathing, several authors, including no less an authority than Chauliac, believed that the plague could be transmitted by sight, literally, the "evil eye." According to another physician from Montpellier, an "aerial spirit" passed from the sick to the well who looked upon them, especially in their death throes. The Carmelite friar Jean de Venette, writing from Paris, declared that people could imagine themselves into the plague, in other words that the Black Death could quite literally invade their thoughts. Medieval physicians liked to call this form of contagion the "accidents of the soul" and believed that fearful thoughts about the plague would inevitably come true. This is probably the reason why the cities of Pistoia and Tournai forbade bells to be rung or black to be worn at funerals, and why Boccaccio's ten protagonists who flee from the plague in *The Decameron* pass their time telling love stories; taking their minds off the illness could be a matter of life or death. Retreat from human habitation was, in fact, the only sure advice doctors could give against infection but was no guarantee that the plague would not suddenly strike. The sad fate of Duke Giovanni, as recounted by Michele da Piazza, a Franciscan friar and chronicler from Sicily, is telling: Wandering aimlessly like a fugitive "through wild and uninhabited places," carefully avoiding the cities and their "infected air," the duke nevertheless died in April 1348, only a few months after the Black Death had arrived in Italy.

Chroniclers and surgeons were also quite accurate in describing the plague's symptoms. In general, their accounts are remarkably consistent from author to author. Descriptions of the buboes, or swellings from bubonic plague, range in size from a lentil (Piazza's description) to a "common apple" (Boccaccio's). Chauliac became acquainted with the plague symptoms at first hand, since he contracted it. (Fortunately he later recovered.) Louis Heyligen, also based at Avignon, reported that the pope authorized dissections that revealed "infected lungs." Other authors who make the distinction between bubonic and pneumonic plague include the Greek emperor John VI Cantacuzenos and the Irish chronicler John Clynn; a few even note the third, very sudden form we call septicemic. Some add their own, unique details of the disease. Gabriele de Mussis recounts how bubonic sufferers felt at first "a tingling sensation, as if they were being pricked by the points of arrows," followed by the well-known boils and an "acute and putrid fever, with severe headaches." Finally, they fell into what seemed a "drunken stupor," "vomited blood," or "gave rise to an intolerable stench." John Canta-cuzenos describes how victims fell into a coma, from which they might wake but could not speak. Others suffered from a deep depression of hopelessness and despair. The doctor Raymond Chalin de Vinario (writing in 1382) observed bleeding from almost all the orifices of the body—mouth, nose, urinary tract, and bowels. Some victims seemed to go mad, for John Clynn says that they "died in a frenzy, brought on by an affliction of the head." One gets the impression that these chroniclers took great care with their descriptions so that, in Clynn's words, "notable deeds should not perish with time and be lost from the memory of future generations . . . in case anyone should still be alive in the future and any son of Adam can escape this pestilence." In the face of this avalanche of arbitrary death, the best one could do was stand back in awe, and bear witness.

MEASURING MORTALITY

How many people died during the Black Death? For once, our knowledge is no better now than what was recorded at the time. The chroniclers, nearly all scholars agree, were prone to exaggeration. That only a "tenth of mankind" survived—in other words, a death rate of 90 percent—was an oft-repeated shibboleth, while many English chroniclers reported something along the lines of "the living were hardly able to bury the dead." Even if inaccurate, some medieval authors at least were impressive in their descriptions of mortality. Agnolo di Tura of Siena, whose observations begin this chapter, testified to the devastating effects the plague had on his own life. William Dene of Rochester complained of the unbearable stench that arose from cemeteries that contained the mass graves of the dead. The Florentine chronicler Giovanni Villani left an empty space in his account to record the date that the plague ended, but himself died before he could fill in the blank.

The numbers of dead given in the chronicles often seem fantastic, especially when one considers how many people were alive at the time. Boccaccio estimated that within five months in 1348 "over 100,000 human lives were extinguished" in Florence, a city that probably contained no more than 80,000 souls. A Paduan chronicler claimed 100,000 deaths in Venice, whose population numbered at most 150,000; Agnolo di Tura recorded 52,000 out of a possible 60,000 inhabitants in Siena; a Flemish chronicler 62,000 within three months in Avignon; Gilles li Muisis over 25,000 in Tournai; John Clynn 14,000 in Dublin; Jean de Venette 500 daily in Paris; Robert of Avesbury over 200 a day in London.

It may be easy to ignore the more inflated of these figures as products of pure fantasy, but it would be unwise to dismiss them

Survivors burying the dead in coffins, as mandated by a city ordinance, during the plague at Tournai in Flanders in 1349. From an illustration of the chronicle of Abbot Gilles li Muisis. (Courtesy Photothèque Giraudon.)

altogether. If anything, they testify to the impression the Black Death made upon the minds of Europeans, who clearly were awed by the scale of the catastrophe. When it comes to modern estimates of the mortality, there is something distinctly unsatisfying about the nearly universal mantra that between a third to a half of Europeans died of the plague. Would a 30 percent death rate inspire the degree of hyperbole to be found in the medieval chronicles?

The most active researchers into the demography of the Black Death have been historians of England, for the simple reason that the most abundant and fruitful records for such an endeavor have survived there. Of the three main sources for the study of plague mortality, the inquisitions post mortem, conducted after the death of a landlord in order to determine who should inherit the estate, give us a 27 percent death rate for England during the Black Death. These records were kept by the crown because if an heir happened to be a minor, the king had the right to administer the estate (and enjoy its profits) until the heir came of age. There are several problems with this evidence, however, that contribute to what appears to be a surprisingly low mortality estimate for the plague. For a start, the sample is limited to a privileged population, just over five hundred potential plague victims. This group was undoubtedly at lower risk from the disease: They lived in stone houses less infested by vermin, kept their animals in separate outbuildings, enjoyed better hygiene, and owned land that gave them greater isolation from contagion. Still another drawback is that inquisitions did not record the deaths of all members of a family: Behind every surviving heir to a vacant estate, the principal concern of the inquisitions, there may have been several others whose deaths went unrecorded.

A far more accurate and broadly based measure of plague mortality is to be found in the institution lists of ten bishops' registers that survive for this period. When the rector or vicar of a parish church died, his successor had to be presented by the church's patron to the bishop for a formal admission (also known as an institution or collation) to the benefice. Usually an inquest was held by the bishop's officials in order to ascertain if the church was truly vacant. In this indirect way, the deaths of all beneficed priests were recorded in the episcopal register, and by tallying such presentations or admissions, we can find out how many of the clergy were dying during the Black Death.

The great advantage of the bishops' registers is their territorial diversity: Records are available from districts all over England. Diocesan death rates can be calculated for Lincoln, York, Bath and Wells, Winchester, Exeter, Ely, Norwich, Worcester, Hereford, and Coventry and Lichfield. The scribes' entries tend to be remarkably regular, even when death raged all around them and the sheer number of vacancies must have made it hard to keep up. We also can gain a fairly accurate idea of the total number of benefices from which to factor a percentage of mortality, something that is extremely difficult to do for the population at large. Provided that one exercises caution in these calculations—such as by eliminating nonresident clergy as well as those who resigned or exchanged their benefices—the registers are perhaps the best sources we have as to plague mortality (see table 5, page 272).

Clerical mortality figures, calculated in 1930 for all ten dioceses and more recently recalculated for Coventry and Lichfield, Ely, and Hereford, point to a total average death rate during the plague of almost 50 percent. This is much higher than the 30 percent commonly repeated as the mean plague mortality. Of course, there was considerable local variation in the potency with which the Black Death struck. In some areas, the disease demonstrated that it was perfectly capable of wiping out nearly all the inhabitants. Mortality reached 70 percent, for example, in the deaneries of Tamerton, Kenn, and Honiton in the diocese of Exeter; 75 percent at Repton, Wisbech, and Hampstead in the dioceses of Coventry and Lichfield, Ely, and Exeter respectively; 76 percent at Irchenfield in the diocese of Hereford; and 77 percent at Totnes in the diocese of Exeter. An indication of the severity of the Black Death is the sheer number of benefices that saw more than one incumbent in 1349 alone. In the diocese of Winchester, for example, thirty-five benefices became vacant two or even three times that year, of which seven saw two vacancies within a month of each other. Exeter was almost as hard hit, with thirty-one benefices vacant two or three times, of which six pairs occurred within a month. Moreover, the episcopal registers allow

a month-by-month analysis of the plague's advance. In many dioceses the disease seems to have waxed during the summer
months, particularly July and August 1349, pointing to the
strong presence of bubonic plague. Yet there are exceptions,
especially in the South: Death was strongest in December
1348 and January 1349 in Bath and Wells; in February
and March 1349 in Exeter; and in March and April 1349
in Winchester. Perhaps in these places pneumonic plague
was the killer.

Though these statistics are revealing, whether a death rate
among the clergy is indicative of a similar death rate among the
population at large has been much debated. On the one hand,
clerical mortality during the Black Death may have been higher
than normal if priests were conscientiously performing their
duties of administering last rites to the sick, and that mortality
was high among the clergy suggests they were doing just that. On
the other hand, if the beneficed clergy enjoyed better living conditions than the typical peasant, housed in stone rather than mud,
for example, they should have had a better chance of escaping
infection. The stone Priest's House that survives from the early
fourteenth century at Muchelney, Somerset, originally had a
large, two-storied hall in the center of the building, with rooms
at either end. In 1344 the vicar of West Harptree in Somerset was
described as living in a house consisting of a hall with two chambers, or "solars," above, and a kitchen, together with a grange,
stable, and dovecote. Likewise the vicar of Kingston-on-Thames,
Surrey, in 1352 was provided with a dwelling containing a hall
surmounted by two chambers, each with its own privy, and a
kitchen with oven and hearth, along with a stable with tiled roof
to house six horses. Many more vicarages probably were built
around a timber frame, but an important difference from parishioners' houses would have been separate buildings for grain and
animals. In the end, the arguments for greater or lesser exposure
of the clergy to the plague balance themselves out: Priests may
have been at increased risk for pneumonic plague as a result of
their higher than average human contacts, but at less risk to
bubonic plague as a result of their lower than average contacts
with rats.

In any case, a third type of evidence that records deaths among the peasantry points to a plague mortality just as high, if not higher, than that of the clergy. By counting up the death taxes, known as heriots, paid by serfs to their lords before property could be inherited, historians can estimate the mortality of tenants based on the total number of holdings on the estate. Such information is available in manorial court rolls and other manorial records. Like inquisitions post mortem, they may underestimate mortality by failing to record deaths of any potential heirs who died before the estate passed to a survivor, although some researchers adjust their figures accordingly. The picture of the plague's ravages thus produced is restricted to a small area, but it is at a more common level than either of the two methods examined above. Furthermore, enough local studies now have been conducted, representing manors from all over the country, that a national trend can be discerned. Death rates of anywhere between 40 and 70 percent have been found on estates in Cornwall, Somerset, and Worcestershire in the West; Suffolk, Norfolk, and Cambridgeshire in the East; Hampshire, Wiltshire, Essex, and Oxfordshire in the South; and Durham in the North. As with some deaneries, the worst-affected manors saw nearly their whole population succumb: 70 percent of tenants died at Oakington, Cambridgeshire; 72 and 78 percent at Nether Heworth and Jarrow in Durham; and 80 percent at Aston in Worcestershire.

Other calculations based on more minor evidence yield no lower figures. The survival rate of monks at twelve houses, including the very large establishments at St. Albans and Christ Church, Canterbury, indicates an average mortality of 45 percent. Reductions in the number of payments of frankpledge dues, a tax levied upon peasant households, points to a 43 percent death rate in Essex and 55 percent in Somerset. And finally, one study of death rates among coroners, revealed in the crown's orders for their election upon the deaths of incumbents, comes up with a 40 percent die-off between 1348 and 1350.

The upshot of all this is to suggest that historians have been far too conservative in the past in their estimates of mortality during the Black Death. Whereas previous estimates confined themselves to between a third and a half, I suggest that the range be revised upwards to between 40 and 60 percent. If we accept the mean of the best calculations of England's total population on the eve of the Black Death—roughly five million people—this would point to the deaths of between two and three million from the disease, as opposed to the 1.5 to 2.5 million commonly accepted, a difference of half a million persons. Perhaps the impressions of contemporary English chroniclers were not that far off when they said barely enough souls survived to bury the dead. If roughly half of England was dying, the other half left alive would, almost without exception, know firsthand the pain of losing someone they had loved.

What little evidence survives from the Continent suggests that death rates there were no lower than in England. At Givry in eastern France, the parish register records a death rate of approximately 50 percent between July and November 1348. At Albi in southern France, two tax assessments conducted in 1343 and 1357 indicate that 45 percent of its propertied citizens lost their lives during this time. In several towns belonging to the Hanseatic League in northern Germany, council records point to a higher than normal mortality during the Black Death, though this varies widely, from 27 to as much as 76 percent. At San Gimignano in Italy, household census returns from 1332 and 1350 show a population decline of nearly 59 percent in the city and 45 percent in the surrounding district. At Perpignan, at the time part of the northeastern Spanish kingdom of Aragon, between 58 and 68 percent of all scribes and legists disappear from the records during the plague. Also in northeastern Spain, in the diocese of Barcelona, the episcopal register of Bishop Michael Ricomá yields a death rate among the beneficed clergy of 60 percent between May 1348 and April 1349, with most of the deaths occurring in July and August 1348.

The final piece of the demographic puzzle to fit into place concerns the epidemics that came after the first plague visitation of 1348–49. Our knowledge of the existence of these succeeding epidemics comes initially from chronicle accounts. Several English chroniclers, for example, mention a "general mortality" or "great pestilence" that struck in 1361, targeting especially children and men. By July of that year, many parts of the country had been "rendered empty" by the plague, according to Robert Stretton, bishop of Coventry and Lichfield, who ordered prayers and processions to avert its advance before it reached his own diocese. Further national outbreaks during the fourteenth century are attested to have occurred in 1369, 1374–79, and 1390–93. For the fifteenth century, a variety of testimony, including chronicles, parliament rolls, bishops' registers, and private correspondence, point to no fewer than seven and as many as eleven national outbreaks of plague, particularly during the 1420s, '30s, '60s, and '70s. The most serious mortality, judging by the number and kind of references to it, occurred in 1479–80. The Continent seems to have followed a similar pattern, with plague striking at least once a decade from the 1360s right up to the end of the fifteenth century. Nor was plague the only scourge during these years. In England, at least, a malady known as the "stich," perhaps pleurisy, which causes sharp pains in the side, became a national epidemic in 1471, followed by the "flux," probably dysentery, in 1473. In 1475 the soldiers of King Edward IV came down with something called the "French Pox" that resulted from the "lust of women." A particularly horrible disease, it caused a burning sensation in men's penises until these "rotted away and fell off, and they died." This most likely was gonorrhea; syphilis was not to be imported into Europe from Africa and the Americas until the 1490s. In 1485 a mysterious disease known as the "sweat" or the sweating sickness made itself known first in London and then in East Anglia. Accompanied obviously by profuse sweating, this disease is thought to have been the respiratory epidemic influenza, better known as the flu, which is characterized by high fevers.

If we wish to be more precise than the chronicles, we have the evidence, yet again, of the bishops' registers. Mortality rates among the beneficed clergy of Hereford and York were indeed higher than normal during the plague years recorded by the chronicles (see table 6, page 273). The death rate averaged around 11 percent in 1361–62, 13 percent in 1369, and about 7 percent throughout the 1390s. Only in the 1370s does no significant mortality seem to occur. However, inquisitions post mortem and manorial records both record death rates of about 12 percent in 1375, while coroners experienced an average yearly mortality of 17 percent between 1375 and 1379. Moreover, in other plague years these sources record slightly higher death rates than among the clerical population.

For the fifteenth century, we have the obituary lists of Christ Church Priory in Canterbury. Extending from 1395 to 1505, the lists are unusually descriptive as to the cause of death of each monk, and considering the expert medical attention the monks received, are probably accurate. The most important conclusion to be drawn from this evidence is that many more epidemics struck the population of fifteenth-century England than is revealed in the chronicle accounts, perhaps because these epidemics were local rather than national in scope. Abnormal mortality occurred at Christ Church no fewer than twenty-seven times in a little over one hundred years, seventeen times alone between 1395 and 1450. Plague probably was the killer in a third of these outbreaks, but other diseases also killed, some seemingly unknown to most medieval authors. Tuberculosis, for example, rivaled plague, being responsible for another third of the deaths recorded, followed by the "sweat," contributing 21 percent of deaths. Also occurring in significant numbers were dropsy, a neurological disorder causing a "drop," or sagging of the face, at 10 percent, and strangury, marked by a painful inability to urinate, at 7 percent. Similar evidence from Westminster Abbey supports Christ Church's picture of continuing population decline well into the fifteenth century.

On the Continent, one of the most fruitful sources of mortality statistics comes from the Florentine contado. There, a detailed census for tax purposes called the Catasto was compiled in 1427 and yields population figures that are remarkably lower than those for a century earlier. Between 1338 and 1427, population in the city fell by 69 percent and in the countryside by between 62 and 67 percent. Comparable statistics are available for other regions in Tuscany: San Gimignano lost more than 75 percent in the city and 70 percent in the country between 1332 and 1427; Pistoia lost between 62 and 68 percent between about 1244 and 1427; and Prato lost over 62 percent between 1290 and 1427.

Farther north, monnéage or hearth tax records point to a population decline of more than a third between 1365 and 1424 in Flanders, and in eastern Normandy a 50 percent decline between 1347 and 1374, another 50 percent decline between 1415 and 1422, and a 30 percent decline between 1436 and 1442. The French sources, however, are complicated by the fact that plague made not the only assault on its population. War, and the famine that came in its wake, were perhaps equal partners in the harvest of death.

Throughout England and the Continent, population held steady, and may even have slightly declined, in the 150 years after the first arrival of plague in the mid-fourteenth century. As the statistics make clear, the Black Death and other diseases that followed, even if they did not approach the mortality of the first epidemic, continued to take substantial tolls on Europe's inhabitants. It seemed the hand of God weighed heavily on the men and women of the later Middle Ages, for behind all the faceless numbers of the dead lay the sufferings and upheavals of a beleaguered society.

RETRENCHMENT AND REVOLT

The death of half the population in two or three years was bound to have serious and long-lasting repercussions for the social and economic fabric of England and Europe. The Black Death threatened to sever the bonds that held society together. One contemporary author after another declares that even family ties began to break down from fear of contagion, as, in Boccaccio's words, "brothers abandoned brothers, uncles their nephews, sisters their brothers," wives their husbands, and parents their own children. In addition, laws were disregarded; doctors refused to tend the sick; priests feared to administer last rites; the sick and dead were treated no better than animals; any relative of a sick man was avoided; whole families were walled into their houses once the plague struck one of their members; no one could be found to bear away the stinking bodies of the dead, except unscrupu-

lous grave-digging fraternities who blackmailed those still living; no one attended or cried at funerals, but rather fled from
them or made them the object of jests; and so on. In economic
terms, the evidence provided by chroniclers such as Henry
Knighton, a canon of Leicester, is that immediately after the
plague of 1349 the wages of laborers rose, while the price of
food and other necessities fell. The result was economic chaos,
as rents and traditional labor services were not paid, "crops rotted unharvested in the fields," and "livestock wandered about
without a shepherd."

If this situation had persisted, it should have been a boon to
peasant laborers and a bane to their masters. The growing
unprofitability of direct farming should have forced lords to
commute the traditional labor services of their tenants into fixed
money rents, while the greater leisure time and landholdings of
the peasantry should have increased their productivity and their
wealth. In other words, the standard of living of the poorer elements of society should have improved. And the records of some
landlords, such as Eynsham Abbey near Oxford, or the city's earl,
John de Vere, indicate that they indeed were forced to renegoti-
ate labor contracts on a wide scale in the wake of the Black Death.
Plague, for the peasantry at least, had a silver lining despite its terrible mortality; the historian A. R. Bridbury has compared it to
"a sort of Marshall aid on a stupendous scale."

However, there are several conundrums that bedevil this
overly neat picture. According to the economic models, the better prospects for most people should have translated into a growing population in the decades after the Black Death. But this did
not happen. In actuality, population seems to have held steady or
gently declined for at least the next hundred years. Why? Part of
the answer may be that living standards for the peasantry did not
in fact increase all that much after the plague. The evidence from
England and elsewhere in Europe indicates that while wages rose,
so too did food prices in the aftermath of the Black Death. From
1349 on, the price of grain produced on the estates of the bishop
of Winchester and the abbey of Westminster, whose manorial
records survive in good number, remained high compared to
what it fetched two decades before the plague. In 1369 grain

prices reached stratospheric levels not seen since the famine years of 1315–16. Thus the peasants' cost of living, measured in terms of units of work needed to buy a quarter of wheat or barley, actually rose in the 1350s and 1360s as their wages, measured in piece rates, increased by only a penny or less. Laborers only began to substantially increase their buying power in the 1370s, when prices fell. Why this should have occurred has been the subject of some speculation—whether it was because of a shortage of coin, bad weather, or simple laziness of workers is not exactly clear. What it means, though, is that at least until 1370 peasants had little more economic recourse to support large families than before the plague.

One theory holds that, perhaps because of changes in the economy after the Black Death, many late medieval men and women deliberately decided not to marry or have children, leading to a low birth, or "replacement," rate that may be revealed in inheritance records. Some historians even hypothesize that medieval couples practiced contraception and abortion, by using extracts from plants such as ferula (fennel), pomegranate, juniper, rue (a member of the evergreen family), pennyroyal, "squirting cucumber," and Queen Anne's lace, taken orally or as a suppository. It is extremely doubtful, however, that contraceptives, much less abortion-inducing substances, were widely used in the Middle Ages, considering that the Catholic Church's position was, and still is, that sexual intercourse exists for the purpose of procreation and that abortion is equivalent to murder. Several medieval authors do demonstrate a familiarity with contraception and abortion, nearly always getting their information from classical and Arab sources. Yet this does not necessarily mean that they approved of these practices or thought about them in more than a theoretical way. Church and secular law, in fact, was to grow more restrictive toward birth control and abortion as the Middle Ages progressed. Indeed, by the fourteenth century, birth control was associated with the Cathar heresy, a dualistic belief system prevalent especially in the south of France that identified two gods, a benevolent god who ruled over a purely spiritual world up in heaven, and an evil god who reigned here on earth. Hell was therefore regarded by the Cathars as the material world that we live in every day, and consequently procreation, which led to the production of more of the devil's matter, was to be shunned by its "perfect" leaders and regulated by the rest of the believers. But it is to be wondered how effective contraception was if, according to a female Cathar from the village of Montaillou in Languedoc, it consisted of wearing an "herb" on a long cord around the neck so that it hung down "between my breasts, as far as the opening of my stomach." Modern laboratory tests on rats have proven that certain ancient plants, if taken internally, could prevent ovulation or implantation of a fertilized egg. But there seems to have been some confusion in the medieval West as to how to use such contraceptives, indicating that on the popular level they were unfamiliar and therefore rarely used. While family planning may seem second nature in the modern West, it was by no means so to our medieval forebears.

Contemporaries, on the other hand, claim that both marriages and births increased in the aftermath of plague. In England, Ralph Higden, a Benedictine monk from St. Werburgh's Abbey in Chester, and John of Reading, a monk from Westminster Abbey, note that after the plague of 1361 widows took almost anyone as husbands, including foreigners, "imbeciles," and kinsmen, and that they "shamelessly gave birth to bastards." Similar trends were noted on the Continent. Gilles li Muisis, for example, reported that after the plague of 1348–49 the men of Tournai married their concubines in obedience to a city proclamation, while Jean de Venette claims that in Paris, "When the epidemic was over, the men and women still alive married each other. Everywhere women conceived more readily than usual. None proved barren; on the contrary, there were pregnant women wherever you looked." Statistical evidence on this is mixed: High marriage rates and low age at marriage were the norm among the inhabitants of Halesowen, Worcestershire, and Lewes, Sussex, in the second half of the fourteenth century, while the opposite trend is argued for Essex during a similar time period.

For the fifteenth century, the evidence seems to favor fecundity. Court depositions of a small sample of Yorkshire couples indicate that they waited longer than in the previous century to marry, typically until their mid-twenties, but an analysis of wills in

the eastern counties demonstrates a high rate of marriage, generally above 75 percent. The latter evidence also suggests that during periods of heavy mortality, both marriage and replacement
rates tended to rise. Similar conclusions have been reached for the
Florentine contado, where tax surveys dating mostly from the fifteenth century again point to high marriage and fertility rates
(and low age at marriage) immediately following rampant mortality, and the opposite trend only when life expectancy improved.
At Lyons in southeastern France, 63 percent of those who made
a will between 1340 and 1380 had no children to leave their
inheritance to, while those with large families of four children or
more made up just over 8 percent. By the end of the fifteenth century these numbers were nearly reversed.

All this is not to deny that lower fertility, in some instances,
may have been a factor in the fate of Europe's declining population. But the intent to have fewer children is very difficult to document, particularly in medieval society. If some women were
indeed giving birth less often than before, this was probably more
by accident of age and availability of spouses than by choice. As
young couples were killed off, especially in later plagues that
apparently targeted the young, a surplus of older men and
women, in a ratio that perhaps favored the latter, may have been
left behind to shoulder the burden of reproduction. On balance,
I believe it is far more likely that the stagnant or declining population of the second half of the fourteenth and of the fifteenth
centuries was due to rampant mortality rather than lower fertility.
This era of an unending series of epidemic diseases has aptly been
called the "Golden Age of the Germ." Even if, as seems likely, a
healthy replacement rate was sustained, such mortal blows coming one after another never gave the population of England a
chance to recover.

A second conundrum of the medieval economy in the wake of
the Black Death returns to the relationship between living standards and population. Let us suppose that living standards
depend on population, rather than the other way around. If population declined or remained stagnant for the rest of the fourteenth century, why did wages not rise more significantly as a
result of the continuing shortage of workers? Pay of threshers,

reapers, and mowers in England increased by only a penny or two between 1350 and the end of the century (an improvement of approximately 15 to 30 percent). The answer may be that the medieval economy did not necessarily operate by the modern laws of supply and demand. Before the Black Death had run its course, King Edward III of England, in June 1349, issued the Ordinance of Labourers that fixed wages to their levels in 1346, three years before the plague. This legislation was reissued in 1351 as the Statute of Labourers, which set very specific wage and piece rates for a whole host of workers, ranging from laborers in the field to those in the towns and cities, such as carpenters, masons, roofers, cordwainers, shoemakers, goldsmiths, tanners, tailors, and others. Similar legislation was enacted throughout Europe in the decade after the Black Death. If upheld, and there is some evidence that in England it was enforced to the limits of medieval administrative capacity, peasants would not have been able to benefit from demand for their services as much as they could expect in a free-market economy.

Yet the practical effect of such wage legislation was flatly denied by many contemporaries. In the words of an English Commons' petition of 1376:

> although various ordinances and statutes have been made in several parliaments to punish labourers, artificers and other servants, yet these have continued subtly and by great malice aforethought, to escape the penalty of the said ordinances and statutes. As soon as their masters accuse them of bad service, or wish to pay them for their labour according to the form of the statutes, they take flight and suddenly leave their employment and district, going from county to county, hundred to hundred and vill to vill, in places strange and unknown to their masters. . . . for they are taken into service immediately in new places, at such dear wages that example and encouragement is afforded to all servants to depart into fresh places, and go from master to master as soon as they are displeased about any matter. For fear of such flights, the commons now dare not challenge or offend their ser-

vants, but give them whatever they wish to ask, in spite of the statutes and ordinances to the contrary.

The only solution to this alarming situation that the Commons could come up with was that the labor legislation be enforced more rigorously. Other fourteenth-century authors complained that after the plague peasants enjoyed more food and drink from their employers, something specifically forbidden by the 1351 statute, and greater leisure time, which they spent doing nothing. Admittedly, such poets and polemicists wrote for a largely middle-class audience—consisting of country gentry and urban burghers—who probably delighted to hear ill of their inferiors, and they used stock characters that passed from one author to another. Nevertheless, the very popularity of their works testifies that they struck a responsive chord among their contemporaries.

The most famous, and perhaps the most representative, of such authors are William Langland and John Gower. Langland, a priest from Worcestershire probably living in London, wrote the first two versions of his great poem *Piers Plowman* during the 1360s and 1370s, within living memory of the first plague and at the time of subsequent outbreaks. Langland employs the allegorical character of "Waster" to symbolize the lazy peasants, the archenemy of his hardworking hero, Piers:

> Then would Waster not work, but would wander
>   about,
> Nor beggar eat bread wherein beans had a part,
> But flour of the finest, and wheat of the whitest;
> Nor halfpenny-ale would in any wise drink,
> But the best and the brownest the borough could
>   sell.
> Then labourers landless, that lived by their hands,
> Would deign not to dine upon worts a day old;
> No penny-ale pleased them, no piece of good bacon,
> Only fresh flesh or fish, well fried or well baked,
> Ever hot and still hotter, to heat well their maw.

When ordered to go back to work by the Knight, citing the law, Waster refuses and instead must be brought to heel by Hunger, who knows no mercy.

Gower, a contemporary of Langland, came from the gentry class and owned several manors, mainly in Kent. In his first major prose work, the *Mirour de l'Omme* (Mirror of Man), written in the latter half of the 1370s, Gower implies that workingmen of his day were living the high life compared to their forbears. "In olden days," Gower writes, "the workers were not accustomed to eat wheat bread; instead their bread was made from other grains or from beans. And likewise they drank only water. And they feasted on cheese and milk but rarely on anything else." In a later work, the *Vox Clamantis* (Voice of One Crying), begun around 1377, Gower seems to speak from experience when he says of hired laborers:

> These are the people who behave basely within the house, as long as your food and drink last. Because such a man is hired as a member of your household, he scorns all ordinary food. He grumbles steadily that everything salted is harmful, and that he doesn't like cooked foods much, unless you give him some roast. Neither weak beer nor cider is of any use to him, and he will not return tomorrow unless you provide something better.

The point of these criticisms was that peasants were demanding, and apparently getting, rewards other than higher pay (though Gower says they were getting that too). Such payments in kind would have been attractive to wage earners in an era of rising food prices. By giving their workers more and better food and drink, landlords could satisfy ravenous appetites and yet evade the prying eyes of contemporary and modern readers alike searching for evidence of violations of the wage limits laid down by the law. The manorial records of some manors, however, do in fact record the better food some lords gave their laborers. At Sedgeford, Norfolk, a manor owned by Norwich Cathedral, harvest workers consumed more than twice as much meat and substantially more ale in the mid-fourteenth century than before the plague. Moreover, the rolls of the justices attempting to enforce the Statute of Labourers reveal that substantially higher wages than those recorded in manorial accounts were indeed often paid—even to the carpenter making the stocks to imprison violators—and that extra perks sometimes included more than just food and drink, such as clothing, board, concessionary plowing and pasturing of the peasants' grain and animals, even complimentary banquets. The solution to the conundrum may be that serfs indeed were trying to avoid work, but not for the sake of simple laziness that their masters thought. Greater leisure time for them may have meant greater flexibility and freedom in order to tend their ever-larger private holdings or to take advantage of better pay rates elsewhere. It is entirely possible that what angered and frightened social critics like Langland and Gower the most was not the peasants themselves, but the changing nature of the market: one that anticipated modern capitalism with its inexorable laws of supply and demand and the opportunism of the workforce that went along with it. To the extent that they recognized these greater forces at work, it seems these observers were uncertain as to how to respond. The world was changing, despite the best efforts of the English Parliament to stop it.

The third and final conundrum is this: If the peasants' living standards really were increasing in the decades after the Black Death, why were they so discontent as to revolt? A few contemporaries, such as Langland and Gower, seem to have anticipated a rising of the "cursed shrewes" or the "impatient nettle," those villeins unwilling to work or to know their place in the established order of society. But the Peasants' Revolt of 1381, when perhaps thousands of rebels from Essex and Kent converged on London in June to make some extraordinary demands of the king, took most Englishmen by surprise. And no one seems to have been more utterly dumbfounded by these revolting peasants (understood in both senses of the term) than the government. The king, Richard II, a young boy of fourteen, emerges from the chronicles as the most confident and decisive figure in the crisis. According to the *Anonimalle Chronicle*, considered the best contemporary account of the revolt, the king "called all the lords about him into a chamber, and asked their counsel as to what should be done in such a crisis. But none of them could or would give him any counsel." This was in spite of the fact that men had before their eyes the example of the rising of the Jacquerie in France of 1358, an event to which the Commons of England referred explicitly in a petition against their own rebellious serfs before Richard's first parliament of 1377. These serfs were ordinarily expected to remain on their lord's estates, pay their taxes, perform manual labor when required of them, and not complain. But nothing expected happened in 1381.

The sparks that ignited the revolt were the three poll taxes levied throughout the realm between 1377 and 1380, the last being a flat tax of 3 groats, or 12 pence, per head. Based on the best available evidence, this would represent roughly two to four days' worth of wages to the day laborer, but barely half an hour's worth to a knight banneret with an income of at least £500 a year. The tax was patently unfair, and everyone knew it: The parliament that granted it met at Northampton rather than London because royal officials anticipated its extreme unpopularity. Revenues from the tax were supposed to pay for the fruitless campaign of Thomas of Woodstock, earl of Buckingham (later duke of Gloucester), through northern France, the culmination of a series of military setbacks suffered by the English throughout the 1370s.

Modern historians, however, prefer to see long-term causes of the revolt going back to the Black Death and even further. In effect, the rebellion is made to be a natural outcome of the social and economic dislocations either initiated or greatly accelerated by the first pestilence of more than thirty years before. And indeed, the rising itself can be said to have had a predominately social and economic cast. This can be gleaned from the main demand of the rebels, uttered by their leader, Wat Tyler, to the king at Smithfield on June 15, "that there should be no more villeins in England, and no serfdom nor villeinage but that all men should be free and of one condition." Other agendas, of course, can be found: political, in the targeting of royal officials deemed responsible for the poll taxes and ruinous war policies; judicial, in the rebels' famous proposition "to kill all the lawyers"; and religious, in the sermons of John Ball, a preacher and another leader of the revolt, urging the dissolution of the monasteries, anticipating the English Reformation of the sixteenth century. Yet if the peasants had succedded in 1381, they would have done away at a stroke with the manorial system of customary tenure that had been the bedrock of the medieval economy for centuries.

The reasons for the revolt of 1381 are complex and many. However, historians' explanations of the rising can be reduced to three main theories. One claims that the various ways in which landlords recovered and reimposed tenure after the plague created tensions with their serfs in the decades leading up to the revolt. Some estates, such as those of the bishop of Winchester, Battle Abbey in Sussex, and Christ Church Priory in Kent, were able to carry on after 1349 much as before, perhaps because they had a surplus of tenants before the plague. Other manors, such as those of Westminster Abbey, Ramsey Abbey in Huntingdonshire, and the bishop of Coventry and Lichfield, had a much harder time returning to normal because they had to fill too many vacant holdings created by the Black Death. Consequently, servile conditions ran the gamut, from unfree status in which the serf had absolutely no legal rights and had to perform all kinds of services for his lord, to free tenantry in which the peasant had no obligation other than to pay rent. This unequal situation perhaps created resentment as tenants engaged in the medieval equivalent of keeping up with the Joneses. Thus, at a meeting with Richard II at Mile End on June 14, the rebels demanded that the king grant "that henceforward no man should be serf nor make homage or any type of service to any lord, but should give 4 pence for an acre of land." Basically, this was an attempt to complete the process of commutation that had proceeded so unevenly since the Black Death. Even though their demands went unheeded, history was on the side of the peasants. Renters, for which status the rebels clamored so impatiently in 1381, were to be the universal labor employed on English estates within two or three decades of the revolt.

Another possible cause of the rebellion was the growing awareness of, and demand for, freedom by long-oppressed serfs. Ideologically speaking, this is what the rebels' spokesman, Wat Tyler, seemed to mean when he told the king at Smithfield "that no lord should have lordship in future, but it should be divided among all men, except for the king's own lordship." Freedom, however, had a much different meaning to the man of 1381 than it does to the man of today. Medieval peasants did not necessarily desire freedom of speech, assembly, or religion, as we understand these terms. A villein well knew that he could not say and do as he pleased; indeed, a month after the revolt, in July 1381, John Shirle of Nottinghamshire was hanged for loose talk in support of the former rebel leader John Ball in a pub in Cambridge. Rather, the freedom medieval peasants hankered for was the freedom from arbitrary taxes, fines, and rents that restricted not only the movements of their persons but also of their lands and chattels. From the cradle to the grave most serfs were liable to a whole host of payments in money and in kind, the most notorious being the *prima nocte*, or first night, to which a lord was entitled with the serf's wife on their wedding night (a privilege rarely invoked). Even infidelity was subjected to a tax, known as leyrwite, because any bastard born of such a union was automatically free. Lords imposed these restrictions sometimes quite harshly and unrealistically after the Black Death, but peasants' desire to be rid of them goes back to the beginning of the fourteenth and as early as the thirteenth centuries.

Still another explanation of peasant discontent sees it as the inevitable product of a class struggle between lords and peasants in which the former appropriated nearly all of the surplus labor of the latter. According to this Marxist interpretation, retrofitted to the Middle Ages, the medieval economy was trapped in a vicious circle: Peasants, because they were ruthlessly exploited under the manorial system by means of numerous labor services owed to their lords, were not allowed to plow any surplus time back into their land; productivity of land thus declined; declining productivity led to declining population; and declining population led lords to try to further restrict the mobility of their tenants and extract ever more surplus from them. The result was a "crisis of feudalism" by the end of the Middle Ages in which serfdom was bound to die a natural death and capitalism take its place. In reality, lords and peasants, depending on the economic conditions of the time, did not always play the roles assigned to them in the Marxist model. It may be that, prior to the Black Death, lords were not averse to freeing their serfs, while serfs were not overly keen on being released from bondage; in an era of high land prices and overabundance of tenants, more profit could be extracted from the rents of freemen than from the "rent-controlled" customary tenures of the unfree. Indeed, in some instances lords had to force their peasants to accept their freedom. Obviously this was an economic, not a charitable act, and plenty of other instances can be found of lords arbitrarily imposing and increasing servile status and dues. Nevertheless, it has been estimated that less than half the peasant population of England was still tied to the soil on the eve of the Black Death, and even those who were probably labored under far less onerous conditions than their ancestors had ever known. Moreover, even when lords tried to reimpose serfdom after the economic dislocations created by successive plagues, they had a very hard time doing so.

The idea of class struggle is hard to sustain when one looks closely at who participated in the rising. It was not just peasants who rose in the Peasants' Revolt; indeed, some scholars prefer the term "English Rising" for that reason. A variety of urban dwellers—primarily artisans and tradesmen—joined the revolt, and may have forged a town-country alliance. The urban element was even more crucial to risings on the Continent, such as the Jacquerie in France and the Revolt of the Ciompi in Florence in 1378. The latter uprising of artisans and workers, primarily in the wool industry, overthrew the Florentine oligarchy and set up its own government, largely in protest against the monopoly that the guild system exercised over the city's political and economic life. The targets of the English rebels' attacks were equally varied: In addition to noblemen, they included merchants, lawyers and others associated with the law, doctors, guild masters, foreigners, and anyone, it seems, against whom there was a local grievance. One victim, Roger Legett, had used "iron man-traps," probably akin to spring-loaded animal snares, in order to keep people out of a dike in Fiketts Field, London. Those members of the upper class who were targeted, such as John of Gaunt, duke of Lancaster; Simon Sudbury, archbishop of Canterbury and royal chancellor; Sir Robert Hales, prior of St. John's Hospital and royal treasurer; and Richard Lyons, a wealthy London merchant, were the victims of political rather than class grievances.

Nor was there necessarily class solidarity among the peasants. Some villagers made a habit of ratting on neighbors who tried to run away from their masters, because their departure would mean extra rent to pay and more land to work. Informers were inevitably part of the suppression of the revolt in July 1381, the most spectacular example coming from Essex, where more than five hundred men, fearing Lord Tresilian's "bloody assizes," sought mercy from the king in return for revealing "the names of the more important malefactors and inciters of the previous disturbance." It is also possible that some of the "haves" were sympathetic to the plight of the "have-nots." In *Piers Plowman*, William Langland advises his Knight to:

O'ertax thou no tenant, save Truth will assent!
And though thou amerce them, let Mercy be taxer!
Be Meekness thy master, let Meed go unheeded;
Though poor men should proffer thee presents and gifts,
Decline them, in case that thy claim be denied;
Lest thou yield them again, at the year's full end,
In a perilous place, that is Purgat'ry named!

In a later version of the poem written after the revolt, Langland paints a pathetic picture of the poor, detailing their hardships and miseries and how deserving they are of alms.

All of these explanations of the Peasants' Revolt have merit, yet there is something dissatisfying about all of them. Each fails to draw a definitive connection between the excessive mortality of the Black Death, which recent estimates keep revising upwards, and the events of 1381. Perhaps there is no all-important connection, but one suspects that if there had been no Black Death in 1349, there would have been no Peasants' Revolt in 1381. How can these two great events be more closely linked?

The answer, it seems, may lie in the legislation we have seen enacted in response to the plague: the Ordinance of Labourers issued by the king's council in 1349, ratified two years later as the Statute of Labourers by Parliament in 1351, and finally joined in

1363 by the sumptuary laws that strove to regulate even the clothes that people wore, since some seemed to be dressing above their station. Essentially, in passing these laws, the king's council and Parliament attempted to pretend as if the Black Death had not occurred at all. Wages, prices, and social mores could go on as before. It was a remarkable reaction, a collective denial of economic reality on the part of the nation's ruling classes, and it inaugurated a reactionary revolution just as significant as the peasants' revolutionary attempt to end serfdom.

This is by no means a new explanation of the revolt. As early as 1908, Bertha Putnam, who examined 312 cases of alleged violations recorded on fifty-nine rolls, demonstrated that labor laws were "thoroughly enforced" by specially appointed justices of laborers in the decade after the Black Death, despite Henry Knighton's complaint that "the workers were so above themselves and so bloody-minded that they took no notice of the king's command." More recent research has shown that, on average, hundreds of thousands of offenders of the statute were prosecuted every year, leading the historian E. B. Fryde to declare that "provisions about wages and contracts of servants were, perhaps, the most zealously enforced enactments in medieval English history." From the 1360s on, enforcement was left up to the newly created justices of the peace, who typically hailed from the gentry class and thus had a vested interest in the statute. (In fact, their wages came out of the fines they imposed.) In order to enforce the statute, the justices played off one element of the community against the other, undoubtedly creating tensions in society that helped contribute to the revolt. It may be argued that such evidence proves that the labor laws were regularly flouted, yet the very existence of this evidence also testifies to the often strenuous efforts taken to make that dream a reality.

Such an explanation is particularly satisfying because it accounts for why a variety of people—not just peasants—participated in the rising. For an equal variety of people were prosecuted under the statute. In 1371, for instance, at Kesteven, Lin- colnshire, there were indicted a plowman, thresher, mason, fisherman, oiler, weaver, roofer, and vintner. In addition, the short-lived attempt to enforce the sumptuary legislation of 1363 adds an important social dimension to the economic buildup to 1381. The revolting peasants committed not only the sin of calling for an end to serfdom, but also that of not knowing their place. Perhaps their most socially ungracious act was when a group of them invaded the bedchamber of the king's mother, Joan of Kent, in the Tower of London on June 14 while their compatriots met with the king himself at Mile End. According to various accounts, several of the rebels "asked the king's mother to kiss them," and then they "tore her bed to pieces, so terrifying her that she fainted." Almost as great a faux pas was committed by Wat Tyler at

The death of Simon Sudbury, archbishop of Canterbury, during the Peasants' Revolt of 1381. Joining Sudbury in martyrdom are Sir Robert Hales, prior of St. John's Hospital and royal treasurer (right), and Brother William of Appleton, physician to John of Gaunt, duke of Lancaster (rear). This illustration, from a fifteenth-century Flemish manuscript of Froissart's Chronicles, *has the archbishop beheaded inside the Tower, whereas most English chronicles of the revolt locate his death outside on Tower Hill. (Courtesy British Library.)*

Smithfield, when he shook the king roughly by the hand and called him "brother." In both small and big ways, the rigid and reassuring order to society was being turned on its head.

If the conservative cause needed a martyr from the revolt, it need have looked no further than to Simon Sudbury, archbishop of Canterbury and chancellor of England. On June 14, 1381, Sudbury was dragged by the rebel mob from the Tower of London and beheaded on Tower Hill. According to the most detailed account of his death, it took eight strokes of the sword to sever his head from his body, the second stroke also cutting the tops off some fingers Sudbury had put to his wound as he cried out, "Ah! Ah! This is the hand of God!" What happened next is described in a letter written three months after the revolt from John Finch, prior of Christ Church, Canterbury, to the man who was to succeed Sudbury as archbishop, William Courtenay, bishop of London. The rebels, Finch says, stuck Sudbury's head on a pike and paraded it through the city to the cries of "This is the head of a traitor!" It then was displayed above the gate of London Bridge, a privilege normally reserved for convicted traitors, while the body was left to rot and be robbed for two days. Both Finch and an anonymous poet commemorating Sudbury claim that the mob made sport of his head while it was up on the bridge by nailing a little cap to the scalp, perhaps in mockery of his mitre. The poem also attests that that very day the head was taken down and reverently wrapped in the archbishop's pallium (a collar of cloth with two pendants worn front and back) by a knight called "Walword," almost certainly William Walworth, mayor of London. Apparently, the man who executed the archbishop, John Starlyng, went mad, roaming the countryside of his native Essex with a naked sword hanging from his neck and a dagger at his back. When he returned to London after the revolt was over in order to claim his "reward," he himself was executed. Sudbury's body eventually was taken back to Canterbury for burial. (His tomb, if he had one, does not survive.) Although the anonymous poem claims that the archbishop's "body finally was restored to the head" on the night of his execution, it is more likely that this "head" was in reality a bust of Sudbury that was carried in his funeral cortege. The real head was taken separately to the church of St. Gregory in Sudbury, his hometown, and placed in a special receptacle in the vestry, where it can be seen to this day. Sudbury's skull, with pieces of mummified flesh still clinging to it, bears ample traces around the lower jaw of hack marks from the inexpert strokes of his executioner's sword.

Clearly, the archbishop had been an unpopular man. But there also seems to have been quite a few who believed him to be a true martyr. One of these, a monk and chronicler from the abbey of St. Albans, Thomas Walsingham, describes Sudbury's death in a way that is highly evocative of that of another archbishop of Canterbury and martyr for the Church, Thomas à Becket. According to Walsingham, Sudbury remained steadfast at his prayers even when his murderers burst into the Tower chapel baying for his blood, just as Becket had done in 1170 when four knights claiming to act on behalf of an exasperated king, Henry II, cut him down as he was preparing to celebrate mass in Canterbury Cathedral. And like Becket, Sudbury allegedly welcomed his coming martyrdom, saying, "Let us go with confidence, for it is better to die when it can no longer help to live. At no previous time of my life could I have died in such security of conscience." John Gower, in his more poetic account of the revolt in *Vox Clamantis*, implies that Sudbury is even more worthy of martyrdom than Becket, for whereas "four men plotted an agreement for Thomas' death, . . . a hundred thousand brought about Simon's murder." Once outside on Tower Hill, Sudbury eloquently tried to reason with the raging mob, but to no avail. At this point, his martyrdom is compared to that of an even greater personage. Walsingham describes the archbishop as the calm eye of a storm of grotesque, bestial peasants, all shouting like the "wailings of the inhabitants of hell," which seems to be how some medieval artists conceived of Christ's procession to Golgotha. Gower is more explicit, claiming that Sudbury was a shepherd "crucified" by his own flock, who were inspired by the devil. Finch calls him "champion of the Crucified [Christ]." The rebels, on the other hand, seem to have had a different opinion, for their treatment of Sudbury's severed head was probably intended as a mockery of such an identification.

The Carrying of the Cross *by Hieronymus Bosch, c. 1510. The image of Christ surrounded by grotesque, satanic faces is akin to how contemporaries viewed the martyrdom of Simon Sudbury, archbishop of Canterbury, in 1381. (Courtesy Museum of Fine Arts, Ghent.)*

Like his famous predecessor, Becket, Sudbury was killed for political reasons. As chancellor, he was held responsible for the poll taxes that ignited the revolt, an unfair charge since he had inherited the office as well as the policies of the former chancellor, Lord Richard Scrope, on January 30, 1380, well after the first two taxes had been levied and the impetus for the third already under way. Even so, there is evidence that Sudbury may have stirred up local hatred at Canterbury. In the late 1370s he rebuilt the nave of the cathedral, perhaps too soon after the entombment of the popular war hero Edward the Black Prince, and in 1380 he oversaw the rebuilding of Westgate in the city walls at a time when the expense of such repairs was weighing heavily on the citizens. His skull was preserved no doubt in the expectation that it would become the focus of another pilgrimage cult like the one at Canterbury made famous by Chaucer. But Sudbury's skull had not the cachet of Becket's bones. Nonetheless, Walsingham reports the requisite miracles wrought by the archbishop's severed body, such as restoring sight to the blind or helping a pregnant woman in the birth of triplets.

Despite the overwrought accounts of his martyrdom, neither Sudbury nor the class he represents was entirely blameless of his death. If the archbishop was a symbol of the cruel vengeance of the mob, he also was a symbol of cruel indifference to the people he helped to govern, a trait that Becket had scrupulously avoided. Indeed, this is perhaps the reason Sudbury's cult did not attain the popularity of Becket's. Although Walsingham was convinced that Sudbury was a martyr, even he expressed the reservation that the archbishop's death was brought on by the "tepidity of his cure [of souls]." Perhaps Gower sums up the condescending attitude of his class best, when he personifies the rebels as asses, swine, dogs, cats, foxes, birds, flies, and frogs; no doubt many of his readers took the allegory more literally. The evidence indicates that the Commons in Parliament proceeded more gingerly in the aftermath of 1381, most notably by abandoning any more experiments in taxation. King Richard, on the other hand, with the tacit approval of the lords, seems to have embarked on a more authoritarian rule—one that stressed the obedience due from his subjects—once his initial fears about dispersing the rebels were over. The crown's intransigent attitude is exemplified by Richard's speech, as reported by Walsingham, in reply to the request at Billericay from the men of Essex for their freedom toward the end of June 1381:

> Rustics you were and rustics you are still; you will remain in bondage, not as before but incomparably harsher. For as long as we live and, by God's grace, rule over the realm, we will strive with mind, strength and goods to

suppress you so that the rigour of your servitude will be
an example to posterity.

As Sudbury's skull could well attest (and as the king himself was
to learn in 1399), in the new social and economic climate created
by the plague, such an attitude was adopted at one's peril.

THE PLAGUE PSYCHE

While the exact nature of the social and economic fallout of the
Black Death was and still is hotly debated, the psychological and
religious response to the disease has been much less so. Perhaps
this is because that response is so much harder to pin down. Yet
one also can detect a certain complacency in past histories of the
Black Death that assumes we have learned all we need to know
about the plague's effect on the medieval psyche and religious
outlook. Generally it has been assumed that the Black Death
caused a spiritual lethargy, a moral malaise, even a "crisis of faith"
that, in England at least, eventually led to the Reformation. A
quiet revolution, however, has been taking place over the past
two decades in English religious scholarship that challenges many
of these assumptions.

To begin with, how did contemporaries see the effect the
plague was having on their collective psyche? The classic medieval
account of the psychological response to the great pestilence
comes from Giovanni Boccaccio's introduction to *The
Decameron*, in which he describes three ways that people in his
native city of Florence coped with the disease:

Some people were of the opinion that a sober and
abstemious mode of living considerably reduced the risk
of infection. They therefore formed themselves into
groups and lived in isolation from everyone else. Having
withdrawn to a comfortable abode where there were no
sick persons, they locked themselves in and settled down

to a peaceable existence, consuming modest quantities
of delicate foods and precious wines and avoiding all
excesses. They refrained from speaking to outsiders,
refused to receive news of the dead or the sick, and
entertained themselves with music and whatever other
amusements they were able to devise.

Others took the opposite view, and maintained that
an infallible way of warding off this appalling evil was to
drink heavily, enjoy life to the full, go round singing and
merrymaking, gratify all of one's cravings whenever the
opportunity offered, and shrug the whole thing off as
one enormous joke. Moreover, they practiced what they
preached to the best of their ability, for they would visit
one tavern after another, drinking all day and night to
immoderate excess; or alternatively (and this was their
more frequent custom), they would do their drinking in
various private houses, but only in the ones where the
conversation was restricted to subjects that were pleasant
or entertaining. Such places were easy to find, for people
behaved as though their days were numbered and treated
their belongings and their own persons with equal abandon. Hence most houses had become common property
and any passing stranger could make himself at home as
naturally as though he were the rightful owner. But for
all their riotous manner of living, these people always
took good care to avoid any contact with the sick. . . .

There were many other people who steered a middle
course between the two already mentioned, neither
restricting their diet to the same degree as the first group,
nor indulging so freely as the second in drinking and
other forms of wantonness, but simply doing no more
than satisfy their appetite. Instead of incarcerating themselves, these people moved about freely, holding in their
hands a posy of flowers, or fragrant herbs, or one of a
wide range of spices, which they applied at frequent intervals to their nostrils, thinking it an excellent idea to fortify
the brain with smells of that particular sort; for the stench

of dead bodies, sickness, and medicines seemed to fill and pollute the whole of the atmosphere.

These reactions—isolation, denial, moderation—can be found at almost any time epidemic disease descends indiscriminately upon an unsuspecting population. How much more true was this fear of the unknown for the medieval experience of plague, when, as Boccaccio testifies, "in the face of its onrush, all the wisdom and ingenuity of man were unavailing." Boccaccio's analysis of the plague psyche was perceptive, and it seems no accident that between 1343 and 1345 he wrote what many consider to be the first psychological novel, the *Elegia di Madonna Fiammetta* (Elegy for Lady Fiammetta).

One response commonly attributed to medieval survivors of the plague is a decay of manners and morals. People were supposedly less well behaved after the Black Death. The American sociologist J. W. Thompson, in a famous article, compared the psychological reaction of post-plague Europeans to that of his own generation in the aftermath of World War I. In both cases, Thompson argued, the crisis provoked a psychic release, a throwing off of traditional mores and customs that previously had regulated society. In place of old-world courtesy was behavioral chaos. In effect, medieval survivors of the plague suffered the equivalent of modern shell shock, and in the new atmosphere created, all the emotional floodgates were open, all rules were meant to be broken, and all bets were off. The stale and artificial pseudochivalry of the nouveaux riches who profited from the plague failed to recapture the old ideals.

In the end, Thompson's analogy between the survivors of the plague and the shell-shocked veterans of World War I fails because the later Middle Ages possessed an entirely different set of religious assumptions than those of the early twentieth century. Thompson's "Lost Generation" was well acquainted with the nihilism expressed by the philosopher Friedrich Nietzsche, who famously declared that "God is dead," something that never would have occurred to the medieval mind. Modern man may associate the approach of death with an end to hope, and therefore an end to the need to be well behaved, because he believes nothing lies beyond death. But such was not the case with his medieval counterpart, as we will see in the next chapter when we examine the way medieval man viewed death.

Nevertheless, plenty of chroniclers of the plague accused their contemporaries of moral turpitude. What shocked them most was abrogation of familial loyalties, particularly between parents and their children. Gabriele de Muisis gives perhaps the most heartrending account of the abandonment of the dying when he records what seems to be the last words of a child to a parent: "Oh father, why have you abandoned me? Do you forget that I am your child?" or "Mother, where have you gone? Why are you now so cruel to me when only yesterday you were so kind? You fed me at your breast and carried me within your womb for nine months." In the same way, parents lamented the lack of faith of their offspring: "My children, whom I brought up with toil and sweat, why have you run away?"

Such pathetic cries have an authentic ring to them, and their authors would have counted themselves lucky to have had the comfort of a candle or food and drink by their bedside in their last days. Those to whom the cries were directed undoubtedly acted out of fear, but also from a hard-heartedness induced by the sheer scale of the mortality, as anyone could see who visited the mass graves of the plague dead "stowed tier upon tier like ships' cargo." Death became cheap, and as a result funerals, as Boccaccio notes, were no longer the occasion for "lamentations and bitter tears" but "for laughter and witticisms and general jollification." According to Matteo Villani, another Florentine chronicler, the end of the plague did not bring a close to such disgraceful attitudes; rather, the survivors "gave themselves up to a more shameful and disordered life than they had led before." If such authors are to be believed, the Black Death was to blame for greater sexual promiscuity, a higher crime rate, more gambling and swearing, and, perhaps worst of all, a decline in good fashion sense.

Yet these complaints ring hollow when the very same authors also complain that men had been so bad before the plague that God sent this catastrophe down to rebuke them. Plenty of lamentations about the current state of human affairs can be found prior to 1348. Anonymous *Poems on the Times* dating to the early fourteenth century rail against all manner of ills in English society in a style that was to anticipate similar diatribes by Langland and Gower after the plague. In 1316 Walter Giffard, archbishop of Canterbury, characterized the Great Famine as divine retribution for his countrymen's "wickedness and sin," similar to self-castigations to explain the Black Death. In 1340 Jean de Venette, a friar of the Carmelite order, expressed his horror of "indecent" French fashion, eight years before the supposedly corrupting influence of the pestilence. The "good ol' days" may be a well-worn phrase but is perennially true: Men of whatever age and enjoying whatever fortune always look back to them.

There were other psychological responses to the Black Death, some unique to the medieval psyche. In one, men and women tried to literally whip themselves free of plague. This practice became known as the Flagellant Movement, and it grew out of a feeling of collective guilt about the Black Death, that the disease could only make sense if it was God's scourge upon mankind for his manifest wickedness and sin. The perfectly logical response, then, was to scourge oneself if God's wrath, in the form of the plague, was to be averted. What gave the movement a popular flavor was that not only individual Flagellants were thereby immune from the disease, but towns that welcomed them could share in their penitential benefits.

Flagellant processions probably started in late 1348 in Austria and Hungary, before the plague arrived in those areas, and in the course of the next year spread through southern, central, and western Germany, moving up the Rhine valley until finally reaching Flanders in July 1349, by which time the movement allegedly had grown to almost a million persons. When some Flagellants tried to come to England in late 1349 or early 1350, they seem to have received a less than enthusiastic reception. By that time, rumor had reached Englishmen that "they were doing these things ill advisedly, in that they did not have permission from the apostolic see." They had, in fact, been condemned in October 1349 by Pope Clement VI, on the grounds that "many of them . . . cruelly extending their hands to works of impiety under the color of piety, seem not in the least afraid to shed the blood of Jews, whom Christian piety accepts and sustains." Although some Flagellants are reported to have killed Jews at Frankfurt and Cologne in the summer of 1349, by and large their arrival in various cities does not overlap with the Jewish pogroms that took place throughout Germany and Switzerland during the Black Death. Clement was predisposed to associate the Flagellants with Jewish massacre on the advice of Jean de Fayt, a Benedictine monk who had personal contact with the Flagellants, but only in his native Flanders at the tail end of the movement.

Flagellants, from a fifteenth-century chronicle from Constance, Switzerland. (Courtesy Corbis.)

Flagellants anticipated Christocentric worship by identifying their sufferings with those of Christ on the cross, reflected in the red crosses they wore on their clothes or in the crucifixes they carried before them in procession. The name Flagellants came from the *flagella,* or whips, they used, graphically described by the German chronicler Henry of Herford:

> Each whip consisted of a stick with three knotted thongs hanging from the end. Two pieces of needle-sharp metal were run through the center of the knots from both sides, forming a cross, the ends of which extended beyond the knots for the length of a grain of wheat or less. Using these whips they beat and whipped their bare skin until their bodies were bruised and swollen and blood rained down, spattering the walls nearby. I have seen, when they whipped themselves, how sometimes those bits of metal penetrated the flesh so deeply that it took more than two attempts to pull them out.

These self-inflicted punishments were supplemented by beatings from other brethren and what must have been painful bruising from objects, such as nettles and stones, lying on the ground upon which the Flagellants "dropped like logs, flat on their belly and face, with arms outstretched" in the shape of a cross. That members were supposed to carry on like this at least twice a day for thirty-three and a half days, corresponding to the number of years that, by tradition, Christ had spent on earth, is hard to imagine, especially if they obeyed regulations that forbade bathing or changing of clothes. Yet there also was a strong exhibitionist streak to the movement that depended on audience support for necessities such as food and shelter, and perhaps they reserved their most frenzied scourgings for special performances.

One must keep in mind that the practice of flagellation in the Middle Ages was not unique to the Flagellants, nor did it have the voyeuristic reputation that it does today. Whipping was an accepted and long-established part of the sacramental rite of confession and penance, and a long catalogue of medieval saints tried to outdo each other in the gruesome torments of their martyrdom. Nor was 1348 the first time Flagellant processions appeared. Around 1260 a movement arose in northern Italy in response to a series of disasters there and to belief in the prophecies of Joachim of Fiore, a twelfth-century author and abbot of a Cistercian monastery at Corazzo, Italy, before he founded his own religious order at Fiore. Joachim divided history into three periods that he christened the Ages of the Father, the Son, and the Holy Spirit. During the first age, men had lived under the law of Moses and of the Old Testament. The second age, of which Joachim considered his times to be a part, was characterized by an established Church that adhered to the gospel of Christ. The third and final stage of history, the Age of the Holy Spirit, lay in the future and would see the coming of the Antichrist. According to Joachim, Antichrist initially would triumph, but after his inevitable overthrow, peace and justice would reign. Joachim's writings, therefore, contain both the optimism and pessimism typical of apocalyptic literature. The apocalyptic character of this earlier Flagellant movement, especially when it crossed the Alps into Germany, where a "heavenly letter" claimed divine inspiration for the processions, apparently reemerged among the later Flagellants of the Black Death. It is questionable, however, whether the Flagellants of 1348–49 had millennial expectations. The most radical of them, in Thuringia in central Germany, did sometimes physically attack churchmen who opposed their movement, but this seems to have been an outgrowth of their extraordinary penance (which by implication invalidated that imposed by a priest) rather than any concerted attempt at heresy.

The response of the medieval psyche to the plague also found expression in the pogroms perpetrated against a traditional scapegoat, the Jews. Between September 1348 and February 1351, massacres of Jews accused of spreading the plague to Christians occurred in as many as a hundred towns and cities. Usually the Jews were burned at the stake after being forced to confess under torture to having poisoned the drinking wells of the town on the orders of a visiting rabbi. The accusations were completely without foundation: Pope Clement VI, in two bulls promulgated in

The burning of Jews in an early printed woodcut. Jews were a common scapegoat for the plague in medieval Germany, foreshadowing their fate in the twentieth century. (Courtesy Corbis.)

September and October 1348, forbade persecution of the Jews on the grounds that they were dying of the plague in equal numbers to Christians. Technically these pogroms had little to do with England, since the country had expelled all its Jewish citizens in 1290. However, if we accept the explanation of the historian Gavin Langmuir that medieval massacres of Jews are largely the product of an "irrational" blood libel perpetrated against them for centuries, then England plays a very big role indeed. For it was in England that the first blood libel—accusing Jews of the ritual torture, crucifixion, and murder of a twelve-year-old boy, named William, for the purposes of mocking the Christian faith— was formulated in 1144. It was also in England that the first executions of Jews on the basis of the blood libel took place in 1255. In that year, nineteen Jews were put to death on the charge of having killed a young boy, Hugh, and thrown his body down a well at Lincoln. Thus, although England did not participate in

the pogroms of 1348–51, its draconian reaction to the Jewish "poisoning" of a well with the body of a Christian boy foreshadowed what was to come by nearly a century. Langmuir's argument is that these blood libels were irrational, since no one actually had seen any Jews commit them. On the other hand, it has been argued that the Jewish blood libel, at least from the medieval Christian perspective, was not irrational at all: As early as 1096 crusaders in Germany had witnessed Jews sacrificing their own families, including children, rather than submit to conversion by their enemies, an event that was replayed in England in 1190. Therefore, medieval Christians may have considered it just as likely that Jews would sacrifice *their* children as they would their own kind. Moreover, other explanations can be found for the Jewish pogroms during the Black Death, including the religious perception of Jews as "Christ-killers" and the economically vulnerable position that Jews held in medieval society as moneylenders. From the thirteenth century onwards, Jewish fortunes became more precarious as fresh accusations circulated that Jews during the first century A.D. had *intentionally* murdered Christ, despite knowing him to be the true messiah, and as their more lucrative lending business was taken over by the great Italian banking houses, such as the Bardi and the Peruzzi. Whatever the explanation, scapegoating of minority "outgroups" in response to incurable disease and economic uncertainty has proven no less attractive, and no less deadly, in the twentieth century as in the fourteenth.

A final aspect of the psychological fallout of the Black Death to consider is the religious one, and this aspect is crucial, for religion dominated the medieval psyche. Since most people imbibed their faith from the parish priest they visited every Sunday, one first must ask how the plague affected the priesthood. That the disease did indeed produce a crisis in Church personnel is attested by Ralph Shrewsbury, bishop of Bath and Wells, in a letter to the clergy of his diocese on January 10, 1349:

> The contagious pestilence, which is now spreading everywhere, has left many parish churches and other benefices in our diocese without an incumbent, so that their inhabi-

tants are bereft of a priest. And because priests cannot be found for love or money to take on the responsibility for those places and visit the sick and administer the sacraments of the Church to them—perhaps because they fear that they will catch the disease themselves—we understand that many people are dying without the sacrament of penance, because they do not know what they ought to do in such an emergency and believe that even in an emergency, confession of their sins is of no use or worthless unless made to a priest having the power of the keys. Therefore, desirous as we must be to provide for the salvation of souls and to call back the wanderers who have strayed from the way, we order and firmly enjoin you, upon your obedience, to make it known speedily and publicly to everybody, but particularly to those who have already fallen sick, that if on the point of death they cannot secure the services of a properly ordained priest, they should make confession of their sins, according to the teaching of the apostle, to any lay person, even to a woman, if a man is not available.

Shrewsbury's radical solution to the shortage of clergy created by the plague was confirmed by a papal indulgence that arrived in England in March 1349, authorizing parishioners to choose their confessor in their hour of death. Two centuries before Luther, Shrewsbury and Pope Clement VI were forced by circumstances to experiment with a form of individual religious practice that was to become one of the hallmarks of Protestantism.

For the rest of the fourteenth century, a succession of archbishops of Canterbury issued legislation that was the Church's equivalent to the Statute of Labourers: attempting either to limit the wages priests received or curb their "leapfrogging" to richer livings elsewhere. In his constitution *Effrenata* (Unbridled) promulgated in May 1350, just after the first plague outbreak abated, Archbishop Simon Islip complained that "priests now refuse to take on the cure of souls, or to support the burdens of their cures in mutual charity, but rather leave them completely abandoned and apply themselves instead to the celebration of commemorative masses and other private offices." Islip's criticisms were repeated by Archbishops Simon Sudbury in 1378 and William Courtenay in 1392, the latter railing especially against "choppechurches," or agents who had sprung up to arrange exchanges between priests anxious to improve their income. The archbishops' concerns are borne out by their registers: Exchanges made up over 45 percent of vacancies in the register of Simon Sudbury as bishop of London between 1362 and 1375, as opposed to just 23 percent in the register of his pre-plague predecessor, Stephen Gravesend, between 1319 and 1338. An examination of exchanges granted in three other English dioceses in the decades after the Black Death reveals that Sudbury's register did not record an isolated trend. A turning point seems to have been reached in 1370–71 at Winchester and Exeter and a little later, in 1386, at Hereford. Exchanges at Winchester went from 9 on average between 1350 and 1369 to just over 13 between 1370 and 1400; at Exeter from over four between 1328 and 1368 to 11 between 1371 and 1400; and at Hereford from three and a half between 1328 and 1385 to over eight between 1386 and 1400 (see table 7, page 275).

It was during these decades of high exchanges—the 1360s, '70s, and '80s—that the English poets Langland, Gower, and Chaucer were writing their famous diatribes against churchmen. Langland's complaint in *Piers Plowman* is perhaps the best known:

> The parsons and parish-priests complained to the bishop
> That their parishes were poor since the pestilence year,
> Asking licence and leave in London to dwell,
> To sing there for simony; for silver is sweet.

Gower likewise complains in the *Mirour de l'Omme*, "There are priests who, for our money, serve willingly and have no other benefice. They chant for three-month periods or even for years for the dead; and they are commonly followers of every vice." Finally, Chaucer, in his prologue to the *Canterbury Tales*, upholds his Parson as a model of priestly behavior, thereby indirectly criticizing the many who behave otherwise:

He did not let his benefice out to hire
And leave his sheep stuck in the mire
And run to London to St. Paul's
To seek out a chantry for souls
Or to a guild be beholden
But dwelled at home and well tended his fold.

The gist of all these complaints was that priests were leaving their parishes in order to service richer patrons who were engaging them to say private masses for their souls. In other words, the needs of the community were allegedly being abandoned for the very private needs of wealthy individuals. What was worse, those who remained on the job were less than qualified as the Church scrambled to fill vacancies created by the plague. According to the chronicler Henry Knighton, "A great crowd of men whose wives had died in the pestilence rushed into priestly orders. Many of them were illiterate, no better than laymen—for even if they could read, they did not understand what they read." Moreover, contempt and even violence directed against Church personnel seems to have been the order of the day in the wake of the Black Death. Bishop Shrewsbury and his retinue, for example, were surrounded and besieged for a night and a day at Yeovil, Somerset, in the autumn of 1349 by "certain sons of perdition" armed "with bows, arrows, iron bars, stones, and other kinds of arms." In 1364 this scene was replayed against Robert Stretton, bishop of Coventry and Lichfield, at Repton, where "certain satellites of Satan, the whole commonalty of the town" assaulted him with "swords and staves, bows and arrows, noise and tumult," forcing him to hole up in the priory of St. Wystan from eleven o'clock of one day until one o'clock of the next. The decade 1379–89 in the diocese of Exeter saw thirteen incidents of assault upon the priesthood, including three murders, a blinding, a castration, and a "crucifixion," in which John Calestake, vicar of St. Gluvias, was bound to a cross in the public way of Penryn, Cornwall.

However remarkable these anecdotes are, one should not recite them without recognizing at least three points in the Church's favor. In the first place, the sheer number of churchmen who died of the Black Death attests to the dedication of a substantial proportion of the clergy during the crisis. Yet despite the mortality, the Church carried on much as before. There is no more impressive evidence of this than the fact that bishops' scribes throughout England continued to enter in their masters' registers the mounting toll of vacancies in parish churches. Nevertheless, the Church had to make extraordinary, even heroic, efforts to maintain the status quo. Recruitment of men to the cloth, judging from episcopal ordination lists, experienced periodic surges during the fourteenth century in response to plagues that decimated the priesthood. Overall, recruitment suffered a long, slow decline until the 1460s, but then ordination levels show a surprising rebound and steadily increase thereafter until the eve of the Reformation. How the Church managed to replenish its ranks during times of recurring plagues is a mystery. The most likely explanation is that it lowered its standards for ordination, admitting younger, illegitimate, or less educated men. Yet it also seems that large numbers of recruits voluntarily came forward to be ordained, not all of them for the mercenary motive of advancing their careers in response to opportunities created by the Black Death.

Second, commentators on the Church may have been unduly critical in the self-flagellating atmosphere after 1349. As already mentioned, ample complaints about immoral behavior, both within the Church and in society as a whole, can be found prior to the plague as well as afterwards. The *Poem on the Evil Times of Edward II*, which rails against all classes of English society, complains that priests, no less than their counterparts after the Black Death, neglected their parishes:

> *And whan he hath i-gadered markes and poundes,*
> *He priketh out of toune wid haukes and wid houndes*
> *Into a straunge contre, and halt a wenche in cracche;*
> *And wel is hire that first may swich a parsoun kacche*
> *   in londe.*
> *And thus theih serven the chapele, and laten the churche*
> *   stonde.*

And when he [the priest] has gathered marks and
   pounds,
He rides out of town with his hawks and hounds
Into a strange country, and stops with a wench in
   her bed;
And it is well for her whom first such a parson catches in
   the land.
And thus they serve the chapel, and let the church
   stand [empty].

In 1333, Bishop John de Grandisson of Exeter complained that every year on the Feast of the Holy Innocents (December 28), priests in the cathedral would "not fear to irreverently and damnably give rise to frivolities, laughter, guffaws, and other insolent responses, even to the point of wearing masks, and debase the clerical dignity by such obscene hand play in their gesticulation in full view of the people."

Sometimes, however, this negative attitude was not entirely justified. Whereas most contemporaries were quick to see roving priests motivated by greed, the actions of some clerical survivors of the plague may have been dictated by necessity. Evidence of poverty in the parish created by the shortage of parishioners and their offerings can be found in diocese after diocese. In Winchester in 1361, Bishop William Edington had to appeal to the king for a reduction in tax contributions of thirteen churches "depopulated since the pestilence," and in 1364 he united the two halves of the church of Abinger because neither alone was sufficient for a living. John Trillek, bishop of Hereford, united the churches of Great and Little Collington in 1352, and his successor, Lewis Charlton, united the parishes of Puddlestone and Whyle in 1364. In 1350 Shrewsbury at Bath and Wells granted special license to Robert Crox, rector of Ilchester, to service a chantry in addition to his other duties "because the tithes and other oblations falling to your church are known to be insufficient." At Rochester, Bishop Hamo Hethe in 1349 likewise allowed poor priests to say private masses because "their income is well known to have diminished through the mortality of parishioners so that they cannot live on what remains or support the

burdens incumbent [on their office]." Finally, in the same year at
Ely, Bishop Thomas de Lisle granted John Lynot, vicar of All
Saints in Cambridge, an annual sustenance for two years on
account of the fact that his "parishioners have in the meantime
suffered for so long from the pestilence . . . so that the oblations
of those coming to the said church are by no means sufficient for
[his] necessities." The remainder of the Middle Ages were not to
see any substantial improvement in priests' living standards.
Moreover, the violence that we see directed against the clergy
may not have been the result of anticlericalism but rather may
have been symptomatic of a general trend of increasing disorder
in fourteenth-century England. Examples of such violence can be
found even before the Black Death.

Third, and last, it must be remembered that the severest critics of the Church were themselves churchmen. The episcopal
hierarchy were well aware that many priests, confessors, and other
Church personnel appointed because of the plague were not up
to snuff. What is remarkable is that despite the fact that English
bishops during the later Middle Ages tended to be servants of the
crown as well as servants of God, these "careerist" prelates made
a serious effort to reform the Church in the aftermath of the
Black Death. There is no better example of such a man than John
Thoresby, chancellor of England during the 1350s and, until his
death in 1373, archbishop of York. Despite a lifetime of royal
service, Thoresby resigned the chancellorship in 1356, probably
in protest to a royal infringement of ecclesiastical liberty.
Thereafter he seems to have devoted himself to pastoral work, in
particular to recruiting candidates for ordination, compelling
nonresident priests to return to their parishes, fixing wages of
stipendiary chaplains, and improving the administration of the
sacraments. In addition, Thoresby tried to improve the religious
education of both lay and clerical members of his flock; in 1357
he issued the *Lay Folk's Catechism*, an English translation of a
Latin work Thoresby wrote himself. Nor was such learning always
by the book: Mystery plays put on by merchant guilds in the cities
dramatized for their audience important events from the Bible.
The Towneley Cycle, for example, one of many Yorkshire plays
performed in commemoration of the Feast of Corpus Christi,

may have been written not just to instruct the laity in the meaning of the Eucharist, but also to respond to attacks upon the sacraments by audacious heretics. Thoresby was by no means a lone reformer. Similar efforts to his own—particularly with regard to absentee rectors and unfit confessors—can be found in diocese after diocese. Moreover, greater educational opportunities were to be had for plague survivors at a growing number of reading and grammar schools and university colleges, many of them sponsored by the episcopate. Between 1348 and 1355 alone, Cambridge University saw the foundation of no fewer than four colleges, doubling its institutions of higher learning.

The conduct of the clergy is one thing, but was popular piety any less fervent in the aftermath of the Black Death? Some authors at the time wrote to that effect, yet like the laments about rampant immorality, such complaints are suspect since they imply that the people's faith had to have been tepid even before the plague if they were to merit so great a disaster in the first place. Nevertheless, some English bishops had quite specific and interesting things to say about matters of faith, or a deficiency thereof, in the years after the plague.

Their primary concern was their parishioners' apparent lack of respect for the sanctified precincts of the church. Already in 1348, Bishop Trillek of Hereford complained of the performance in churches of his diocese of "theatrical plays . . . that make coarse jests and rude remarks . . . and other things of a mocking nature, on account of which the hearts of the faithful, which ought to be attending to divine services and saying devout prayers, are distracted toward inanities and their devotion subverted." In 1353, Thomas Hatfield, bishop of Durham, heard report of parishioners in the deaneries of Durham and Darlington who preferred to eat, drink, and be merry rather than attend church on Sundays, a concern that was echoed by Archbishop Simon Islip in 1359. Islip complained to the bishops of the southern province that people, instead of going to Sunday services, frequented markets and other illicit gatherings, where they ate and drank together and did many other "dishonest things . . . from which proceeded quarrels and insults, threats and blows, and sometimes murders." Due to their absence from church, "reverence to God and the saints ceases, the holy mysteries are by no means held in due veneration as is fitting, and the mutual support of prayer is greatly undermined and decreased, in irreverence of God and Holy Church, grave peril of souls, and manifest contempt and scandal of divine precepts as well as Christian religion."

Such complaints would be echoed in the following decades. In 1354 Gilbert Welton, bishop of Carlisle, warned against keeping hay, grain, and animals in the churches of Wetheral and Warwick, while his successor, Thomas Appleby, was concerned in 1372 and 1386 that several rectors and vicars of the diocese failed to join in the traditional procession to Carlisle Cathedral during the week of Pentecost. In 1360, John de Grandisson, bishop of Exeter, heard report of priests who on certain feast days performed with their altar boys "tasteless and offensive games, indecent to clerical honesty, nay in detestable mockery of the true Divine Cult," which caused the congregation to "dissolve into incoherent laughter and illicit amusements." His successor, Thomas Brantyngham, in 1386 admonished the parishioners of three churches, including his own cathedral, to abstain from gossiping, conducting business, and engaging in "extremely filthy and profane conversations" during the service. In 1365 and 1367 Archbishop Thoresby issued prohibitions against the use of churchyards for activities other than going to church, such as archery, wrestling, dancing, singing, feasting, and setting up of markets. In 1384 William Wykeham, bishop of Winchester, had similar concerns about goings-on in the cathedral cemetery, which included playing ball and slinging stones, activities that clerics and laymen alike indulged in and that threatened priceless stained-glass windows. Sometimes churches were even robbed, as happened in January 1385 when the reliquary of St. Etheldreda at Ely Cathedral was despoiled of rings, brooches, and other jewelry.

In recent years scholars have tried to find more comprehensive and rigorous measures of popular piety during the late medieval period. There is much at stake in this effort, particularly with regard to England. Were Englishmen moving away from Catholicism, toward a more Protestant kind of belief, already during the later Middle Ages? Or were they as Catholic as their Continental counterparts right up until Henry VIII's break with

Rome in 1534? Such considerations could affect the way we look at the English Reformation entirely.

The strongest argument in favor of the uniqueness of the English Church, and the inevitability of its split from the Continent, is that the ideas of John Wycliffe, an anti-papist polemicist who died in 1384 (of natural causes, only to be dug up and burned as a heretic thirty years later), constituted a kind of "premature Reformation." This argument first was made by the sixteenth-century Reformation hagiographers John Bale and John Foxe and still holds sway among some historians. There is, indeed, a remarkable similarity between Wycliffe's ideas, especially as reconstituted by his later Lollard followers, and the Reformation program. Lollard heretics (a name derived from their tendency to "loll," or mumble their English prayers), in the course of their trials during the fifteenth century, espoused beliefs that a century later were to become the bedrock of Protestantism: denial of the real presence of Christ in the Eucharist and of the efficacy of the other sacraments; appeal to the Bible (now translated into English) as the ultimate authority; extension of sacerdotal powers to all those who were "righteous"; predestination of the saved and the damned; and rejection (sometimes violently) of images, pilgrimages, feast days, and saint cults. Most presciently of all, Wycliffe and the Lollards advocated dispossession of Church property (to be seized into the hands of the crown), an idea finally realized by Henry VIII's Dissolution of the monasteries in 1536–40. Moreover, through England's contacts with Bohemia as a result of King Richard II's marriage to Princess Anne, Wycliffe influenced the Bohemian reformer Jan Hus, and through him, Martin Luther.

In the end, though, it is difficult to argue that Wycliffe so neatly anticipated the Reformation. In the first place, there is no evidence that Wycliffe intended his movement to be popular and broad-based. Despite the fact that he may have been one of the first to attempt an English translation of the Bible, most of his writings are in academic Latin, clearly intended for the eyes of his rarefied circle at Oxford. Nor is it certain that Wycliffe's contemporaries were as disillusioned as he with Church scandals abroad, such as the Babylonian Captivity and the Great Schism. Much of

Wycliffe's disillusionment with the Church was personal, the result of having been passed over by the pope for ecclesiastical preferment. He himself, in fact, indulged in many of the abuses, such as pluralism, or the holding of many church offices at once, and nonresidence, that he so denounced in others.

In general, the English after 1378 can be said to have been remarkably supportive of a papacy based at Rome. The Great Schism may have led to some disillusionment with the Church, as indicated by a decline in recruitment to the priesthood in several English dioceses after 1380, and the English government seems to have used the Schism in order to have its political wars against Flanders and Spain during the 1380s blessed as crusades by the Roman pope, Urban VI. Nevertheless, by the early fifteenth century, Englishmen, headed by Kings Henry IV and Henry V and Archbishops Thomas Arundel and Henry Chichele, made concerted efforts to help heal the Schism through a series of Church councils known as the Conciliar Movement. Their commitment is shown by their active participation in the councils, by their continual call for prayers to be said for Church unity, and by the stream of English writing that was produced on the subject.

The connection between Wycliffe's movement and the Reformation becomes even more problematic when we look at the later history of the Lollards. From about 1440 Lollardy entered a free-fall decline, which may have begun even earlier in 1414 with the failed revolt of the Lollard knight Sir John Oldcastle (the inspiration for Shakespeare's Falstaff in *Henry IV*). This decline is evidenced by an almost complete halt to the production (or reproduction) of heretical works, which did not pick up again until around 1480, during which time episcopal persecution of Lollards had grown lax, which should have encouraged such activity. Moreover, when Lollardy did revive and was appropriated by the English Reformation, it is clear that this was only after a long and painstaking recovery of outdated texts. The irresistible momentum Lollardy supposedly provided toward an English Reformation was wishful thinking on the part of Reformation authors, who sought to justify their movement with hindsight. It may be, as some have argued, that Lollardy would have caught on if only it had the disseminating power of the printing press or the support of the local nobility, advantages that Luther in the sixteenth century clearly enjoyed. Then again, there is a much more plausible explanation: Lollardy simply was not widely popular. On the eve of the Reformation most Englishmen were strictly, if unimaginatively, orthodox.

Much of what we can know about general religious attitudes comes from parish records, primarily wills proved in one of the Church courts and recorded in probate registers. However, there are caveats to be considered before using the testimony of medieval wills. The bulk of wills survive from the fifteenth rather than the fourteenth century; almost all testators came from the gentry and rich urban elite (in other words, those who owned enough to make leaving a will worthwhile); wills invariably are couched in formulaic language that leaves little room for individual expression; and they are an incomplete record of the pious works of a benefactor, since they do not record deeds done during his or her lifetime. Nevertheless, wills are about as close as we will ever get to a window onto the religious mind-set of the English people.

Medieval wills have been mined from all over England: London, Canterbury, Salisbury, Bristol, Norwich, Bury St. Edmunds, York, and Kingston-on-Hull, to name the most current studies. What this evidence reveals is that secular priests, and the parish churches they served, continued to play a central role in the lives of late medieval Englishmen. Henry's later break with Rome was by no means a foregone conclusion. His subjects, in the years leading up to the Reformation, were not nearly as dissatisfied with Catholicism as Whiggish historians of England once had claimed. Rather, the average testator of the fifteenth and early sixteenth centuries was content enough with the Church to leave it a major beneficiary at his or her death. Local priests were by far the most requested group to participate in the deceased's funeral and, outside of the deceased's kin, were left the most money in order to say masses to speed the deceased's soul through purgatory. Parish churches, the most popular places to be buried among those who could afford it, also received much money for their upkeep, which was only natural since they housed the expensive tombs of benefactors and their ancestors. At Norwich,

95 percent of lay testators and 85 percent of clerical ones between 1370 and 1532 left money to a parish church; 53 percent of testators at Bury St. Edmunds between 1380 and 1399 requested secular priests to preside at their funerals, and 41 percent did so between 1449 and 1530; 81 percent of will-makers at Kingston-on-Hull and an average 88 percent of those among the Kentish gentry between 1400 and 1539 wished to be buried in a local church or churchyard, while 46 percent and over 50 percent respectively invested in some kind of commemorative mass for their souls.

It could be argued that some wills, particularly those that established chantry chapels in which priests were hired to attend solely to the spiritual well-being of a patron, reveal an individual concern for salvation that anticipates the Reformation. Yet even chantry priests contributed—as was intended by founders—to the overall service of the parish, and this sense of community was reinforced in other ways, such as bequests to the poor, directions for prayers to be said for others beyond the deceased's kin, and the efforts of parish guilds or lay fraternities, who hired chantry priests on behalf of all their members. Nor can the spurning of worldly pomp and the self-abasement evoked by some wills opting for simple funerals be used as evidence for Lollard beliefs, since such sentiments were likewise expressed by patrons of unquestioned orthodoxy, both in England and on the Continent. In addition, the perpetual commemoration of the dead provided for by wills, such as obits or masses celebrated on the anniversary of the patron's demise, went a long way toward helping the living cope with their own future deaths. Such obits and celebrations blurred the line between life and death, conferring a certain immortality to the dead and holding out to the living the promise of rebirth and resurrection. The "cult of remembrance" that has been observed among the will-makers of Renaissance Italy therefore can be found equally among the inhabitants of English cities like Bury St. Edmunds. Ordinary Englishmen had more in common with their Continental counterparts on the eve of the Reformation than the makers of that event had led us to believe.

Wills may tell us something of the kind and extent of religious belief held by medieval people, but they cannot tell us anything of the intensity and fervor of such beliefs. For the latter, we must turn to other types of evidence. What is somewhat surprising is that this evidence points to a religious revival—not a decline—in the decades after the Black Death. In England, the advent of the plague coincided with a coming avalanche of mystical writing that was unprecedented in the religious history of the island. The best of these works—the anonymous *Cloud of Unknowing*, Walter Hilton's *The Scale of Perfection*, and *A Book of Showings* by Julian of Norwich—rival in their beauty and simplicity of the English language anything written by Chaucer or Langland. Unlike their more famous contemporaries, the mystical authors excelled in prose rather than poetry, and their pioneering efforts in that medium perhaps have yet to be appreciated. The English mystical tradition was important in a couple of other respects. It made England part of a constellation of mystics who emerged in Europe during the fourteenth century that included Meister Eckhardt, Johannes Tauler, and Heinrich Suso in Germany, and Jan van Ruysbroeck in Flanders. It also provided unprecedented opportunities for religious expression to English women, such as Julian of Norwich and Margery Kempe, who again had their Continental counterparts in the Blessed Angela of Foligno, St. Catherine of Siena, and St. Brigitta of Sweden.

Obviously, not everyone was cut out to be a mystic. But neither does this mean that mystical works went unread by a population growing more and more literate in their native tongue. Nor was literacy strictly required, since some "readers," such as Margery Kempe, had works read to them by spiritual guides, especially priests. The evidence of bishops' registers indicates that Kempe was by no means the only housewife-turned-mystic in late medieval England. Other married or recently widowed women who took religious vows include Beatrix Stronge of Devon in 1329, Margaret Meifolyne of Somerset and Beatrice le Botiler of Worcestershire in 1349, Alicia Brete of Somerset in 1360, Isabel Burgh and Isabel Golafre of Hampshire in 1379, Katherine Bernard of Cambridgeshire in 1385, and Lady Margaret Hakeluyt of Somerset in 1413.

Even though these women took the vows of nuns, this does not mean that they lived like them. For unlike their cloistered counterparts, women like Margery Kempe and, on the

Continent, the Beguines, a movement of lay religious women that flourished during the thirteenth and early fourteenth centuries, moved very much within society and sometimes trod a fine line between heresy and orthodoxy. Yet, it would be a mistake to ascribe modern—particularly Protestant or feminist—sensibilities to these mystics, as some have tried to do. Most of them, including Julian, St. Catherine, and St. Brigitta, operated within a well-established tradition of mystical theology going back to the sixth century A.D. In this "pseudo-Dionysian" tradition, named after an anonymous Syrian monk, the aspiring mystic must enter a darkness, or spiritual silence, surrounding God, whose superlative qualities can never be defined by earthbound attempts at description. Rather, this "cloud of unknowing" can only be penetrated by a complete rejection of material distractions and the constant and repeated act of prayer beating upon the darkness, until God chooses to reveal himself to the mystic in all His overwhelming and unspeakable glory. In the words of *The Cloud of Unknowing*, designed as a manual for the novice mystic and which saw wide circulation during the later Middle Ages:

> But now you will ask me, "How am I to think of God himself, and what is he?" and I cannot answer you except to say "I do not know!" For with this question you have brought me into the same darkness, the same cloud of unknowing where I want you to be! For though we through the grace of God can know fully about all other matters, and think about them—yes, even the very works of God himself—yet of God himself can no man think. . . . Therefore, though it may be good sometimes to think particularly about God's kindness and worth, and though it may be enlightening too, and a part of contemplation, yet in the work now before us it must be put down and covered with a cloud of forgetting. And you are to step over it resolutely and eagerly, with a devout and kindling love, and try to penetrate that darkness above you. Strike that thick cloud of unknowing with the sharp dart of longing love, and on no account whatever think of giving up.

This period of suffering and doubt that must be endured before achieving a mystical union with God can be compared to the more material pains wrought by the Black Death, which many chroniclers assumed were but a prelude to a reunion with their Creator at the Apocalypse.

One may question what other connections can be drawn between mysticism and the Black Death. There is little evidence that the plague directly affected late medieval mystics (except for Richard Rolle, who probably died of it in 1349). Still, I believe that the popularity mysticism enjoyed in England and on the Continent in the later Middle Ages was not unrelated to the onset and continuing presence of the pestilence. If disasters such as the plague were the will of God, what better way to make sense of them than to acquire a mystical knowledge of God's will? Mysticism gave its practitioners a chance to understand, and ultimately transcend, all the sufferings God placed in their path. Illness, for example, plays a significant role in the *Book of Showings* of Julian of Norwich, and sickness was the genesis of Julian's mysticism. As she informs us herself, in May 1373 she lay near death in her bed in Norwich. When the priest brought her a crucifix and held it before her on what she believed to be her last day, she experienced the first of her sixteen "showings," or revelations, on Christ's passion. The showings proved to be the start of Julian's recovery, but what exactly her illness was will never be known. What is clear, however, is that sickness and suffering were an integral part of Julian's unique brand of theology. Indeed, she desired to be ill, by her own account, in order to reenact Christ's suffering:

> There came into my mind . . . a desire of my will to have by God's gift a bodily sickness. I wished that sickness to be so severe that it might seem mortal, so that I might in it receive all the rites which Holy Church has to give me, whilst I myself should think that I was dying, and everyone who saw me would think the same; for I wanted no comfort from any human, earthly life in that sickness. I wanted to have every kind of pain, bodily and spiritual, which I should have if I had died, every fear and tempta-

tion from devils, and every other kind of pain except the
departure of the spirit. I intended this because I wanted
to be purged by God's mercy, and afterwards live more to
his glory because of that sickness.

Pain and suffering had a definite purpose, which was twofold,
as Julian explains in a later revelation, where she contemplates the
existence of evil and sin in the world. On the one hand, the experience of suffering reminds us of the passion of Christ, which was
far greater and of far nobler a purpose. That is, we are reminded
that we are part of a greater whole—that we do not suffer alone—
and that our suffering could always be worse. On the other hand,
suffering gives us the opportunity for personal redemption, by
which we can know the everlasting love of God, a redemption
that will be shared by all mankind at the Last Judgment at the end
of the world. The Apocalypse is key to Julian's religious outlook,
for at that time God will set everything right and take away all our
suffering. As she says in perhaps the most famous sentence in the
Showings, "Synne is behovely [necessary], but alle shalle be wele,
and alle shalle be wele, and alle maner of thynge shalle be wele."
This mantra of optimism is explained more fully in revelation 15,
in which Julian, speaking in the persona of God, relates it to sickness and suffering:

> Suddenly you will be taken out of all your pain, all your
> sickness, all your unrest, and all your woe. And you will
> come up above, and you will have me for your reward,
> and you will be filled full of joy and bliss, and you will
> never again have any kind of pain, any kind of sickness,
> any kind of displeasure, no lack of will, but always joy and
> bliss without end. Why then should it afflict you to
> endure awhile, since it is my will and to my glory?

After witnessing so great a disaster as the plague, any man
would naturally question his faith, whether it be in God or in
some other set of assumptions that gave order and sense to his
world. Medieval mystics embarked willingly upon this difficult
path of uncertainty, passing through a darkness before emerging

into the light of revelation. Their experiences would therefore have had deep resonance with the survivors of the Black Death, or at least with those who pondered the meaning of the catastrophe that had befallen them. Julian, who followed in the pseudo-Dionysian tradition but ultimately pursued her own path to mystical enlightenment, tapped into another response to the plague besides that of psychological doubt and decline. Rather, Julian's theology emphasizes the resilience and recovery of the human spirit after a long illness of the soul or of the flesh. Unlike the chroniclers of the Black Death, who emphasized disease as a punishment for man's sin, Julian turned suffering into a message of hope. It is this optimism that is perhaps the most attractive quality of her work. No doubt for those who lived through the horrible year of 1349, and other plague years thereafter, a faith that "alle shalle be wele" in God's plan for the world gave them the mental and physical strength to carry on no matter how much pain and misery the Black Death wrought.

DEATH

I was a pauper born, then to Primate raised
Now I am cut down and ready to be food for worms
Behold my grave.
Whoever you may be who passes by, I ask you to remember
You will be like me after you die
All horrible, dust, worms, vile flesh.

— Epitaph from the tomb of Henry Chichele, d. 1443

To see the fifteenth-century tomb of Archbishop Henry Chichele in Canterbury Cathedral is to gaze upon the very image of death. On the upper level of the tomb, on a great stone slab, lies the archbishop decked out in all the robes and regalia of his state. But just below it, in what seems an ornate coffin with open, traceried, Gothic windows, appears the archbishop again in quite a different aspect. Except for the pudding haircut, which was the fashion of the times, the discreetly naked cadaver lying on its shroud could be our contemporary: pale, still, emaciated, the bony flesh drawn tightly over the shrunken form, the eyes hollow, the cheeks sunken, the mouth open from the shock of being dead. From an age not known for its realistic portraiture of the living, it seems that the medieval sculptor of this tomb is giving us a privileged glimpse into the grave. Such a portrait of death is duplicated in various forms on hundreds of tombs in England and throughout northern Europe from the end of the fourteenth to the seventeenth centuries. Why did our forebears portray themselves so graphically in death and display the result to posterity for all time?

Needless to say, they had a different attitude toward death than we do today. For the vast majority of us in the modern Western world, it would be utterly inconceivable to pay for the privilege of having ourselves carved on our memorials (should we choose to have one) as a desiccated, rotting corpse. Why bury the dead, only to have the tomb throw up our remains in all their hideous, gruesome deformity for all to see? Even in the Middle Ages, the thirteenth-century theologian St. Thomas Aquinas asserted that burial is "for the sake of the living, lest their eyes be revolted by the disfigurement of the corpse." But unlike medieval men and women, we in the modern West studiously avoid *all* unpleasant reminders of death. The French historian Philippe Ariès has characterized our present attitude as the "death denied," the "dirty death," or the "invisible death." By this he means that nowadays the dying no longer determine their own deaths—indeed, they feel compelled to perpetuate the lie that they are not dying at all—and with the advent of new medical technologies, we have lost the choice to die a natural death.

Our recent repugnance for death perhaps was already evident

by the latter half of the nineteenth century. It was during the Victorian era that authorities at the church of Dalton Holme in Yorkshire ordered that the life-size carved skeleton lying underneath the reclining effigy of Sir John Hotham be removed (not to be replaced until the 1960s) because it "frightened the children" of parishioners. Hotham's tomb, erected at his death in 1689, was the last monument in England to depict a cadaverous or skeletal figure, known as the "transi," a term derived from the Latin verb *transire*, meaning to pass away. Clearly, to the Victorians of Dalton, Hotham's skeleton had infringed upon the comfortable remoteness they now enjoyed from death.

Nevertheless, the transi tomb is evidence of a genre of apocalyptic and macabre art and literature that enjoyed great popularity, especially in northern Europe, during the later Middle Ages and for centuries beyond. From illuminations and other depictions of the Fourth Rider of the Apocalypse to portrayals of interactions between death and man, to the enshrinement of cadavers in the transi tombs, these expressions of mortality are all closely dependent on each other. One can trace a natural progression as, at each stage, death assumes an ever more personal aspect, allowing us a valuable and revealing window onto the mentality of late medieval man.

THE FOURTH RIDER OF THE APOCALYPSE

Go to almost any great Romanesque cathedral in France, and the first sight that greets you as you approach the immense portals is a vision of the Apocalypse. Just above the main doorway will loom most likely a reenactment in stone of the Last Judgment at the end of the world. Christ resides in the middle of the heavenly spheres, often surrounded by the four evangelists, the twelve apostles, and a host of saints, preparing to separate the saved from the damned. In the words of St. John:

> And I saw a great white throne and the one who sat upon it; from his face the earth and heaven fled away, and there

was found no place for them. And I saw the dead, the great and the small, standing before the throne, and scrolls were opened. And another scroll was opened, which is the book of life; and the dead were judged out of those things that were written in the scrolls, according to their works. And the sea gave up the dead that were in it, and death and hell gave up the dead that were in them; and they were judged each one, according to their works. (Apocalypse 20:11–13)

This scene is essentially the same, whether carved in the tympanums at Moissac, Vèzelay, St. Denis, or Chartres. At Beaulieu and Bourges the dead rise at the sound of the angels' trumpets by actually lifting up the lids of their tombs. At Autun and St. Foy-de-Conques devils and angels vie to tip the scales that weigh men's souls. Yet in all these examples the message is clear: Entrance to the church is the entrance to a better world.

As it was outside the church, so it was inside. The Doom, or Last Judgment of Christ, was painted on the walls of many a parish church in England during the fourteenth century. Traces of the subject, if not the whole scene itself, survive in no fewer than twenty-four examples, usually painted over the chancel arch, just above the entrance to the sanctuary containing the high altar. Most of these show the dead rising from their graves and either the weighing of souls or the separation of the saved from the damned. Again, the message is clear: Participation in the sacrament of the mass is the gateway to paradise.

Our focus, however, is not on the climax of John's Revelation, but on the beginning: the opening of the seven seals that will unleash God's destructive forces upon the land and that eventually will lead to the Second Coming. In particular, we are concerned with the Fourth Rider of the Apocalypse, Death, heralded by the opening of the fourth seal. How should Death be portrayed? Medieval artists' attempts to grapple with that question led to the earliest depictions of the cadaver in art: The Triumph of Death theme became one of the most awe-inspiring subjects in Western painting.

Around the middle of the thirteenth century a remarkable group of manuscript illuminators emerged in England. From

about 1240 to about 1280 these artists produced a series of beautifully illuminated editions of the Apocalypse of St. John.
Commissioned largely by the court of Henry III and later by that
of the young Prince Edward and his wife, Eleanor of Castile, the
manuscripts, thought to have been produced mainly in London,
typically contain a half-page illustration above a text in Latin or
French. Why did the Apocalypse emerge at this time to be the
subject of such sumptuous illumination?

The answer, in part, goes back to the twelfth-century writings
of one of the most apocalyptic authors of the Middle Ages,
Joachim of Fiore. According to Joachim's periodic view of history, the third and final Age of the Holy Spirit would see the
coming of the Antichrist and the final reckoning of mankind. By
his numerical calculations, the visionary predicted that this apoc-

*The Doom, or Last Judgment, over the chancel arch at Lutterworth Church in
Leicestershire. Note how some of the dead rise as skeletons, some as naked cadavers,
while the rest rise fully clothed in their earthly garments. (Courtesy A. F.
Kersting.)*

alyptic age would begin in the year 1260. Joachim's ideas probably first began filtering back to England after September 1190, when Richard the Lionhearted landed at Messina, Sicily, on his way to the Third Crusade. It was at Messina, according to the chroniclers, that the English king was granted an audience with the mystical abbot. There Joachim expounded his prophecies regarding the approaching Apocalypse and the Antichrist, whom he believed to be allied with the man who would become Richard's greatest enemy: Saladin, sultan of Egypt and Syria. In the succeeding decades, English authors such as Ralph of Coggeshall were to demonstrate a thorough familiarity with "Joachism." By the 1240s, when the English Apocalypse manuscripts were being produced, the countdown to 1260 was fast approaching.

With its emphasis on a confrontation between good and evil, the Apocalypse may also be seen as a heroic adventure story full of angelic knights fighting ferocious dragons and many-headed beasts. In this respect, the Apocalypse has many affinities with the romances of King Arthur, whose cult was to be particularly favored by King Edward I. The reign of his father, Henry III, was, with the exception of Richard's exploits on the Third Crusade, the most intense period of England's contributions to the crusading movement. In 1240 Richard, earl of Cornwall, Henry's brother, and Simon de Montfort, earl of Leicester, left for the Holy Land with eight hundred knights. In 1250 Henry himself took the cross (for a second time), and between 1270 and 1272 his son campaigned in the East with a small contingent of fellow crusaders. The men who commissioned the Apocalypses may very well have seen themselves as the embodiment of resistance to overwhelming evil.

The artists who executed the English Apocalypses did not make them in isolation, but were undoubtedly in contact with Continental artists, particularly in France. This is not to say that the English style was not distinctive, but communication across the Channel was common, and English models influenced French work and vice versa. In some cases a single manuscript may have been produced jointly by workshops in both countries. Politically speaking, relations between England and France after 1254 were strong. In that year, Henry III visited the French capital at the invitation of Louis IX, and in 1259 the Treaty of Paris was concluded between them. Ten years later, Prince Edward, the son of Louis's sister, also came to Paris to prepare for the Eighth Crusade. Such political contacts could not but help facilitate artistic ones as well.

The vast majority of the Apocalypse manuscripts produced in England and France during the thirteenth and early fourteenth centuries depict the Fourth Rider, Death, as a man. Usually he is bearded, wearing a turban, pointed cap, or hooded cloak, and he is riding a pale horse, carrying either a sword or a brazier of fire in his hand and issuing from, or dragging along by a harness, the mouth of hell in the form of a great beast's head. Often the hell mouth contains burning souls, among whom can be recognized kings, bishops, and the tonsured heads of monks. But within this group, a handful of illuminations depict Death in quite a different aspect: as a decaying, skeletal cadaver.

The oldest such illustration can be found in the so-called Burckhardt-Wildt Apocalypse (named after its eighteenth-century owner, Daniel Burckhardt-Wildt, who compiled an album of the illustrations only, after these had been cut out of the original manuscript). The manuscript was made around 1280 by a workshop located within the county of Lincoln or York in England. The Fourth Rider is shown with the hollow eyes, fleshless nose, and sunken jaw of a skull. (See the illustration that opens this chapter.) He carries a silver sword with a golden handle in his right hand, while in his left he holds the reins of a pale horse. Except for his extremities, on which his flesh is decaying, the corpse is clothed in a hooded mantle, perhaps meant to represent a shroud. Death issues from a double-headed mouth of hell, from which peer the faces of burning souls presided over by a demon. An almost exact copy of this image, down to the repeating diamond background, survives in another Apocalypse manuscript thought to have been painted by the same artist a decade later in the 1290s. Finally, a very similar example, with a cadaver emerging from a hell mouth, carrying a sword and wearing a mantle but with no hood, and riding what appears to be a leaping rather than cantering horse, appears in an Italian Apocalypse whose text is thought to have been composed in the early decades of the four-teenth century. The illuminations, however, are ascribed to an English artist working between 1280 and 1290. All three manu-scripts, in fact, are attributed to the same illuminator, an identifi-cation greatly strengthened by their common use of the cadaver to represent Death.

Why did a small group of illuminators in late-thirteenth-cen-tury England suddenly decide to draw Death as a corpse, rather than as most contemporary illuminations would have him, in the form of a living man? Showing the Fourth Rider as a cadaver or skeleton aligns the figure with his role as the harbinger of death and suits the narrative context of the Apocalypse story, where Death makes a dramatic entrance as a corpse, setting himself apart from the other three riders. And in the Apocalypse, this is indeed Death's role: He is more powerful than the other horsemen, for he can kill with all their weapons—Plague, War, and Famine—combined. Death has a license from God to kill with every disas-ter that may be commanded. He thus can wreak havoc upon

The Fourth Rider of the Apocalypse, Death. From a manuscript dating to the 1290s in the British Library. (Courtesy Conway Library, Courtauld Institute of Art.)

humanity far more sweeping and terrifying than that of any of the riders alone.

The use of the cadaver in the Apocalypse story by these English illuminators represented an artistic leap that was to have lasting effects. It now is thought that the original Burckhardt-Wildt series inspired a famous tapestry of the Apocalypse made for Louis, duke of Anjou, between 1377 and 1380. Originally comprising eighty-four *tableaus,* or scenes, on six *pièces,* each measuring approximately 20 by 75 feet, the Apocalypse Tapestry of Angers (restored twice during the nineteenth century) still

The Fourth Rider of the Apocalypse, Death. From an Italian manuscript in the Laurentian Library, Florence. (Courtesy Conway Library, Courtauld Institute of Art.)

dazzles with its vivid colors and monumental figures. It was woven in the workshop of Nicholas Bataille of Paris, based on cartoon drawings by Jean Bondol, painter to the French royal court. In 1380 it was recorded that the king, Charles V, had lent to the duke an illuminated manuscript of the Apocalypse, now known to have been painted in England around 1250. Nonetheless, art historians long have been dissatisfied with this manuscript as a model for the tapestry because the two display quite different artistic styles. Indeed the manuscript King Charles lent shows the Fourth Rider as a bearded man carrying a brazier of fire, while the Apocalypse Tapestry at Angers features Death riding out as a skeleton wielding a sword. The image, down to the position of the sword on Death's shoulder, is instead very similar to the Burckhardt-Wildt series and may have been transmitted through English contacts with France.

The fifteenth century saw a second artistic leap in the representation of the Fourth Rider. In 1413 Jean, duke de Berry, of France commissioned a trio of Dutch illuminators known as the Limbourg brothers to make a book of hours that would surpass all others in his collection. Left unfinished at the deaths of the duke and his artists in 1416, the *Très Riches Heures* was not to be completed until 1485 under a new patron, Charles, duke of Savoy. To finish the manuscript, he hired an illuminator from Bourges named Jean Colombe, who already had done similar service for the duke on an illustrated text of the Apocalypse.

On folio 90v. of the *Très Riches Heures*, Colombe portrays the horseman of Death. The rider himself has been returned to human form as an elegant nobleman mounted on a white steed and brandishing a sword. However, he is preceded by an army of skeletal corpses dressed in winding sheets worn in the style of Roman togas. Before them flees in terror another, human army, whose armor avails them little as they retreat from the scene of battle, a graveyard, back toward the town beyond. Cadavers appear in Colombe's Apocalypse no doubt because by that time

This elaborate rendition of Death is from the Angers Apocalypse Tapestry, c. 1377–80. Compare this image to that at the beginning of this chapter from the Burckhardt-Wildt Apocalypse. (Courtesy Centre des Monuments Nationaux, Paris.)

a long tradition had established that this should be so. But where Colombe departs from tradition is in his multiplication of the corpse, to the point that it overawes the viewer with the power of Death.

Artistically and psychologically, this effect was to achieve its most sublime expression in the next century with Pieter Brueghel the Elder's *Triumph of Death* masterpiece of circa 1562. Cavorting across an apocalyptic landscape in an orgy of activity, the skeletal Death invades every imaginable space of the painting. We see him, for example, in the lower left-hand corner riding a tired old nag leading a cart full of skulls, reminiscent of illustrations of Petrarch's poem *Triumphus Mortis* (Triumph of Death). Directly above, a chorus of cadavers don winding sheets as togas as they baptize stone-weighted bodies in a river, while in the lower right-

hand corner a handful of knights vainly draw their swords against their skeletal adversaries, both evoking Colombe's illumination. At the thematic and spatial center of the painting, Death on his horse herds the living into a giant coffin, whose trapdoor swings open like a mousetrap, as the only avenue of escape is blocked by a horde of skeletons armed with sepulchral shields. With the mortality of all mankind here on display, never has the overwhelming power (and terror) of Death been so convincingly portrayed.

In all of these images, from the Fourth Rider of the Burckhardt-Wildt Apocalypse to the triumphal skeletons of Brueghel's painting, Death is an impersonal force. He mows down all regardless of rank. His work leaves little room for compassion or contestation. There is no appeal beyond Death. As the late medieval English poet John Lydgate describes him:

> *In the Apocalips of Seyn John*
> *The chapitlys whoo so can devyde*
> *The Apoostyl thoughte that he sawn oon*
> *Upon a paale hors did ryde,*
> *That poweer hadde on every syde.*
> *His name was Deth thorugh cruelte,*
> *His strook whoo so that durste abyde.*

> In the Apocalypse of St. John
> In one of the chapters into which it is divided
> The Apostle thought that he saw one
> Upon a pale horse did ride
> Who had power on every side
> His name was Death, because of his cruelty
> Whose stroke no one dared abide.

It was a terrifying message: Death was uncomfortably godlike in his all-encompassing might. Yet Death's terror was mitigated by the close relationship between the Fourth Rider and the Last Judgment that was to come at the end of the Apocalypse story. The opening of the fourth seal meant that eventually Christ was to come again to separate the saved from the damned. Justice

The Fourth Rider and his army of skeletons, as depicted by Jean Colombe in the Très Riches Heures, *fifteenth century. (Courtesy Photothèque Giraudon.)*

The Triumph of Death, *by Pieter Brueghel the Elder, c. 1562, a masterpiece of apocalyptic imagery. (Courtesy Museo Nationale del Prado.)*

would reign at last. In preachers' sermons, the pale horse of Death symbolized the arrival of incorruptible and unbiased justice. This was an attractive theme, particularly to late medieval Englishmen, who lived at a time when the bribery of judges, the depredations of sheriffs, and the flouting of the law were all too common. Indeed, the outlaw ballads popular in England during the later Middle Ages, such as the legend of Robin Hood, can be considered apocalyptic. The hero overturns the old, corrupt order and a new, more equal justice reigns. To the modern reader such apocalyptic visions may seem threatening, but to the medieval mind there was comfort to be found in the aftermath of the Apocalypse, where good finally triumphs over evil and everyone meets with the fate that he deserves.

THE THREE LIVING AND THE THREE DEAD

Another way in which medieval men softened the impact of Death was by engaging with him directly, drawing him into conversation in which the personality of both Death and the dying assumed greater importance. An emerging personal rapport with Death was related in the medieval mind to the Apocalypse, particularly to the Fourth Rider and the Last Judgment. By conversing with Death, man took some of the terror out of his coming and could better prepare for the final end. This engagement with death ultimately took shape in the legend of the Three Living and the Three Dead. According to the legend, three men are walking in the woods one day and stumble upon three rotting cadavers. Confronted with this gruesome sight, each of the three men speaks his mind. But what is even more remarkable, the dead talk back. For the first time in the medieval West, Death speaks to man.

This story has a long and rather unusual pedigree. Strange though it may seem, it probably originated in the life of Buddha in India during the sixth and fifth centuries B.C. The story of Siddharta Gautama, the pampered son of an Indian bigwig who left his father's palace to confront the miseries of the world and eventually lead a life of asceticism, was christianized into the legend of Sts. Barlaam and Josaphat. The similarities between the lives of Buddha and Josaphat illustrate the influence of the East on early Christianity, particularly on the Desert Fathers whose careers as hermits closely paralleled those of the heroes of these stories.

The inspiration that the Barlaam and Josaphat legend may have provided to that of the Three Living and the Three Dead is thought to come at the point where the hermit Barlaam converts the young prince Josaphat to Christianity. Following the example of Christ, Barlaam tells Josaphat a series of parables. Among them is the story of the good king who made four caskets, two of them covered with gold but filled with the stinking bones of the dead, the other two covered with tar but filled with precious stones and pearls. The caskets are used to instruct the king's entourage that those of rich appearance secretly are filled with vice, while the poor emanate the sweetness of virtue. Another parable tells of a man with three friends. The first two, symbolizing riches and family, whom the man loved the most, abandon him in time of need, at the hour of death. But the last friend, symbolizing good works and whom the man loved least, comes to his aid. Traditionally, the story of Barlaam and Josaphat is ascribed to John of Damascus, a Syrian theologian writing around A.D. 730. It is thought to have passed to the West through a Latin translation of a Greek manuscript made at Constantinople during the middle of the eleventh century. The story then made its way to southern Italy through that region's close connections with Byzantium at this time.

In one version of the legend, the living come upon the dead lying in their caskets or tombs. There is no dialogue between the two realms; rather, the living draw the appropriate moral lessons from the hideous specimens before them. The dead act as a mirror for the living, reminding them of the transitory nature of the world and the inevitability of death, which spares no one, rich or poor, young or old. This version of the legend is thought to have come down to us in the Latin poem *Cum Apertam Sepulturam* (When the Tomb Is Opened). Three kings or men gaze upon a rotting cadaver lying in a mass grave. Each of the living draws his own lesson from the macabre spectacle. The first laments the passing glory of the world and reminds his companions that they will end up like the corpse, just as it was once like them. He urges repentance and preparation for the afterlife, for no one can escape death. The second king, repulsed by the sight and smell of death, dwells on all the material things that the dead have lost. Rotting bones inspire the third man to deliver a sermon on the futility of pride and human desires, echoing the moral tone of the first king.

Among early Italian frescoes of the Three Living and the Three Dead theme are some that show the living, usually mounted on their horses, before the dead in their coffins in varying stages of decomposition. Such images were painted on the walls of the church of Poggio Mirteto in the Monti Sabini region toward the end of the thirteenth century, in the gallery of the University of Goettingue in Florence at the beginning of the fourteenth century, and at the monastery of Sacro Speco in Subiaco during the 1360s. But the masterpiece, indeed the finest painting of them all, is the fresco attributed to Francesco Traini in the Campo Santo in Pisa, thought to date to the middle decades of the fourteenth century. Traini's *Triumph of Death* shares many elements with other Italian paintings of the subject: the dog sniffing out the corpses, also present at Goettingue, and the hermit pointing out the moral of the dead, undoubtedly a reference to the Barlaam and Josaphat story, also present in frescoes at Vezzolano, Atri, and Montefiascone, all of which predate Traini. Yet the artistic genius of Traini's painting is evident in the masterly way he depicts the psychological reactions of the assemblage of male and female riders to the three corpses, ranging from disgust and fear to curiosity and moral posturing.

For our purposes, the real genius of Traini's *Triumph* is the way it brings together the legend of the Three Living and the Three Dead with other Christian themes, particularly the Fourth Rider and the Last Judgment of the Apocalypse. Originally the fresco adorned the southern wall of the cloister along which people had to pass in order to go from the cathedral to the cemetery, and it is useful to look at the painting as if passing by it in procession. If one follows the painting from left to right, one sees first the moral of the Three Living and the Three Dead, as a troop of finely mounted noblemen come upon three coffined cadavers in varying stages of decay. Then one sees the act of death itself, in the form of an old woman armed with a scythe who, while ignoring the sick and lame begging for death, is about to invade an unsuspecting party of pleasure seekers in a garden. Finally, just above Death, Traini shows what happens afterwards, as angels and devils play a tug-of-war with souls at the Last Judgment. Thus the spectacle of cadavers confronting the living points to a higher, more epochal event: to a time when all men must confront their own deaths and the fate of their souls forever after.

It is quite clear in the *Triumph of Death* and other paintings like it that the dead lie mute in their tombs. But already by the end of the thirteenth century, the dead were beginning to find their voice. In one of the earliest paintings of the Three Living and the Three Dead, a fresco in the church of Santa Margherita de Melfi in Italy, perhaps dating to the early thirteenth century, the living encounter the dead as upright skeletons. A similar scene occurs at the cathedral of Atri in the Abruzzi region from the second half of the thirteenth century and at the church of San Flaviano in Montefiascone, also in Italy, from the early fourteenth century.

In literature, the dead begin talking as well as walking in French poems of the legend. The first and perhaps most accomplished of these poems was written by Baudouin de Condé, minstrel to Marguerite d'Anjou, countess of Flanders. Condé lived during the second half of the thirteenth century, and his poem, *Li Troi Mort et li Troi Vif* (The Three Dead and the Three Living), probably influenced later versions composed in France, England, Germany, and Italy. In the poem, three young noblemen come face-to-face with three decomposing cadavers crawling with worms. Predictably, each of the three living men reacts differently. The first is almost driven mad with fear; the second wishes to profit from this "mirror" sent by God; and the third enumerates in gruesome detail the various parts of the body missing from the dead. Such a range of responses had already been encountered in the *Cum Apertam Sepulturam*. But if the dead begin to speak, what do they say? They too have their roles. The first dead introduces himself and his companions. They were once

The Triumph of Death, *attributed to Francesco Traini, in the Campo Santo, Pisa, mid-fourteenth century. (Courtesy Archivi Alinavi/Art Resource, New York.)*

noblemen like their living counterparts, he informs them, and God sent them to the living to mend their ways. Somber is the second dead. Death is cruel when he bites; he spares no one, high or low; the pains of Death are the evil result of Adam's original sin. Finally, the third dead ends the poem on what one might say is a happier note. He addresses the living as "brothers and friends." He warns them to turn to good works rather than remain in sin for one hour, for this is nothing compared to the endless pain of death. He requests their prayers and wishes them well.

The Three Living and the Three Dead can be considered a medieval ghost story, part of a literary genre that dates back to at least A.D. 1000 and that speaks to a universal urge to trespass the bounds of Death and communicate with the other world. In most medieval ghost tales, the dead are there to hector the living into a better remembrance, usually through prayers and other rituals designed to shorten the dead's time in purgatory. Yet the three dead are more than just ghosts of former individuals wishing to return to their earthly haunts. They speak on behalf of Death and all the dead, and therefore their message is of a far greater scope and import than that of ordinary ghosts. These dead are here to terrify us and console us. They remind us that we too will die but tell us how to triumph at the end. They show us the agony of death and point us to the ecstasy of the eternal. Ironically, it is the dead who must teach us how to live.

In the only English-language version of the legend, "gostis ful grym" appear to three kings out of the mist. The poem, *The Three Dead Kings*, from a fifteenth-century manuscript attributed to John Audelay, portrays these ghosts as not unfamiliar to the living:

> "*Nay, are we no fyndus,*" *qoth furst* [dead], "*that ye before you fynden. We wer your faders of fold that fayre youe have fonden.*"

> "Nay, we are no fiends," said the first [dead], "that you before you find. We were your fathers of old that once you deemed so fair."

As the above passage indicates, *The Three Dead Kings* is highly alliterative, and it employs an extremely elaborate rhyme scheme. In this respect it is similar to the French poems of a century earlier, although similarities also have been noted with German versions of the legend. Among the latter is the setting of the poem where the three living meet the three dead in the course of a hunt in the woods, a feature that is typical of English wall paintings of the subject. After the usual exchanges, the poem ends with the living kings making a minster, or church, in order to avoid the fate of their fathers and to profit from their advice.

Wall paintings of the Three Living and the Three Dead became quite common in England. Nearly forty such frescoes are known to have existed, of which hardly more than half can still be seen in varying states of preservation. The majority were executed during the fourteenth century. The earliest of them, at Widford, Oxfordshire, and Charlwood, Surrey, are dated to the early part of the century, before the plague. Nonetheless, the theme seems to have picked up only after the arrival of the Black Death in 1349.

Artistically speaking, these paintings do not compare with Traini's masterpiece at Pisa. In particular, the figures of the dead, usually skeletons, tend to be stiff and awkwardly drawn. But clearly, the sheer number of the frescoes in England attests to the popularity of the subject, and it seems that each painting played a large and important part in the decoration of the local church. One of the most complete and best-preserved examples is the painting in the church of St. Andrew at Wickhampton, Norfolk. One enters the church and immediately sees on the opposing north wall a monumental Three Living and the Three Dead. It fills the entire field of vision: three skeletal cadavers on the left, three hunting kings on the right, and underneath a huntsman with his hounds chasing a hare in the woods. The Wickhampton Three Living and the Three Dead dates to about 1380 and was thus made within living memory of the Black Death, which is known to have carried off the rector of the church in 1349. Why, in the middle of the flat, bleak Norfolk Broads, was such a large and prominent painting commissioned?

The answer, I believe, at Wickhampton as elsewhere, lies in the atmosphere of death created by the plague, which kept recurring throughout the later Middle Ages. The Three Living and the Three Dead, already well established in European art and literature, imparted a message that may have helped people cope with death. Even though the dead provide a mirror of mortality, they also remind the living that the body, riddled with disease and decay, will be resurrected in its pristine form at the Last Judgment. One of the most important lessons the three dead teach the three living is to prepare for this event. Traini's fresco made clear the connections between the legend and the Apocalypse. The message was also driven home in the English parish church. The huntsman and hounds pursuing the hare in the lower border of the painting at Wickhampton, for instance, is thought to symbolize the single-minded pursuit man should have of the spiritual world. At Lutterworth church in Leicestershire, over the chancel arch the dead rise from their tombs at the call of Christ's trumpet, while on the south wall the three kings of the legend are still visible from a painting made in the mid-fourteenth century. At the church of St. Andrew in Pickworth, Lincolnshire, a depiction of the Doom, or Last Judgment, again dominates the chancel arch while on the north wall to the west fragments of the Three Living and the Three Dead survive next to an equally damaged painting of the Weighing of Souls. The last dead in Audelay's poem of *The Three Dead Kings* advises his audience to "Do so ye dred not the dome"—in other words, see to it that you approach the end of the world with a clear conscience. The appearance of the dead and the coming of the Last Judgment, when man would triumph over death, were inextricably linked.

Medieval man wanted to talk to Death and have Death talk back. Undoubtedly, this easy familiarity with Death made the Fourth Rider less arbitrary and awe-inspiring. It gave Death a human face, a personality. The Three Living and the Three Dead provided one of the first and simplest means to humanize Death, not only in art, but also in dramatic settings. Perhaps the clearest evidence that the legend was reenacted for popular audiences comes from a fifteenth-century German poem from Strasbourg: Its lines are illustrated with drawings of the dead standing on top of tombs with their arms and forefingers extended in dramatic gestures. Could not paintings of the theme inside churches inspire reenactments without? By rehearsing death, medieval man may have been far less terrified when it came time to play the real thing.

DANCE OF DEATH

Of all the cadaverous art and literature produced during the later Middle Ages, that of Death dancing with a series of partners culled from the whole range of the medieval social hierarchy was perhaps the most popular. Texts and images of the Dance of Death, or Danse Macabre, penetrated nearly all countries of Europe and inspired some of its most famous authors. In fifteenth-century Paris, a painting of the Dance in the cloisters of the cemetery of Les Innocents led François Villon to contemplate life's fleeting pleasures in his *Testament*. About a century and a half later it appeared in Shakespeare's *Measure for Measure* and Cervantes's *Don Quixote*. The motif has continued to appeal in modern times. Camille Saint-Saëns composed a musical tone poem called *The Danse Macabre*, Hermann Hesse describes it in his novel *Narcissus and Goldmund,* and Ingmar Bergman brought it to life in the finale to his film *The Seventh Seal.*

The Dance seems ready-made for the stage, for both entertainment and didactic purposes. The first reference to a performance of the Dance of Death comes from Caudebec in Normandy, where it was acted out in the parish church in 1393. Johann Bischoff, writing in 1400, hints at a Dance of Death performed among twenty different kinds of dances in Vienna at Easter. In 1449 a Dance of Death was acted out before the duke of Bourgogne at Bruges in Flanders, and in 1453 the Franciscans of Besançon, France, staged a Dance of Death in the church of St. Jean. The Catalan *Dansa de la Mort* from Spain is still sung and danced to this day.

One of the reasons why the Dance of Death has endured is that it seems to have tapped into the mixed and complex responses to widespread mortality, becoming especially a pictorial and poetic summation of the plague. In origin, the Dance may have been forged in the crucible of pestilence. One theory holds that the Dance was first written down by a Dominican friar from Wurzburg, Germany, almost immediately after the Black Death, in 1350. Other scholars date the earliest mention of the Dance to 1376, when a French poet, Jean le Févre, composed *Le Respit de Mort* (A Reprieve from Death), in which he boasts, "Je fis de Macabre la danse," or "I made the Danse Macabre." Le Févre perhaps implies that he wrote a poem entitled *La Danse Macabre*, or that he himself "danced with Death," when he had a close brush with the plague that was making the rounds of Europe in that year. Contemporary chroniclers likewise relate the Dance to plague. According to the *Grand Chroniques* compiled by the monks of St. Denis in Paris, during the Black Death of 1348 men and women danced to the accompaniment of drum and bagpipe in order to ward off the pestilence. Two monks from the abbey who witnessed this spectacle in the course of their travels asked the people the reason for its practice, to which they replied, "We have seen our neighbors die, and are seeing them die daily, but since the plague has not entered our town, we hope that our merrymaking will keep it away, and this is why we are dancing." A German chronicler relates that in 1374 groups of dancers, sometimes five hundred strong, would dance for half a day in towns along the Rhine and then fall to the ground and allow people to trample on their bodies, in the belief that this would cure them of the disease. There may, in fact, have been a physiological explanation for the dancing. Bubonic plague eventually attacks the nervous system, perhaps resulting in chorea, sometimes known as St. Vitus's Dance, which produces involuntary contractions of the muscles in the face and limbs that may be characterized or masked by a dance. In this respect it may be akin to the ergotism, or St. Anthony's fire, that was contracted by many people eating moldy grain during the Great Famine.

Another reason for the Dance of Death's popularity is its suitability for dramatic presentation. Before the Dance acquired a secular audience, it may have been used by preachers to dramatically illustrate their sermons on death. Such is indicated in

a fifteenth-century English translation of a French poem, in which
Death comes to the Cordelier, or Franciscan Friar, with the words:

Sir cordeler, to yow myn hand is rawght
To this daunce, yow to conveie and lede
Whiche in youre preching, have ful ofte tawght,
How that I am moste gastful for to drede.

Sir Cordelier, to you my hand is extended
To convey and lead you to this dance
Which in your preaching, you have often taught
That I am most fearfully to be dreaded.

In 1429 in Paris, a Friar Richard preached apocalyptic sermons to
thousands for five or six hours with one of the most famous frescoes of the Dance as a backdrop.

Lastly, we must not discount the appeal of the social message
of the Dance of Death. Death here is the Great Leveler, the dem-
ocratic spoiler who comes for one and all regardless of wealth,
rank, or power; no one is exempt, a point that must have been
forcibly driven home during time of plague. Of course, this
theme was not new: We already have seen it in representations of
Death as the Fourth Rider of the Apocalypse and in the poems of
the Three Living and the Three Dead. The close connections
between these three forms is demonstrated by the frequent prox-
imity of their images. In Paris in 1408, the legend of the Three
Living and the Three Dead was sculpted on the doorway of the
church of Les Innocents on the orders of the duke de Berry,
shortly before the Dance was to adorn the southern wall of the
cloister that enclosed the adjoining cemetery. At Clusone in
Bergamo, Italy, a fresco dated 1485 depicts King Death and two
skeletal attendants shooting down the high and mighty, including
three men on horseback interpreted as the three living, while
below is an elaborate round of the Dance of Death. A sumptu-
ously illuminated manuscript from France, also dating to the late
fifteenth century, combines in its first twenty-three folios images
of the Dance of Death, the Three Living and the Three Dead,
and the Fourth Rider of the Apocalypse.

Yet the Dance of Death clearly represents an advance on the simple personification of the Grim Reaper. The dialogue with Death now is greatly extended, to thirty or more figures, and Death tailors his message to each of the living. Consequently, the Dance, through the mouthpiece of Death, reveals some uniquely medieval Western worldviews. For example, in a version of the poem printed by Guyot Marchant in 1485 the Patriarch is informed by Death that he never will become pope, a clear slap at the Greek Orthodox Church. The Usurer is likewise chastised, by both Death and a Poor Man, because he coldheartedly extracts profit from the interest on his loans, a practice condemned by canon law and usually associated with the Jews. In the Dance of Death, death also plays a more sinister role than in the Three Living and the Three Dead. He does not just speak to his observers, he carries them away. Though the living resign themselves to the Dance, the rich meekly resist and the poor stoutly submit, a formula ripe with social meaning. The Archbishop throws his head back in fear at Death's approach, and the King's Sergeant threatens rebellion. The Laborer, on the other hand, welcomes a rest from his toil, and the Hermit dies secure in the riches of God's grace, an expression that prompts Death's only reply, commending his attitude.

The earliest surviving image of the Dance, accompanied by a poem, was arguably the most influential: the fresco that once adorned the southern cloister of the cemetery of Les Innocents in Paris. Painted in 1424–25 during the English occupation of the city in the course of the Hundred Years War, the elaborate mural at Les Innocents was destroyed in 1669 when King Louis XIV ordered that the neighboring boulevard of la Féronnerie be expanded. The inscriptions that accompanied the painting survive in two manuscripts from the abbey of St. Victor in Paris, and in 1485 the printer Guyot Marchant issued the first of many editions of the same poem, containing woodcut illustrations thought to be updated versions of the original mural. In the next century, the Dance of Death was to be revived by the famous woodcuts of Hans Holbein the Younger, perhaps inspired by the cycle painted at Basel, Switzerland.

The poem from Les Innocents, which through cross-Channel contacts was to be so influential in England, tells of thirty partners who dance a reel with Death: Pope, Emperor, Cardinal, King, Patriarch, Constable, Archbishop, Baron, Bishop, Squire, Abbot, Bailiff, Astronomer, Bourgeois, Canon, Merchant, Carthusian Monk, Sergeant, Monk, Usurer (accompanied by a Poor Man), Physician, Lover, Advocate, Minstrel, Priest, Laborer, Franciscan Friar, Infant, Clerk, Hermit.

The plague may very well have inspired the artists of Les Innocents to document this macabre procession. Between 1414 and 1439 the pestilence visited Paris no fewer than eight times, and in England national epidemics raged for several years during the 1420s and 1430s. Despite the apparent good government of the English duke of Bedford in the city, the other Horsemen, namely War and his close attendant, Famine, also may have played a role. According to the anonymous *Journal of a Bourgeois*, which records the painting of the mural, Paris suffered in 1421 from high taxes, a long winter, famine, and the depredations of wolves, most of which the author attributes to the Hundred Years War. Perhaps it is a war weariness that makes the Constable lament:

> My whole intention has been
> To assail castles and fortresses
> And bring them to my subjection
> To acquire honors, riches;
> But I see that all prowess
> Death lays low, which is a great vexation.

Nor should we discount the possibility of the very surroundings of the cemetery inspiring the Dance, just as they inspired Villon, who observed the bones of all the dead mingled so equitably in the charnel houses just above the cloisters.

The painting at Les Innocents would inspire other renditions. In 1426 a Benedictine monk from Bury St. Edmunds, Suffolk, John Lydgate, was in Paris, then still occupied by the English, where he could observe at first hand the freshly painted Dance at

Les Innocents. According to the opening and concluding stanzas of his version of the poem, Lydgate freely translated the Dance from the French at Les Innocents with the help of some native clerks in order to transport it back to England. This would have been done at least by 1436, the year the English were forced to evacuate Paris. By 1440 the pictures and words of the Dance, as transposed by Lydgate, seem to have been re-created on painted boards in the north cloister of the Pardon Churchyard at St. Paul's Cathedral, London, under the patronage of Jankin Carpenter, town clerk. To the original thirty dancers with Death, Lydgate added six others: the Empress, the Lady of Great Estate (or noblewoman), the Abbess, the Amorous Gentlewoman, the Juror, and the "Tregetour," identified as John Rikill, formerly personal jester to Henry V, who apparently died at the time Lydgate made his translation. In a later, inferior revision of the poem, known as the B text, ten new characters were added, including the Mayor, the Canon Regular, the Judge, the Doctor of both Canon and Civil Law, the Nun, the Artificer (or crafts-man), and the Servant, or Officer, while the Lady of Great Estate, the Bailiff, the Bourgeois, the Monk, the Usurer (and Poor Man), the Squire, the Tregetour, the Priest, and the Clerk were left out.

There are several characteristics of Lydgate's poem that are distinctly different from the original in Paris. For one thing, the connections with plague are much stronger. This is made clear immediately, in the first stanza of the Translator's Introduction, where Lydgate informs his audience what lessons they should learn from the Dance:

> O yee folkes, harde herted as a stone
> Which to the world, have al your advertence
> Liche as it sholde, laste evere in oone
> Where is your witte, wher is your prudence
> To se a-forne, the sodeyne violence
> Of cruel dethe, that be so wyse and sage
> Whiche sleeth allas, by stroke of pestilence
> Bothe yonge and olde, of lowe and hie parage.

O you people, hard-hearted as a stone
Who devote all your attention to the world
Which you think should last forever and anon
Where is your reason, where is your wisdom
To see in advance the sudden violence
Of cruel Death, who is so wise and knowing
Who slays all of us, by the stroke of pestilence
Both young and old, of low and high degree.

Later, in stanza 54 of the poem, the Physician bewails his impotence in the face of plague:

Ful longe a-goo, that I unto phesike,
Sette my witte, and my diligence
In speculatif, and also in practike
To gete a name, thurgh myn excellence
To finde oute, agens pestilence
Preservatives, to staunche it and to fine
But I dar saie, shortly in sentence
Agens deeth, is worth no medicine.

A long time ago, I studied medicine,
Applying to it my reason, and my diligence
In theory, and also in practice
To get a name, for my excellence
To discover, against pestilence
Medicines, to halt and cure it
But I dare say, briefly in this sentence
Against death, medicine is of no worth.

The doctor's words no doubt were borne out by bitter experience, as no remedy seemed to cure the Black Death. Such explicit reference to pestilence is missing in the original French version of the Dance; the closest *le Médecin* comes to uttering the word is *maladie* (malady). England may well have had the pestilence more on its mind. In addition to the plagues of the 1420s, already mentioned, the 1430s were a time of cold weather and

disease: National epidemics and famines broke out between 1433 and 1435 and between 1437 and 1440. This apparently was the very time when Lydgate returned to England from Paris and when the Dance at St. Paul's in London was being made.

In addition, there is a heavy judicial overtone to the English Dance. The A and B versions together introduce four new representations of the legal profession—Judge, Doctor of Laws, Juror, and Officer—to the Bailiff and Advocate of the original French procession. The Judge is ashamed of having obstructed justice; the Doctor of Laws is admonished by Death of any guile in his disputations; the Juror admits that he would "hang the trewe and the theeff acquyte"; the Officer gives the parting advice, "in office lat no man doon outrage." Essentially, their message is: The men of law are corrupt, but they will get their just sentence before the one, true Judge. This righteous tone can be found in the French poems as well, but it waxes in the English verses.

Death warns the Bailiff that he will be judged at a "new assise" for the "extorcions and wronges to redresse," crimes of which he is not accused at Les Innocents. The Advocate, or Man of Law, is threatened with the "dome," or the Last Judgment, a punishment he does not face from the French Death. Lydgate's Dance of Death thus shares with the Fourth Rider an apocalyptic sense of ultimate justice that proved so attractive to late medieval Englishmen.

What is remarkable is that, despite the auspicious early influence from France, the Dance of Death adorns so few of English churches, far fewer than the Three Living and the Three Dead. Traces of the Dance survive at Hexham and Newark-on-Trent in the North of England, where it was painted on rood screens during the late fifteenth or early sixteenth century. Aside from the example at St. Paul's, frescoes of the Dance that once existed but since disappeared include examples at Stratford-on-Avon; Wortley Hall, Gloucestershire; the archbishop of Canterbury's

Death as a Chessman: checkmating a bishop at St. Andrew's Church, Norwich, late fifteenth or early sixteenth century (previous page), and in Ingmar Bergman's The Seventh Seal *(1957). (Courtesy Royal Commission on Historical Monuments in England and Svensk Filmindustri.)*

palace at Croydon, Surrey; Henry VIII's castle at Whitehall, London; and perhaps the Hungerford Chapel in Salisbury Cathedral. A minor series of the Dance was carved in the misericords (ledges for support attached to the underside of seats in choir stalls) of Windsor Castle and of Coventry Cathedral. The latter's images, however, were already defaced before being destroyed in bombing during the Second World War, while those in the retro-choir rib vault of Rosslyn Chapel, Scotland, have also much suffered from time. In the church of St. Andrew, Norwich, a stained-glass panel, one of an original set of forty-four from the late fifteenth or early sixteenth century, displays a cadaverous Death draped in his shroud checkmating a bishop on a chessboard. In Lydgate's poem, Death checkmates the Empress and the Amorous Gentlewoman (rather than the Bishop), while the theme of man playing a chess game with Death returns as the central conceit of Bergman's film *The Seventh Seal.*

It may well be that England has a paucity of these images of the Dance of Death because they are more elaborate and therefore more expensive to execute. But I do not think that we should discount the possibility that the message of the Dance may have been socially unpalatable to many an English country parson. In the wake of the Peasants' Revolt of 1381 and Lollard activity in the decades thereafter, English authorities were particularly sensitive to the leveling themes that the rebels and heretics propounded. In both the French and English poems of the Dance, nearly the entire Church hierarchy is accused of being worldly. Aside from the Cardinal, Archbishop, and Bishop, all rich, proud men, the Abbot is fat from high living, the Canon clutches at his many benefices, the Monk wallows in vice. Not even the Parson, a sympathetic character in Chaucer's *Canterbury Tales*, is above cherishing his tithes. On the other hand, the Dance does, in a macabre way, preserve a rigid hierarchy. Yet even this may have been offensive, particularly to the later reformers who saw a pope and a cardinal precede their king. In the A version of Lydgate's poem, the Pope is given "soverente over the churche and states temporal," whereas in the B version his authority is limited to the Church. Although Henry VIII apparently had a tapestry and fresco of the Dance commissioned (but exactly when in his reign is uncertain), in 1549, after his death, the lord protector, Edward Seymour, duke of Somerset, pulled down the cloister containing the Dance at St. Paul's.

The last intriguing question concerning the Dance is what relationship exists between Death and the dancers. Are the cadavers simply replicated images of almighty Death? Or is each cadaver a mirror image of its living counterpart, as he or she will appear at death? There is nothing in the Dance poems themselves to suggest that the living are addressing their dead selves. Sometimes, in both the French and English versions, Death is addressed by male dancers using the feminine article or pronoun. Moreover, the images do not tally: In the case of the obstreperous Sergeant, for example, two dead escort him to his grave, while the Infant is carried away by an adult corpse. Nor do the Three Living and the Three Dead juxtapose two stages of the same body. In the Latin poem *Cum Apertam Sepulturam*, three kings address a single corpse, and Traini's ten riders gaze upon three decomposing dead. Not until cadavers are carved on tombs themselves do we see living individuals masquerade as Death.

VADO MORI AND *ARS MORIENDI*

Vado mori, je vois morir, I wende to dede—such is the refrain of the *Vado Mori* poems appearing in several languages, the earliest of which date to the thirteenth century. Like the Three Living and the Three Dead and the Dance of Death, the message of *Vado Mori* is clear—there is no escape from death. To prove its point, members of all classes of society, from Pope to Poor Man, repeat its mantra: "I go to die." Each dying man has barely enough time to tell how he dies in a manner suited to his station. The Knight, for example, who had conquered in life, is conquered by Death. The Logician is out-argued by Death; the Cantor cannot sing his notes through his tears; the Sailor is shipwrecked by Death; the Butler is poisoned. In one version of the poem, probably dating to the fourteenth century, there is a dialogue of sorts between the dying and an anonymous speaker, either a moralizing hermit or Death itself. In response to each man's lament of "I go to die," his companion answers, "Live in God," meaning, amend your life so that you may have a "future life, a celestial future" after death. Like the Dance of Death, the *Vado Mori* poems parade a variety of participants whose deaths are tailored to their occupational or social classes. The poems are unusual, however, for their favorable view of the Lawyer: He is called the "defender of the poor."

Although Death plays little part in the poems, the English illustrations of *Vado Mori,* or variations of it, usually depict Death as a skeleton or cadaver coming to claim the speaker. One such illustration, from an English manuscript of the fifteenth century, shows Death with a dart in each hand stinging a king, a bishop, and a knight, all of whom recite: "I wende to dede." Later in the same manuscript, a harp player is about to be shot at by Death, who draws back his bow. The harpist laments:

Allas ful warly for wo may I synge
For into sorow turned is my harpe
And my organ into voyce of wepynge
When i rememyr the deth that is scharpe.

Alas, full warily in woe may I sing
For to sorrow is devoted my harp
And my voice [is turned] into one of weeping
When I remember death that is sharp.

Arming Death with a bow and arrow is a particularly English touch. It also appears in a window at the parish church of Stanford-on-Avon, Northamptonshire, whose vicar, Henry Williams, dying in 1501, had himself commemorated next to an image of Death with his longbow rising out of a tomb "shoting at me." Englishmen conceived of Death claiming them with the same weapon with which they dealt so much death to their enemies in war. Finally, in a memorial brass to James Gray, park-keeper at Hudson, Hertfordshire, who died in 1591, Death hunts the hunter with his dart, reminiscent of the earlier *Vado Mori* poems, in which men die as they lived.

The *Vado Mori* poems anticipate the *Ars Moriendi* manuals that became so popular throughout Europe during the fifteenth century. Also called the *Art of Living Well and of Dying Well* (for the two, in the medieval mind, naturally go together), the *Ars Moriendi* (Art of Dying) survives in over two hundred manuscripts. As with the use of the pronoun "I" in the *Vado Mori* poems, the *Ars Moriendi* shifts the focus to the individual. Man is no longer concerned with Death in general but with one particular death: his own. He is especially concerned about what will happen to him after death, where he can end up in one of three places—heaven, hell, or purgatory. Consequently, it is not the act of dying that is most important, but rather how the bedridden man behaves up to the very moment of death. Of the eleven scenes typical of the printed editions of the genre, five show the

Vado Mori: *Death taking aim with a favorite English weapon, the longbow, at a harp-player. From a fifteenth-century English manuscript. (Courtesy British Library.)*

temptations before death—unbelief, despair, impatience, pride, and avarice—followed by five angelic inspirations to counteract the temptations, and, at the very end, the good death, wherein the soul ascends to paradise. Such a sustained examination of death illustrates a more introspective exercise than any of the previous macabre genres.

What the *Ars Moriendi* does share with the Three Living and the Three Dead and the Dance of Death is its suitability for the stage. An allegorical reenactment of the deathbed scene became popular in fifteenth-century England as the play *Everyman*. In the play, Everyman, symbolizing any man about to die, is abandoned in short order by his friends, symbolized by Fellowship; his family, symbolized by Kindred and Cousin; and by his material possessions, symbolized by Goods. Not even his natural qualities—Knowledge, Beauty, Strength, Discretion, Five-wits (or senses)—can accompany him on this "pilgrimage." His only steadfast companion, even unto the grave, is Good Deeds, sym-

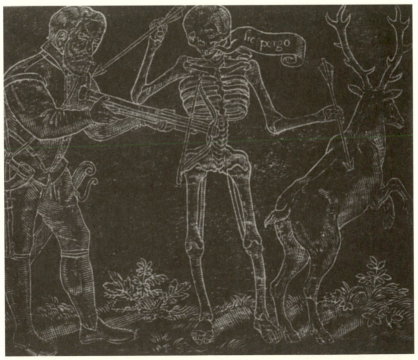

Vado Mori: *Memorial brass for James Gray (d. 1591), park-keeper, at Hudson, Hertfordshire. (Courtesy Conway Library, Courtauld Institute of Art.)*

bolizing Everyman's charitable works, which he had hitherto neglected. A key part also is played by Confession, symbolizing the necessity to do penance that sets Everyman on the path to salvation.

What is striking about the play is the prominence given at the beginning of the drama to Death, who has a much greater role here than in any other *Ars Moriendi* form. (Interestingly, Death does not appear at the end, when Everyman dies.) Indeed, he speaks more in *Everyman* than he ever has before. Death is commissioned by God to take Everyman unawares, when he has his end "least in mind." Then ensues a long conversation between Death and Everyman, consisting of no fewer than ninety-nine lines, the essence of which is that Everyman desperately pleads with Death to grant a stay of execution. First he offers Death £1,000, but Death cannot be bribed. Next, Everyman begs for a moratorium of twelve years in which to settle his spiritual accounts, but Death is impatient. Finally, Everyman requests a single day to amend his life, but Death denies even this. What is remarkable, though, is that in the end, Death does grant a delay, however fleeting:

> And now out of thy sight I will me hie:
> See thou make thee ready shortly,
> For thou mayst say this is the day
> That no man living may 'scape away.

For the first time, Death stays his hand, if only briefly; the personal face of Death is nowhere more evident, and much drama remains. How long this *mortus interruptus* lasts—several minutes, hours?—we do not know, but without it, the play cannot go on.

At one point Everyman asks Death if he will ever return from the pilgrimage he is about to undertake. Death answers:

> No, Everyman. And thou be once there,
> Thou mayst never more come here,
> Trust me verily.

Death does not tell the whole truth, however. A little later on in the play, Fellowship asks the same question as Everyman asked Death: Will they ever come back from their journey to the other world? Everyman answers, "Nay, never again, till the day of doom." So, in actual fact, man *will* return from death: at the Last Judgment of the Apocalypse, when his body will be reunited with his soul. This point is reemphasized by the Doctor, who comes on the stage at the very end of the play to explain its meaning:

> And he that hath his account whole and sound,
> High in heaven he shall be crowned,
> Unto which place God bring us all thither,
> That we may live body and soul togither.

The ancient belief in the resurrection of the body at the end of the world can be traced in the Judeo-Christian tradition back to the Old Testament, especially to the Book of Job, where Job says, "I know that my redeemer liveth, and that He shall stand at the latter day upon the earth. And though after my skin worms destroy this body, yet in my flesh shall I see God" (19:25–27). In the New Testament we have, above all, the example of the resurrection of Christ himself. In addition, the Apostle Paul explains the resurrection to the Corinthians using the beautiful image of a seed sown in the ground that sprouts forth "in incorruption" (I Corinthians 15:35–44). Then, of course, there is the famous vision of St. John in the Revelation, where he sees the dead rise up from their graves at the coming of Christ in judgment (Apocalypse 20:11–13). But what *Everyman* demonstrates is that, at the popular level, people came to the same conclusion as did schoolmen in the university: Even with an immediate judgment of the soul upon death, the Apocalypse still holds an important place for its power to redeem the body. At the Last Judgment, medieval men believed, the physical forms we had enjoyed in our youth, despite any ravages from famine, war, plague, and death, will be restored to us in order to rejoin our souls. Even in the midst of the crises of the Apocalypse, there is hope that a full recovery is imminent. *Everyman* attests to the enduring necessity of the resurrection to the medieval psyche.

The dying man of the Middle Ages therefore believed that he could have it both ways, that he could take his body, hale and whole, with him after death. (In what condition the body would be resurrected is a question we will explore later.) But in order to do this, he had to first humiliate his body, humiliate his pride, so that he might be deemed worthy by God to enter paradise. For it was no good resurrecting the body if it was to end up in hell suffering real, physical torments for all eternity. Even though Dante denies "Suicides" their bodies in canto 13 of the *Inferno* in his great poem *The Divine Comedy*, the Church made it quite clear that the resurrection of the bodies of the damned will be no different from that of the blessed. Therefore, it became fashionable to express contempt for the body, as the fourteenth- and fifteenth-century French poets Eustache Deschamps and Pierre de Nesson do so well. Sometimes borrowing from the Book of Job, they describe the body as the repository of dung, filth, spittle, urine, excrement, menstrual blood, and other assorted and repulsive bodily fluids. Yet this was simply a means to an end. Man could have his soul and his body too, and enjoy them both in a future paradise, provided that he played his cards right.

BODY AND SOUL

It became fashionable in the later Middle Ages to express a twofold concern for the body and the soul in the form of a "dialogue" between them. The Latin poem *Dialogus inter Corpus et Animam* (Dialogue between the Body and the Soul) was very popular in England during the thirteenth century and served as the basis for a more poetic English version. By the middle of the fifteenth century, a prose version appeared in a northern English dialect under the title *A Dysputacion betwyx the Saule and the Body when it is Past Oute of the Body*. The verses are accompanied by illustrations of a soul in human form conversing with a decomposing corpse lying in a shroud. Proof that the disputation became part of the macabre genre is Guyot Marchant's publication of a *Debate of the Body and the Soul* in his 1486 edition of the

Danse Macabre. Likewise, the French poet of death, François Villon, wrote a *Debate of the Heart and of the Body* loosely based on that between the body and soul.

The soul begins the *Dysputacion,* as it does in the earlier poems of the debate, by abusing the body and accusing it of leading the soul into corruption. The body is "horribille and fowle stynkyng wormes mete," whose misgovernance led the soul to "gret disese and hevynes." But in the next lines, as is true of other debate poems, the body holds its own against the soul's opening barrage. In fact, the body is quite a skillful debater, parrying the soul's bitter attacks by quoting from Ezekiel and Aristotle and turning the soul's arguments against it. Whether the metaphor be a smoky fire, a smelly candle, or a narrow sack, the body reverses the reference to itself by pointing out that it is but the outward form of the "actyfe" flame, wick, or enclosed contents within. Ironically, the body argues against the soul by diminishing its own importance and exalting the powers of its other half: It was but the faithful subject of its sovereign who "suld hafe drawne me to the [thee] with thi goode governance aftyr Gods lawe." Other bodies that were better ruled have lain in the ground miraculously "alle hole withouten corrupcion in thair grave or sepulkyr [sepulchre]."

The *Dysputacion* is finally ended by an angel, who in the last illustration of the verse looks down upon the antagonists, pleading:

Pes and stynt of your pleyng, for it is not your avaylyng betwyx yow twoo to stryfe on swylk maner of wyse be swylk wordes and to be mefed. For ye ar predestinate to salvacion and hereafter sal be ioyned agayn togeder.

Be peaceful and stop your arguing, for it is unavailing for you two to debate in such manner using such words and to be so moved. For you are predestined to salvation and hereafter will be joined again together.

Feuding between these two cantankerous spouses is thus put to rest by the promise of the resurrection, when they will be wedded in a perfect union, a solution already hinted at by the body in its first response to the soul: "Thu sal in bones cum to thi jugement at the general resurreccion of me and of al other that ar ded." Such a reconciliation is not found in earlier poems of the debate, where both the body and soul are doomed to eternal torment as a result of their mutual failings. By means of an apocalyptic denouement at the Last Judgment, body and soul in the *Dysputacion* are counseled back together.

A singular variation on the debate theme occurs in the same manuscript in *A Disputacioun betwyx the Body and Wormes*. Here the body debates not with the soul but with worms that are about to devour her flesh. The poem begins like other debate poems with a dream vision by the poet. Yet in this case the dream vision is unique in two important respects. In the first lines of the poem, the poet immediately relates his vision to a time of plague:

> *In the ceson of juge mortalite*
> *Of sondre disses with the pestilence*
> *Hevely reynand whilom in cuntre*
> *To go pylgramege mefed by my conscience.*

> In a season of huge mortality
> Of various diseases including the pestilence
> Which once upon a time ruled strongly over the land
> To go on pilgrimage was I moved by my conscience.

The poet dreams his disputation partly because he enters a church to pray for relief against the apocalyptic horseman of Plague. It would be fair to assume, then, that this poem was inspired by the sickness and death caused by such a disease and that it was meant to provide some comfort in the face of rampant mortality.

The second important aspect of the prologue to the poem is its use of a "towmbe or sepulture" inside the church for inspiration. The tomb effigy is of a great lady, "ful freschly forgyd, depycte, and depynte." The poet then falls asleep beside the tomb and dreams that the woman it depicts engages in a dialogue with worms that eat her dead body. The first manuscript page of the

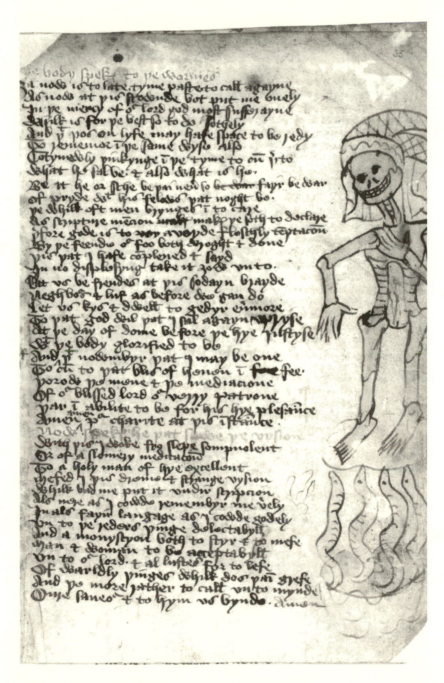

A Disputacioun betwyx the Body and Wormes, *fifteenth century. In the poet's dream, a lady's corpse lying underneath her elaborate tomb (opposite) engages in a debate with the worms crawling through her rotting flesh. (Courtesy British Library.)*

poem is illustrated by a colored drawing of a woman's tomb, the effigy decked out in elaborate headdress and robes, while underneath is a skeletal corpse in a shroud riddled with what look like worms, toads, and newts. This central illustration is followed by others in the margins of the poem showing the woman's naked corpse, standing up and still in her headdress, addressing an assemblage of wriggling worms.

Unlike the dialogue between the body and the soul, the body and worms do not engage in a true debate between two evenly matched antagonists; the worms win here hands down. The woman pleads with the worms to stop gnawing her body and calls upon the knights and squires who so admired her in life to come defend her from these inconsiderate vermin. But the worms will not be denied. They have conquered far more powerful adversaries in the past, men like Judas Maccabaeus, Julius Caesar, Godfrey of Bouillon (first crusader king of Jerusalem), Alexander the Great, David, Hector, King Arthur, and Charlemagne, among others. The worms send their advance guard of lice and fleas to pick at her while she is alive and are swiftly followed by a rearguard of the cockatrice, basilisk, dragon, lizard, tortoise, snake, toad, mole, scorpion, viper, adder, ant, caterpillar, spider, maggots, newt, water leech, and others not far "behynde."

Nevertheless, the *Disputacioun* ends in a similar way to that between the body and soul: with the promise of the resurrection. In this way, the body is reconciled with the worms because it knows it will be made whole again. As the body says to the worms:

This that I hafe complened and sayd
In no displesyng take it yow unto
Lat us be frendes at this sodayn brayde
Neghbours and luf as before we gan do
Let us kys and dwell to gedyr evermore
To that God wil that I sal agayn upryse
At the day of dome before the hye justyse
With the body glorified to be
And of that nownbyr that I may be one
To cum to that blis of heven in fee

Thorow the mene and the mediacione
Of our blissed lord our verry patrone
Thar in abilite to be for his hye plesaunce
Amen, Amen pour charite at this instaunce.

At what I have bemoaned and said
Do not you take offense
Let us be friends after this sudden uproar
[Let us be] neighbors and love each other as we did
   before
Let us kiss and dwell together forevermore
Because God wills that I will rise again
At the day of doom before the High Judge
When my body will be glorified
And of that number may I be one
Who enters by right into the bliss of heaven
By means of the intervention and mediation
Of our blessed Lord [Christ] our savior
There at his almighty pleasure will I be with my [bodily]
   faculties
Amen, amen, may He be charitable in this instance.

If the debate poems argue for the resurrection of the body, the question remains: Exactly what kind of body will be resurrected? This sort of problem has been addressed throughout the centuries of medieval Christianity. There are three main authorities on the subject: St. Augustine of the fourth and fifth centuries A.D., Peter Lombard of the twelfth century, and St. Thomas Aquinas of the thirteenth century. Some of these authors' specific concerns (which also were those of many Christians) were, quite frankly, bizarre. How will our bodies be resurrected if they happen to be eaten and digested by cannibals? (The flesh will simply be given back, as if on loan.) Will aborted fetuses be resurrected? (Yes, even though they cannot be "born again" since they were never born in the first place.) Will all the hair and nails we have shaved or pared off be restored? (No, only what does not result in ugliness.) Will all the food we have eaten form a part of our bodies? (No, only what is permanent will rise.) Will we be married in heaven? (No, nor will we have any intercourse despite the presence of our genitals.) Will we all be the same sex and height? (No, we will be resurrected with our individual proportions.) At what age will we be resurrected? (At around thirty, the age of Christ, even for those who died young.) Will the resurrection occur during the day or the night? (At night, when Christ was resurrected.)

Despite such learned explanations, there remained some confusion at the more popular level about what the resurrection would look like. Even though William Durand, a thirteenth-century liturgist, declared that we would be fully clothed at the "day of judgment," and Aquinas asserted that man would be "remade perfect in all his members," John Lydgate imagined the dead at the day of doom standing on their tombs showing "a dredful foul figure . . . with boonys blak and donne." Paintings and sculptures of the Last Judgment often have the dead rising naked out of their graves at the sound of the angels' trumpets, yet Christ in his majesty is shown surrounded by the saved in all the accoutrements of their former lives. A considerable amount of variation and imagination thus accompanied artists' rendering of the climax of the Apocalypse.

What concerns us here, and what probably interested Englishmen who lived through the crises of the later Middle Ages, is how the resurrected body will overcome mutilations and deformities of various sorts brought on by famine, war, and plague. Peter Lombard, the twelfth-century theologian, makes it clear that the body will be resurrected perfectly whole. Basing himself on Augustine, he writes in the fourth book of his *Sentences*: "Therefore the bodies of the saints will rise without any blemish, without any deformity, as it were without any corruption, affliction, difficulty." But it was left up to Aquinas to explain exactly how this will occur. Drawing from Aristotle, Aquinas states in his *Summa Theologiae*:

The soul stands in relation to the body not only as its form and end, but also as efficient cause. For the soul is compared to the body as art to the thing made by art . . . and whatever is shown forth explicitly in the product of art is all contained implicitly and originally in the art. In like manner whatever appears in the parts of the body is all contained originally and, in a way, implicitly in the soul. Thus just as the work of an art would not be perfect if its product lacked any of the things contained in the art, so neither could man be perfect, unless the whole that is contained enfolded in the soul be outwardly unfolded in the body. . . . Since then at the resurrection man's body must correspond entirely to the soul . . . it follows that man also must rise again perfect, seeing that he is thereby repaired in order that he may obtain his ultimate perfection.

This elegant statement solves the problem of dismemberment and disease that may have afflicted the temporal body. The soul is conceived by Aquinas as a kind of blueprint for the resurrection of matter, which becomes a perfect expression of man's inner beauty. By borrowing Aristotle's analogy of art, Aquinas also calls to mind the importance of physical elaboration of these ideas, especially for the vast majority of the illiterate. The two-tiered transi tombs of England are one, perhaps the greatest, such artistic expression of Aquinas's theory of the resurrection.

THE TRANSI TOMBS

Tomb effigies of the deceased lying in a recumbent position, commonly known as "gisants," may date to as early as the tenth century in Europe and became common from the late eleventh and twelfth centuries. These images appear to be of the deceased as they may have looked in life (the so-called *representacion au vif*). Yet the presence of angels at the head of Edward II (d. 1327), for instance, suggest that the effigy may also have been intended as an idealized figure depicted at the resurrection. Certainly the contents of some tombs indicate a preparation for such an event: The exhumed grave of a twelfth-century bishop of Paris, for example, revealed that he was buried with a note on his chest proclaiming his assurance that he would rise again. A number of fourteenth-century English tombs portray angels presenting the naked souls of their patrons to Christ or the Holy Trinity. In addition, some portrayals of the Last Judgment show bodies being resurrected in full regalia. Giovanni Pisano's tomb of Margaret of Brabant (d. 1311) in Genoa, Italy, actually has two angels on either side of the deceased lifting her up in her earthly garments to her heavenly fate.

What the transi tomb did, of course, was contrast or replace altogether the idealized effigy with its opposite: a decomposing or desiccated cadaver (the *representacion de la mort*, or representation of death). Among the first to be so represented were the physician Guillaume de Harcigny (d. 1393) at Laon, France; François de la Sarra (d. 1363 but tomb erected in the 1390s) at

The two-tiered transi tomb balanced the representacion au vif, *in life, as in this armored figure of John Fitzalan, earl of Arundel, with the* representacion de la mort, *in death, the cadaverous figure below. (Courtesy Royal Commission on Historical Monuments in England.)*

La Sarraz, Switzerland; and Cardinal Jean de Lagrange (d. 1402) at Avignon. Lagrange's tomb was an especially elaborate monument consisting of ten stages, including an effigy of the deceased just above his transi, that may have served as a model for the first double-decker tomb in England. The macabre was an important element of these tombs, but their main purpose was as preparation for the Apocalypse, not as moralizing message or appeal for prayers. Humiliation of the body in the service of God was not new: One can find it already well established in the medieval mystical literature. What was new about the two-tiered transi tombs was their perfectly balanced union of two sensibilities, mortification and glorification, fear and hope, that made up the process of death and resurrection. This did no more than reflect medieval man's mixed emotions at the coming of the Apocalypse.

Several examples from tombs of the English deceased during the fifteenth century amply illustrate this harmonious (rather than adversarial) dialogue between two bodies, one of death and the other of resurrected life. Reflecting their patrons' high status, these tombs are among the most sumptuous and beautifully carved in the country. Their transis are gruesome, and their inscriptions certainly call attention to this fact. But the strong presence of angels on the tombs points to a triumph over sickness, mutilation, and death. For some whose lives were directly touched by one of the horsemen of the Apocalypse, this must have been a great comfort.

Archbishop Henry Chichele

On August 31, 1422, Henry V, king of England and heir to the kingdom of France, died at Vincennes, near Paris. The king had taken ill at the siege of Meaux, just thirty miles from Paris, and he probably died of dysentery caused by some intestinal infection or disease. He was undoubtedly a wasted man in his last days: hollow eyes, sunken cheeks, skeletal frame, the very image of death on the transi tombs.

When Henry's body arrived in England in late October or early November, it was met at Dover by the archbishop of Canterbury, Henry Chichele. Chichele, who owed his primacy to his sovereign's patronage, had been a key figure in the royal administration. From at least 1406 he had acted as diplomat to France on behalf of the then Prince of Wales, and he continued to serve in this capacity under the new king. In 1414 he was translated to Canterbury from the relatively minor Welsh see of St. David's, at a time when schism in the papacy made the king's wishes in ecclesiastical preferments law. On November 17, 1415, Chichele received the victor of Agincourt at Canterbury, and from 1418 he himself took part in Henry's French campaigns leading up to the Treaty of Troyes of 1420. The archbishop obviously was a member of the war party: Shakespeare put into his mouth the arguments for going to war with France just before the French ambassadors arrive at court. When it came time to prepare for his own death, Chichele willed that his chantry colleges at Higham Ferrers, Northamptonshire (where he had been born), and at All Souls College, Oxford, pray for the soul of his friend, "the illustrious Prince Henry, late king of England."

Undoubtedly Chichele's tomb, the first to employ the double-decker style, was inspired by the premature death of his royal namesake. Henry V died at thirty-five, a monarch who seemed on the verge of conquering France for the first time since the days of the Angevin Empire in the twelfth century. For English patriots, his demise was a cruel blow, leaving behind a baby son to carry on the cause. We know that the tomb was completed by early 1425, less than three years after the king's death, as in that year a goldsmith by the name of Bernard took refuge behind the iron railings of the "new monument" in order to escape a mob seeking his arrest. In artistic terms, Chichele may have been inspired by Lagrange's tomb at Avignon, where he probably visited as ambassador. On the other hand, it is equally possible that the two-tiered tomb was in imitation of the double image of effigy and coffin paraded at state funerals. This processional technique was first performed in 1327 at the funeral of Edward II and subsequently was used at those of Henry V and Chichele himself.

Chichele's epitaph, carved in Latin in an abbreviated Gothic script, runs along the top and bottom verges of the tomb, but it is unlikely that it was read by many. (Not even the pilgrim in *A Disputacioun betwyx the Body and Wormes* read the inscription on the tomb that inspired his dream: "The Epytaf to loke was I not faynte," or "I was not inclined to look at the Epitaph.") The lower epitaph around Chichele's transi emphasizes mortality, but the upper one around his effigy proudly describes his worldly career up to and including his appointment as archbishop. His tomb, especially the surrounding canopy with its statues of the apostles that had been destroyed during the seventeenth century, has been heavily restored. Yet it illustrates well how medieval monuments originally were richly decorated. Every fifty years the fellows of All Souls College in Oxford must repaint the tomb in accordance with Chichele's foundation charter, a tradition that continues to this day.

The most interesting fact about Chichele's tomb is that, for at least eighteen years until his death in 1443, he could have looked

The tomb of Henry Chichele, archbishop of Canterbury, at Canterbury Cathedral. The tomb was completed by 1425 but the archbishop did not occupy it until his death in 1443. (Courtesy Royal Commission on Historical Monuments in England.)

down at his transi and seen himself portrayed in death. In this "portrait as prediction," Chichele could gaze into the future at his approaching end. Whereas other macabre art depicts Death as a separate entity, discrete from the viewer, here one is presented with a far more intimate mirror: the spectacle of one's own mortality. For the first time in England, a patron masquerades as Death, imagining how he would decompose in the grave. Why would Chichele ever have wanted to have such an image carved and displayed?

The answer, I believe, is that the tomb proclaims a hope in the resurrection of the body at the Apocalypse, not just a morbid meditation on the theme of corruption and decay. In this dialogue between two bodies, one of the deceased as a living, resplendent effigy, and the other as a rotting, naked corpse, one is tempted to "read" only downward, from the effigy to the cadaver, and see the end of man as nothing but "dust, worms, vile flesh." But for medieval patrons like Chichele, death was not the end. Rather, it was the beginning, the gateway to a better world. Death, who triumphs as the Fourth Rider of the Apocalypse, now at the Last Judgment bows down in defeat before the triumph of the resurrected body. We must read upward in the two-tiered tombs, not to a *representacion du vif* (representation of life), but to a *representacion de l'après-vif* (representation of the afterlife). The upper effigy is a pristine body resurrected out of the mere skin and bones lying underneath. Thus, as Chichele read down his tomb, he viewed his humility before God: the corruption and decay that would come upon all earthly status and goods. But when he read back up, he saw his reward: his restored body, around thirty years of age, dressed in his pontifical vestments, rising up like a phoenix out of his ashes below. Two angel supporters on either side of his head, and angels bearing heraldic shields in the canopy, escort him upwards to the heavenly host, to rejoin his beloved king.

Bishop Richard Fleming

Richard Fleming, bishop of Lincoln, died in 1431 and left his two-tiered transi tomb to posterity in Lincoln Cathedral. Fleming probably was inspired by the example of his colleague at Canterbury in the making of his monument. The two have several similarities. Fleming's tomb, like Chichele's, was designed as part of a chantry chapel and still forms part of the original structure in the north aisle of the choir. Also following Chichele, Fleming attached an inscription, likewise in Latin rhyming couplets, to his tomb. Fleming's epitaph, originally inscribed on a tablet that is no longer extant, is much longer than Chichele's (no fewer than twenty-six lines) but has much the same theme. Once again, there is the reminder of voracious worms, the transitoriness of life. "Of what use is the height of a Doctorate?" Fleming asks, a question that still may be on the lips of many a graduate student. And yet once again there is a biographical element behind which one can detect, despite the self-flagellation, a hint of pride. Fleming was an Oxford man, he tells us, then a master of canon law, chamberlain to Pope Martin V, bishop of Lincoln (1420–31), and finally archbishop of York for a brief time (1424–25). He was

Transi tomb of Richard Fleming (d. 1431), bishop of Lincoln, at Lincoln Cathedral. The tomb forms part of the chantry chapel of the Fleming family. (Courtesy Royal Commission on Historical Monuments in England.)

retranslated back to Lincoln at his own insistence, perhaps a practical application of the humility shown in his transi (now much
defaced). The inscription ends, as does the lower one of Chichele,
with an appeal for prayers, but this function was far better fulfilled
by the chantry foundation.

In his youth Fleming had been a Lollard sympathizer, but his
days as bishop were to see him a hunter of heretics. In this regard
he may have had some contact with Chichele, who was especially
active in the suppression of Lollardy in 1428. In 1430, shortly
before his death, Fleming founded a college at Oxford, just as his
primate was to do seven years later. The express purpose of
Lincoln College was to combat the Lollard heretics "who profane
with swinish snouts its [the Bible's] most holy pearls." It is
doubtful if a man who was as much an enemy of heresy as
Fleming would have built a tomb that was itself heretical. (Quite
the opposite is suggested by the dragon crushed under the
effigy's feet.) Yet that is the impression one gets from scholars
who focus on the castigation of the body that these tombs seem
to portray. If such was the sole intention of the bishop, his tomb
would have flirted dangerously with the extreme self-abasement
of those very Lollards he had spent his life trying to root out.

I believe that Fleming, like Chichele, used the presence of
angels to signify the resurrection of his body on the upper level
of his tomb rising up from his cadaver below. Two angels on

*Fleming chantry, at Lincoln Cathedral. (Courtesy Royal
Commission on Historical Monuments in England.)*

bended knee with overlarge hands and feet cradle Fleming's curly locks in a more intimate gesture than on Chichele's monument. In addition, there are two angels pendent from the arches above Fleming's piously gesturing body. The left angel, faring better than its neighbor from mutilation, can still be seen clasping its hands in prayer and directing its gaze heavenward in an appeal for the resurrected bishop's reception to paradise.

Earl John Fitzalan

On November 16, 1857, the Reverend Canon Tierney, chaplain to the duke of Norfolk, excavated the tomb of John Fitzalan, seventh earl of Arundel. Fitzalan had died in France during the Hundred Years War, and everyone assumed that he had been buried there. However, Tierney came across the will of Fulke Eyton, Arundel's squire, in which he mentions "the bones of my Lord John . . . that I broughte oute of France" in exchange for a reward of over £1,000. This led Tierney to believe that Arundel actually had been buried in the family chapel, and sure enough, directly underneath the tomb, in a vaulted chamber, lay the skeletal remains of what had once been a large man, over six feet tall, missing one of its legs.

Fitzalan had died in 1435, a hero (for the English side) of the later period of the Hundred Years War. So great was his reputation for capturing towns and castles in northern France that he was styled the "English Achilles." He was honored with the title of duke of Touraine and entrusted with the captaincy of Rouen Castle. But in May 1434 Fitzalan's military career came to an abrupt end. He was shot in the leg by a culverin, a primitive gun, while besieging the castle of Gerberoy in Normandy. Taken prisoner by the French, Fitzalan was conveyed to the nearest big town, Beauvais, where his leg was amputated. A year later, on June 12, 1435, he died of his wound. He was alleged to have been buried in the Franciscan church at Beauvais, but even if he had, his squire, Fulke Eyton, apparently exhumed his body and arranged to have the remains brought back to the family's resting place at Arundel. This would have been in accordance with the earl's wishes expressed in his own will of 1430, in which he desired to be buried in the chapel for the canons of Trinity

College, Arundel, that had been founded by Richard, the fourth earl, fifty years before.

Nevertheless, a section of the wall on the north side of the chapel had to be removed to make room for Fitzalan's double-decker tomb. Originally, the tomb and chapel were part of the church of St. Nicholas, considered a safer venue than the castle since the latter was a potential target of marauding Frenchmen during the Hundred Years War. Under the Dissolution of religious houses in the sixteenth century, Henry VIII sold the collegiate chapel to the duke of Norfolk, under whose protection it remains to this day a Catholic place of worship (as well as serving as the private mausoleum of the Norfolk/Arundel family). The western half of the church became Anglican. One now can stand behind its high altar and look through the original fourteenth-century iron grill that had separated the chancel from the nave into what once had been the high altar of the entire Catholic building. Since that great divide of the sixteenth century, there

Tomb of John Fitzalan (d. 1435), seventh earl of Arundel at Arundel Castle, West Sussex. A hero of the Hundred Years War, the earl appears in his full armor, with his amputated leg restored in this depiction. The earl's body was discovered underneath the tomb in the nineteenth century. (Courtesy Royal Commission on Historical Monuments in England.)

have been only six occasions when the grille was opened and one could pass from one religion to the other.

What remains unclear is if Fitzalan himself commissioned the transi of his tomb or if his executors saw it as the modish style of the day. Undoubtedly, the restorative power of the resurrection would have held some appeal to the fractured body of the earl, and it was not unknown for the English nobility to think in such religious terms. In 1354, seven years before his death, Henry of Grosmont, duke of Lancaster, close friend to King Edward III, and one of the most militarily successful and chivalrous figures of his day, composed a devotional work in French, *Le Livre de Seyntz Medicines* (The Book of Holy Medicines). In it, Lancaster uses many analogies to battle scars and field hospital remedies, such as Fitzalan himself received, in order to describe the state of his soul. He compares his sins to seven wounds on his body, and one of the bandages that will help him rise from his sickbed is the Virgin Mary's joy at her Son's resurrection.

Whether Fitzalan intended it or not, his tomb shares elements of angelic resurrection that also appear at Canterbury and Lincoln. Two angels, their heads decapitated probably by Cromwell's soldiers quartered in the chapel during the English Civil War, hold Fitzalan's pillow in a very similar pose to those at the head of Chichele. Angels also hold shields on corbels attached to the wall at either end of the tomb. Meanwhile, Fitzalan's elegantly armored body (originally painted) rises up above his emaciated cadaver on its shroud. In both instances, the earl's missing leg, so cruelly blasted by the new technology of war, is once again made whole.

Bishop Thomas Beckington

More than any other patron noted above, Thomas Beckington, bishop of Bath and Wells, left behind documentation concerning the disposal of his corpse. In his will drawn up in 1464, the year before he died, Beckington bequeathed his body to Wells Cathedral to be buried under his double-decker tomb in the chantry chapel, "which I have already fully and perfectly disposed and prepared for that purpose." In line, perhaps, with the humility demonstrated by his transi, Beckington also willed that his

The wasted image of the transi tomb of Thomas Beckington, bishop of Bath and Wells, depicts the hollow eyes, sunken cheeks, and skeletal frame of death. (Courtesy Royal Commision on Historical Monuments in England.)

funeral be a modest affair, more "in the recreation and relief of the poor than in the solace of the rich and powerful." On January 15, 1452, on "about the fifth hour in the morning," according to his episcopal register, Beckington consecrated his tomb before an audience that included the "dean and some canons of the cathedral and many other men and women." Finally, among his official correspondence is a letter to Beckington from Master Thomas Chandler, dated October 1449, that praises the bishop for his tomb and its "perpetual memory of death." Thus, like Chichele, Beckington could have seen himself portrayed as dead for as long as sixteen years before he actually died.

Unfortunately, there is little explanation of why Beckington built the monument that he did. In his early career he was official to Archbishop Chichele, and surely he knew about the

Details from the tomb of Bishop Thomas Beckington (d. 1465). (Courtesy Royal Commission on Historical Monuments in England.)

Canterbury tomb. After he became bishop, Beckington served as secretary and emissary to France for King Henry VI during the 1430s, when England began suffering defeat after defeat in war. Whatever his motivation may have been, Beckington followed the pattern of his mentor, Chichele, but not in every respect.

This time there are no angels holding vigil by the head of the bishop, whose effigy and transi, once painted, suffered damage to face, hands, and feet. But this does not mean that angels heralding the resurrection play no role in the tomb; they very much do. At the top of each of the six columns supporting the effigy's bier is a cross-crowned angel, his elaborate feathered wings wrapping themselves up and around the pendulated arch to almost touch the wings of his neighbor. And in the canopy that originally surmounted the whole tomb, two angels with similar cruciform crowns and elongated wings hang down in the style of Fleming's tomb. Each angel holds in his hands a shield bearing a wounded heart, the symbol of Christ's passion. This most beautiful and intricately carved canopy, its inner surface decorated with stars, seems to depict the very heavens toward which the resurrected body, gazing up, looks forward at its day of doom.

Duchess Alice de la Pole

The two-tiered tomb of Alice de la Pole, duchess of Suffolk, at the church of the Virgin Mary in Ewelme, Oxfordshire, is the only one of its kind to portray a female transi in fifteenth-century England. It also is one of the most richly carved and thematically significant of the tombs. In its layout and use of angelic imagery, Alice's monument provides the strongest affirmation yet of the resurrection of the body.

Alice de la Pole was born Alice Chaucer, granddaughter of the poet. At least two of her husbands (she had three) succumbed to the violence of the age. Thomas Montagu, earl of Salisbury, her second husband, was shot to death at Orléans in 1428, shortly before Joan of Arc was to arrive to raise the English siege. His place, both as commander of English forces at Orléans and at Alice's side, was taken by William de la Pole, fourth earl of Suffolk. For the next two decades Pole was to assume a leading role in English politics. In 1437 he was made high steward of the duchy of Lancaster, north of the Trent, in effect commanding the king's lands in the North. That same year, he and Alice cofounded an almshouse for twelve poor men at Ewelme. The chapel of St. John the Baptist was added to the church as part of the foundation and was to play an important part in Alice's tomb iconography. In 1448 Pole was created duke, but two years later he was exiled by the Yorkist faction and murdered at sea en route to France. His death, largely the result of his unpopular match-making between King Henry VI and Margaret of Anjou, and of his efforts to make peace with France, was a harbinger of what was to come in the War of the Roses. He was buried apart from his wife in the Carthusian monastery of Kingston-on-Hull. Alice, a very wealthy widow, never remarried and survived her husband by twenty-five years until her death in 1475.

Alice's cadaver image, although beautifully carved and quite dramatic, is barely visible, hidden as it is by two arcades of eight small Gothic arches. Her transi shows a wizened and wrinkled duchess: her face shrunken and drawn, her breasts pendulent and withered. Its ugliness almost seems an act of penance, like the almshouse, due to God. By contrast, the upper effigy depicts a handsome and dignified woman, a coronet on her head, widow's weeds around her face and neck, her wedding ring on the fourth finger of her right hand, and the symbol of the Order of the Garter on her left forearm. Traces of red, blue, and gold paint still survive on this magnificently opulent tomb, yet the inscription sim-

The tomb of Alice de la Pole (d. 1475), duchess of Suffolk, at Ewelme, Oxfordshire. (Courtesy Conway Library, Courtauld Institute of Art.)

Angels depicted on the tomb of Alice de la Pole. (Courtesy Royal Commission on Historical Monuments in England.)

ply asks the reader to pray for the soul of "the most serene princess, Alice, duchess of Suffolk, patroness of this church and foundress of this almshouse."

The most impressive aspect of the tomb, however, is the overwhelming presence of angels of two kinds—gowned and feathered. Four feathered angels, two on each side, hold the duchess's pillow, while underneath the elaborate canopy sheltering her head two gowned angels hold heraldic shields. Sixteen angelic weepers, both gowned and feathered, array themselves directly above each of the openings giving in to Alice's transi. Twenty angelic busts in an attitude of prayer range along the canopy of the entire tomb, surmounted by eight wooden carvings of full-figured gowned and feathered angels, their arms raised to heaven, on crenellated mounts. The wooden ceiling of the chapel of St. John

the Baptist, just to the south of Alice's monument, is alive with more half-figured angels holding scrolls and shields. Finally, directly above the transi, painted on the underside of the sarcophagus, are two images. The first, over the cadaver's head, is a painting of the angel's annunciation to the Virgin Mary; the second, over the feet, is a depiction of Mary Magdalene and John the Baptist. The whole effect is of a multitude of the heavenly host bearing and welcoming Alice's resurrected body up to paradise, leaving behind the corruption and decay of a turbulent life.

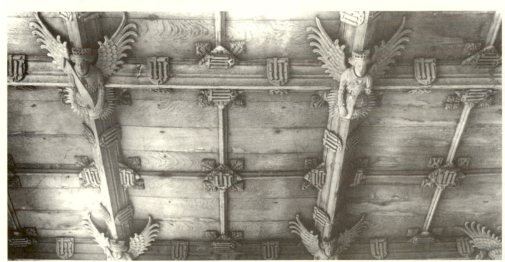

SINGLE TRANSIS AND SHROUD BRASSES

Most of the "macabre" tombs carved in England during the late medieval, and continuing into the early modern, period consist of a single image—the cadaver. The double-decker monument seems to have been a luxury afforded only by the very rich, usually the prelates or the nobility. A single transi, on the other hand, was a more economical alternative favored by the gentry and merchant classes or the minor clergy. There were, of course, exceptions to this rule. John Barton, a wool merchant who became wealthy from the trade with Calais, the only French town to remain in English hands after the Hundred Years War, built a double-decker tomb at the end of the fifteenth century in the church of Holm-by-Newark, Nottinghamshire, consisting of the effigies of Barton and his wife above and the cadaver of Barton alone in the alcove below. Richard Fox and Stephen Gardiner, both bishops of Winchester during the sixteenth century, opted

for single transis in their chantry chapels, despite the fact that they were bishops of the richest diocese in England.

In at least some instances, what appears to be a single transi was originally intended to be a double tomb. The cadaver of Thomas Heywood, dean of Lichfield, who died in 1492 and was buried in the cathedral, looks to be a single monument of the much weathered transi of the dean lying on his shroud. But we know from drawings done of the tomb before the destruction of the Civil War that Heywood was originally portrayed a second time in an upper painted effigy of the dean in a red-and-white hooded gown. John Wakeman, last abbot of Tewkesbury in Gloucestershire, who died in 1549, was cheated out of his intended funeral by Henry VIII's Dissolution of the monasteries. Before Tewkesbury was dissolved in 1539, Wakeman built his chantry and tomb in the abbey, but he was not to be buried there. Moreover, the cenotaph, which has a single transi on its upper level, houses an alcove below that looks as if it originally was meant to receive Wakeman's cadaver image, while his effigy, never carved, would have replaced it beneath the elaborate, filigreed canopy.

Assuming, however, that in most cases the single transi tombs were designed that way, this still does not obviate the importance of the resurrection and the Apocalypse to their making. The most famous single transi, that of John Baret, a rich clothmaker who died in 1467 and was buried in the church of St. Mary in Bury St. Edmund's, Suffolk, may have the founder castigate himself on his tomb as a "ful rewli wretche" (a very despicable creature). But this profession of humility, as indicated above, was perhaps a clever ruse to ensure one's place in heaven once the body was reunited with the soul at the sound of the angels' trumpets. Angels still make their appearance on single transis, as they do so prominently on the double-decker tombs. One such example comes from Ireland, the sixteenth-century tomb of Sir Edmond Goldyng and his wife, Elizabeth, in the churchyard of St. Peter's, Drogheda. Eight angel weepers bear the arms of Goldyng,

The details of the transis of King Louis XII of France (d. 1515) and Anne of Brittany (d. 1514) are realistically rendered, down to the depiction of embalming stitches. (Courtesy University of California Press.)

Elizabeth, and his two other wives, Blanche and Joanna, on tablets that originally supported the transis. Goldyng's tomb is the only one from the British Isles that shows both husband and wife in the dual matrimonial pose of decomposing corpses.

Shroud brasses were an even more inexpensive route to the macabre that was employed especially by the urban middle class. The best known of these brasses is that of Ralph Hamsterley, rector of Oddington in Oxfordshire, whose shrouded skeleton is crawling with worms. Yet even among these "bargain" brass tombs, the double-decker image and the resurrection can be found. The brass of Bernard Brocas, Esq., from 1488 at Sherborne St. John in Hampshire, depicts the kneeling effigy of the squire above his shrouded skeleton. Richard Willoughby of Wollaton, Nottinghamshire, who died in 1471, combined for his tomb an upper brass effigy of himself and his wife, inset with seven brass shells symbolizing the resurrection, and a carved stone transi below. Thomas Spryng of Lavenham, Suffolk, was commemorated at his death in 1486 by a brass showing himself, his wife, and his three children all rising up from a communal tomb at the Last Judgment. Sir Ralph Wodford, who died in 1498, is depicted on an incised slab at Ashby Folville, Leicestershire, standing in his shroud as just above his head a scroll proclaims the passage from Job relating to the resurrection. Both William Feteplace and his wife cast off the covers of their tombs as they rise up at the end of the world on their brass installed in 1516 at Childrey, Berkshire. All these examples foreshadow by at least a century the resurrection monuments that were to become so popular in England.

RENAISSANCE AND RESURRECTION TOMBS

The Renaissance may conjure up a time of emerging modern sensibilities in art and politics, but the tombs of three pairs of French kings and queens who are said to typify the age are carved in the medieval English style of the double-decker monument. Kathleen Cohen, the art historian of transi tombs, has characterized the sixteenth-century French examples as expressing a "new spirit" of the "triumph of worldly glory," as opposed to the old spirit of "anxiety and humility" that marked the fifteenth-century English types. But that division is an artificial one. Medieval English tombs have more than their fair share of bodily resurrection, while the French ones, despite some classically Renaissance features, still try to approach the resurrection through a show of humility. The two were closely linked. England's two-tiered plan served as a model for France, whose modified designs then traveled back across the Channel during the seventeenth century to influence the double-decker tombs of Robert Cecil and John Hotham.

Between 1515, marking the death of King Louis XII of France, and 1589, the year of the demise of Catherine de Medici, widowed queen of King Henry II, three magnificent tombs were

Renaissance transi tomb of Henry II (d. 1559) and Catherine de Medici (d. 1589). The idealized effigy of Catherine by Germain Pilon, modeled after Botticelli's The Birth of Venus, *was substituted for the original and more realistic sculpture by Girolamo della Robbia of 1565, now in the Louvre Museum. (Courtesy Centre des Monuments Nationaux, Paris.)*

added to that royal mausoleum known as the abbey of St. Denis in Paris. Spanning three-quarters of a century, these tombs, built by Renaissance princes and princesses, have a medieval quality. On the upper level are their effigies as they seem to have been in life and perhaps as they would like to be when resurrected. On the lower level are their transis, naked in the rigor mortis of death. The message is essentially the same as in the medieval double-decker tombs: Humility is the path to eternal glory. Nevertheless, there are some important differences. The French effigies are shown kneeling, usually before a prie-dieu, in an attitude of prayer and humility before God. Classical elements have been added in the form of columns on rectangular porticos, and on two of the tombs, those of Louis XII and Anne of Brittany and of Henry II and Catherine de Medici, the four virtues of Force, Temperance, Prudence, and Justice appear on the corners in the guise of ancient goddesses.

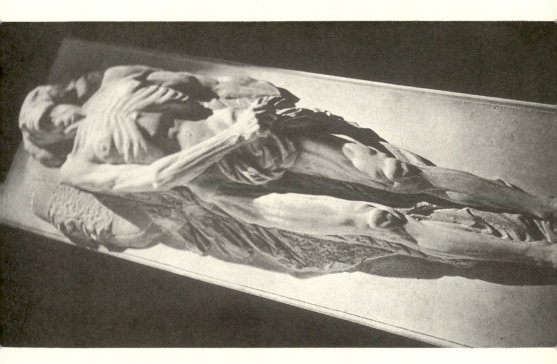

The unused transi of Catherine de Medici, by Girolamo della Robbia, 1565. (Courtesy Centre des Monuments Nationaux, Paris.)

But it is the cadavers lying on their burial urns in the alcoves below that are most remarkable. They are carved in the Renaissance style—anatomically correct and fine in the attention paid to every detail of the body—yet this newfound realism is allied to a most grisly depiction of death. The transis of Louis XII (d. 1515) and Anne of Brittany (d. 1514) show embalming stitches used to repair the body after its being eviscerated just after death, a procedure undertaken to preserve the royal corpse for the funeral, which for the sixteenth-century Valois kings could be elaborate rituals, sometimes lasting as long as eleven days. Yet despite this new fascination with the human body, even a dead one, it was the resurrected version that was more important. The corpses of Francis I (d. 1547) and his wife Claude (d. 1524) are,

The tomb of Sir John Hotham (d. 1689), the last monument in England to depict the transi figure below, now a gruesome skeleton. (Courtesy Royal Commission on Historical Monuments in England.)

like those of Louis and Anne, superbly rendered images of mortality. Their lifeless gaze, however, is directed literally toward the resurrection: On the underside of the vault that houses the transis is a carved relief of Christ rising triumphant from his tomb. Clearly, Francis and Claude were looking to share a similar fate.

The only exception to the realism of the French royal cadavers is the transi of Catherine de Medici. While her husband, Henry II, who died in 1559 in a jousting accident, is portrayed in the previous tradition of rigid rigor mortis, Catherine is given a beautified pose similar to Botticelli's *The Birth of Venus*. Nonetheless, the original transi of Catherine designed for the tomb is quite different. In 1565 Girolamo della Robbia, one of the Italian artists frequently commissioned by the French Renaissance kings, was ordered to sculpt the queen "as she would look a few days after death." Catherine, who was to outlive her husband by thirty years, was at the time forty-five years old. Robbia's sculpture, now in the Louvre, shows the queen in the more typical pose of death: stiff limbs, shrunken belly, prominent ribs, and flaccid breasts. Apparently, Catherine became offended by Robbia's transi and substituted the current one by Germain Pilon. Of these royals, she is the only one to have insisted on two idealized figures for her tomb, defying the humility thought due to God.

The format of the French royal tombs was to return to England on the monuments of Robert Cecil, first earl of Salisbury (d. 1612) and Sir John Hotham (d. 1689). Their tombs, respectively at St. Etheldreda's Church in Hatfield, Hertfordshire, and at Dalton Holme in Yorkshire, both display the classicized virtues of Force, Temperance, Prudence, and Justice bearing on their shoulders the effigies, now recumbent in the traditional English manner. However, these tombs also borrowed from Renaissance monuments in the Low Countries, which had a long history of trade with England. For instance, the kneeling position of the virtues as they support the effigy is thought to have been derived from Tommaso Vincidor's monument to Engelbrecht II of Nassau at Breda, Holland, constructed sometime during the 1520s. The skeletal transi probably was influenced by that on the double tomb of Reynout III (d. 1556) at Vianen, also in the Netherlands. Whatever the medium of its transmission, the persistence into the seventeenth century of the two-tiered tomb structure testifies to the enduring power of the meaning behind this type of monument.

The seventeenth century in England is more famously known for its resurrection monuments, over thirty of which were carved and erected in parish churches throughout the country. Typically, they show a standing figure in its shroud rising up out of its burial urn, the standard being set by the monument to the poet John Donne (d. 1631) at St. Paul's, London. The overall imagery may be quite different, but there continue to be connections between these tombs and the earlier double-decker style. Sir John Denham, a judge who died in 1638, is commemorated at Egham, Surrey, in a remarkable monument in which he rises half-naked in his shroud at the sound of the angels' trumpets above a charnel house or ossuary full of shrouded skeletons, among which can be discerned the fleshly features of Denham and his second wife, Eleanor. The juxtaposition of resurrection and decay recalls the medieval tombs, although Denham's memorial seems more directly inspired by a passage from Ezekiel referring to the reassemblage of dry bones in a valley. Angels, who play such an important role in medieval double-decker tombs, haul Henry Howard out of his grave in his wall monument installed at Ewelme after his death in 1647. The familial resurrection featured in shroud brasses over a century earlier reappears in the tomb of Sir John Astley (d. 1639) and his wife and parents, all shown standing in their shrouds at All Saints Church in Maidstone, Kent, or in the wonderfully intimate monument to Edward Noel, Viscount Campden, and his wife, Juliana, erected in 1664 at St. James Church in Chipping Campden, Gloucestershire.

Though there are strong links down the centuries within the English memorial arts, the seventeenth-century images favored the resurrected body, while the fifteenth-century examples emphasized the macabre cadaver, especially on the single transi tombs. Perhaps this can be explained by what one might call the

Resurrection tomb of Sir John Denham (d. 1638) at Egham, Surrey, and (opposite) of John Donne (d. 1631) at St. Paul's Cathedral. Among the bony figures below Denham's resurrection can be distinguished the faces of Sir John and his wife, Eleanor. (Courtesy A. F. Kersting and Royal Commision on Historical Monuments in England.)

arrogance of the new religion. To the medieval mind, the humility of the decaying corpse helped one on the path through purgatory preparatory to the Apocalypse; the cadaver was therefore representative of the program of piety, penitence, and good works that went along with faith in order to achieve salvation. After the Reformation, and particularly after the Puritan version of Protestantism took hold, this humility was eliminated. What was required now was membership of the elect (to which one was chosen by God, regardless of merit), which the patrons of these effigies, rising so confidently from their tombs, seemed to believe they had attained.

THE LAST WORD

There have been numerous attempts over the years to explain the transi tomb. The oldest and most widely accepted interpretation argues that the decaying corpse or skeleton expressed a deep psychological fear of death, wherein the patron's "anxiety" and "humility" concerning his supernatural fate is on public display. Tomb inscriptions impart either a moralizing message against pride and vanity along the lines of "I was what you are, I am what you will be," or take the form of a humble appeal for prayers from the onlooker to speed the patron's soul through purgatory. Thus the transi tomb embodies, on the one hand, a morbid obsession with death, and on the other, a self-centered concern, despite the lip service to humility, with the soul's afterlife. This interpretation is largely derived from the the famous Dutch historian Johan Huizinga. In *The Waning of the Middle Ages* Huizinga argues that late medieval culture, particularly its unhealthy preoccupation with death, had assumed a sterile rigidity of expression. In the morbid gloom that descended on Europe during the fourteenth and fifteenth centuries, all of man's most tender and subtle feelings became swallowed up in "the too much accentuated and too vivid representation of Death hideous and threatening."

However, Huizinga's overly

dark view of the *memento mori,* or "remembrance of death," theme in art and literature of the later Middle Ages ignores the message of hope and recovery from misfortune that was juxta-posed with a reminder of man's mortality. Some inscriptions on medieval tombs do suggest an anxiety for the deceased's soul, but these were almost always written in Latin and probably were not intended for public consumption. Judging from the complacency and tranquil self-assurance evinced by Englishmen whose wills survive from the late medieval period, such an anxiety does not seem to have been widespread. Rather than a morbid obsession with death, these tombs provided a redemptive power that was apocalyptic in character. They are a grand summation of not just the macabre art of the corpse, but of the whole medieval psyche that endured the four apocalyptic horsemen of Famine, War, Plague, and Death. Only by exploring the uplifting message behind all the gruesome imagery of "skeletons and worms" can we understand how the late medieval psyche coped with rampant death and engendered a rebirth of culture during the Renaissance.

The cadaver is but a transitional figure to the time when that individual will reinhabit his complete, young body at the resur-rection: Such would have been the consolation proffered during the Middle Ages for the decay that so disfigured an earthly form. It was certainly a consolation for Englishmen and Europeans who faced the crises of the Apocalypse during the fourteenth and fif-teenth centuries. At the end of the world during the Last Judgment, bellies distended by famine would be reduced to their proper proportions, limbs hacked and scarred by war would be restored, and skin ruptured and swollen from the plague would resume its true complexion. In all this, we should not discount an element of humor, even if it be a morbid one, in the ability of medieval man to picture himself in death. Death became familiar, and therefore less frightening. Perhaps tomb patrons like Chichele smiled a little at their dead selves, and in that amuse-ment banished some of the terror of their impending death.

Though one is unlikely today to depict oneself carved as a cadaver on a tomb, and only suicidal cultists would insist that we welcome death by looking forward to the Apocalypse, we can perhaps transcend our mortal prison through an appreciation of the art of our ancestors, especially tombs, through which the dead survive. Sadly, destruction of church monuments, including tombs, was particularly severe in England during the reign of Edward VI in the sixteenth century and during the Civil War in the seventeenth. Like Milton's fallen angels, the iconoclasts attacked what they could not understand, defacing what had been created in a time and place now wholly alien to them.

Coutesy of National Monuments Record Centre

EPITAPH

When we recall the amazing pestilence which lately attacked these parts and which took from us by far the best and worthiest men, those of us who have survived and have been mercifully spared by Providence (although we do not deserve it), must break forth in praises and devout expressions of gratitude. . . . For these reasons, order the seven penitential psalms and the litany to be specially recited twice every week in parish churches for the peace of the realm, for the lord king and for the obedience of the people, and the usual processions around the churches and churchyards to be carried out on the same days, by which means the people, sincerely contemplating the past and present gifts of God, should be better able to serve and please him. And thus those of us who remain alive should pray for the good state of the world, for the lord king, for us and for you, so that God, having mercy on the prayers of the just, should turn away his anger and in response to our prayers show us how to serve him more devotedly.

— Letter from Archbishop Simon Islip to Bishop
Ralph Stratford of London, December 28, 1349

So Simon Islip, archbishop of Canterbury, gave thanks for England's deliverance from the Black Death of 1349 and from a French attack upon the English-held town of Calais. Islip's gratitude was premature, however, as plague would recur again and again and England's fortunes in war would decline during the remainder of the century. But Islip's letter illustrates Englishmen's resilience in the face of a nationwide catastrophe: Life persisted, even after the scourges of war and plague, and, if the words of their spiritual leader are at all representative, the people's faith seemingly emerged intact.

As we enter the third millennium, our world is still visited by famine, war, plague, and death, but certainly not with the concentrated fury of the later Middle Ages. If the Four Horsemen were destined to ride together upon the earth, perhaps at no other time were men and women better equipped to endure the ordeal; culturally and psychologically they were imbued with the assumption that everything happened by design in accordance with the will of a beneficial God. Indeed, this was their religion, and it served them well.

In the case of famine, fourteenth-century Englishmen learned by bitter experience at the hands of the Scots that the calamities of nature could be greatly exacerbated by the ravages of war. The lethal combination of these two horsemen in the north of the country led to severe depopulation and dislocation for several decades. Famine reappeared in the North during the winter of 1587–88, when the registers of several parishes record two to four times as many deaths as in an average year. The coming of the agricultural revolution during the eighteenth and nineteenth centuries finally relieved the problem of feeding growing populations in Europe, but even in modern times communities, especially in the Third World, continue to starve when food supplies are disrupted by war. The men and women of the later Middle Ages, as evidenced by their poetic and legal complaints, understood the connection between the scourges of famine and war, a lesson that remains valuable today.

Nevertheless, the fourteenth and fifteenth centuries saw new technologies and tactics in warfare that led to an unprecedented shedding of human blood. Casualties from one battle could number in the thousands, a death toll previously unfathomable, and the powerful weapons of the longbow, cannon, and firearm did not spare even the nobility equipped with the latest suits of armor. A more modern, and far more ruthless, way of waging war had been unleashed, one that significantly made no distinction between civilians and soldiers. But toward the end of the fourteenth century, public opinion in both England and France turned firmly against the warmaking policies of the past, and new efforts were made to permanently resolve the conflict. Clearly, these initiatives were a response to the financial hardships and miseries that the Hundred Years War had wrought on both sides of the Channel, and although largely unsuccessful, they reflected the beginnings of a gradual shift from a warloving culture in favor of a peacemaking one.

In the face of plague, it seems, medieval man was powerless. The Black Death of 1348–49 can now be said to have carried off at least half of England's and Europe's populations, but this was merely the beginning of a century and a half of recurring epidemic disease. During the later Middle Ages, death was, sometimes quite literally, always in the air. Even so, a remarkable resilience can be detected in the flowering of mysticism that occurred throughout England and the Continent at this time. Both men and women sought a closer, more personal rapport with God, perhaps in part because they wanted to better understand his will, even if that meant death on an unimaginable scale. But if God's ways remained mysterious, it was enough to know that a supremely wise and benevolent deity was fulfilling his own plan for the history of the world and for man's place within it. Even the coming of the Apocalypse held out the promise of a better tomorrow.

For many of us in the modern world, death represents a finality, the end. But for medieval men and women it was only the beginning. The far more important journey was to take place in the next life, as our souls were dispatched to heaven, hell, or purgatory. When the end of Creation truly arrived with the Apocalypse, our bodies would be rejoined to our souls, to dwell together for eternity. With such a vast expanse of time before us, it did not really matter much if we suffered horribly from famine, war, plague, and death in this life. All would be redeemed at the resurrection, when our bodies would be made whole. The gruesome cadaver images that survive from the late medieval and early modern eras were not nearly so frightening to contemporary audiences as they are to us. Our ancestors knew that those grinning skeletons were looking forward to their apocalyptic fates. If there be no other permanence to our existence, it should at least be found in the sometimes magnificent art and literature of this period, which preserves its patrons' memories.

Because it was beset with so much catastrophe, the later Middle Ages has been popularly understood as a morbid, depressed, decadent era, during which society and culture were in collapse. The historian perhaps most responsible for this view, Johan Huizinga, wrote at the end of his classic work, *The Waning of the Middle Ages*:

> Profound pessimism spread a general gloom over life. The gothic principle prevailed in art. But all these forms and modes were on the wane. A high and strong culture is declining, but at the same time and in the same sphere new things are being born. The tide is turning, the tone of life is about to change.

Even Huizinga recognized that Europe was in transition, rather than decline, and that without the upheavals of the later Middle Ages there would have been no Renaissance, no Reformation. Yet Huizinga dwells overmuch, I believe, on the darkness of late medieval life, and not enough on its light. Without the existence of a vigorous, even exuberant strand to late medieval culture, Europe could never have reinvented itself in the early modern period. Lately the scholarly consensus seems to be that the line between late medieval and early modern has in the past been too sharply drawn. In their widely read volume *Western Europe in the Middle Ages*, Brian Tierney and Sidney Painter conclude:

> In the last century of the medieval era, the peoples of Europe had to cope with an unprecedented combination of plague, war, schism, and economic decline, all occur-

ring simultaneously and all interacting with one another.
In the face of these disasters, medieval people did not
lose their nerve. They did not succumb to a "death wish."
Instead, they kept working at their problems, solved them
as best they could, and in doing so, brought into existence the institutions of the early modern world. Thus the
"time of troubles" of the late Middle Ages did not lead
to a disintegration of Western civilization but to a new era
of expansion and achievement. Unlike the population of
ancient Rome, the peoples of medieval Europe conducted
themselves with enough sense and courage to avert the
threat of a new Dark Age. That was the greatest achievement of medieval civilization.

It is possible now to present another picture of the later Middle
Ages besides one of "waning" or decline. Though Englishmen
and Europeans faced a wrenching series of crises, by the close of
the medieval era they had launched a new peace, liberated serfs,
rediscovered mysticism, and developed a literature and art that
became the foundation for the Renaissance. At the brink of the
Apocalypse, they had wrested hope from despair.

TABLE 1: CLERICAL MORTALITY DURING
THE GREAT FAMINE, 1307–26

Year	DEATHS*		
	Diocese of Hereford	Diocese of Winchester	Diocese of Exeter
1307	19	24	1
1308	30	14	22
1309	13	29	61
1310	25	16	48
1311	13	13	32
1312	24	16	35
1313	24	29	36
1314	19	24	31
1315	13	22	18
1316	33	22	20
1317	incomplete	22	25
1318	13	29	33
1319	1	incomplete	17
1320	26	incomplete	17
1321	14	18	29
1322	13	19	27
1323	5	incomplete	19
1324	9		23
1325	7		12
1326	10		incomplete

*Figures adjusted in order to account for the probable death dates of incumbents, usually one month prior to the institution of his successor.

Sources: *Registrum Ricardi de Swinfield, Episcopi Herefordensis*, A.D. *1283–1317*, ed. W. W. Capes (Canterbury and York Society, 6, 1909), 539–46; *Registrum Ade de Orleton, Episcopi Herefordensis*, A.D. *1317–1327*, ed. A. T. Bannister (Canterbury and York Society, 5, 1908), 385; *Registrum Henrici Woodlock Diocesis Wintoniensis*, A.D. *1305–1316*, trans. and ed. A. W. Godman, 2 vols. (Canterbury and York Society, 43–44, 1940–41), 2:722–47; *The Registers of John de Sandale and Rigaud de Asserio, Bishops of Winchester*, A.D. *1316–1323*, ed. F. J. Baigent (Hampshire Record Society, 1897), 119–58, 428–528; *The Register of Walter de Stapledon, Bishop of Exeter*, A.D. *1307–1326*, ed. F. C. Hingeston-Randolph (London and Exeter, 1892), 184–271.

TABLE 2: ABUSES OF PURVEYANCE—LINCOLNSHIRE, 1334–39

VICTUALS AND MONEY EXTORTED BY PURVEYORS

YEAR	Grain Qrs.	Bs.	Sacks	Animals Per head or side	Cheese Stone	Salt Qrs.	Bs.	Money £	s.	d.
1334				45						
1336	200									
1337	161	2		270	106	80		1402	11	1
1338	2488ᵃ	2	36	884ᵇ	252	73	2	127ᶜ	17	7
1339	1263ᵃ		255ᵇ			32ᶜ			11	8
none given	1204	4	10	37.5	168	3		41	1	11
TOTAL	5317	46		149.5	526	156	2	1604	2	3

VICTUALS RECEIVED BY CROWN

Grain Qrs.	Bs.	Pecks	Animals Per head or side	Cheese Stone	Salt Qrs.
2630					
1865	.5	7	107.5	407	137
4495	.5	7	107.5	407	137

ᵃ The 1,000 quarters of grain said to have been taken by Herbert de Gresseby and his deputy, Robert de Severby, in 1338 and 1339 are evenly divided between these two years.

ᵇ The 200 large animals said to have been taken by John de Podenhale in 1338 and 1339 are evenly divided between these two years.

ᶜ The £45 said to have been extorted by John de Podenhale in 1338 and 1339 is evenly divided between these two years.

Sources: Public Record Office, London. JUST 1/521, mm. 3–19; E358/1, m. 6; E358/2, mm. 3d, 11, 29; E358/4, m. 8; *The 1341 Royal Inquest in Lincolnshire*, ed. B. W. McLane (Lincoln Record Society, 78, 1988), 2–110.

	VICTUALS AND MONEY EXTORTED BY PURVEYORS								VICTUALS RECEIVED BY CROWN			
	Grain				Animals	Money			Grain			Animals
YEAR	Qrs.	Bs.	Strikes	Sacks	Per head or side	£	s.	d.	Qrs.	Bs.	Baskets	Per head or side
1330	4			8								
1333	15											
1334	10											
1336	424	7	13									
1337	621	4.5	16		134	137	18	2	299	5	.5	
1338	770	1	29	23	65	4	4	2	520			
1339	234		10		4	7	16	10				
1340	22				60		3	4	565			595
none given	219	7	7		15	2	9	10				
TOTAL	2321	3.5	59	39	278	152	12	4	1384	5	.5	595

Source: Public Record Office, London: Just 1/691, mm. 1–9d.; E358/1, m. 6; E358/2, mm. 8, 11d., 12d., 26, 29, 33d.; E358/4, mm. 1d., 18.

TABLE 4: CLERICAL PROPAGANDA DURING THE HUNDRED YEARS WAR, 1337–77

YEAR	DIOCESES	OCCASION	RESPONSE
1337	Ely, Bath and Wells	Peace negotiations between England and France; king's expedition to Scotland	Prayers, processions, masses, publication of "schedule" (in English) concerning peace negotiations
1338	Carlisle	King's expedition to Scotland	Prayers, processions
1339	Worcester, Bath and Wells	King's expedition to France	Masses, processions, fasts, vigils, almsgivings
1340	Winchester, Durham, Ely, Worcester, Hereford, Carlisle	Peace; victory at Sluys; further success of king's expedition to Flanders	Prayers, processions, masses, litanies, psalms, bell-ringing
1342	Lincoln, Winchester, Durham, Worcester, Exeter, Bath and Wells, Salisbury	King's expedition to France and another to Scotland	Prayers, processions, masses, and sermons
1345	Worcester, Bath and Wells	King's expedition to France	Prayers, masses
1346	Ely, Worcester, Winchester, Hereford, Carlisle, Bath and Wells	King's expedition to France and its safe return; King's landing at St. Vaast de la Hogue in Normandy and continued success; capture of Caen	Prayers, processions, masses, litanies, psalms, publication of "schedule" detailing the king's exploits from the landing at St. Vaast de la Hogue to the capture of Caen

Year	Dioceses	Occasion	Response
			Prayers
1348	Bath and Wells, Hereford	King's expedition to France	Prayers
1350	London, Bath and Wells, Hereford	The king at Calais and plague; peace and well-being of king; king's expedition against Spanish pirates	Prayers, processions, psalms, litanies
1352	Bath and Wells, Salisbury[a]	Expedition and victory of Henry of Grosmont, duke of Lancaster, in Prussia	Prayers, processions, masses, sermons
1355	Lincoln, Exeter, Ely	Expedition of king, Black Prince, and Henry of Grosmont, duke of Lancaster, to France	Prayers, processions, masses, litanies
1356	Lincoln, Winchester, Exeter, Hereford, York[b]	Expedition of Black Prince, and Henry of Grosmont, duke of Lancaster, to France; king and Henry of Grosmont going over-seas for peace; victory of Black Prince at Poitiers	Prayers, masses, processions, nocturns, psalms, fasts, sermons, publication of victory
1359	Carlisle, Exeter, Winchester	King's expedition to France	Prayers, processions, litanies, psalms, fasts, almsgiving

[a] No date given, but probably 1352.
[b] Year illegible, but probably 1356.

1361	York	Peace and plague	Prayers, litanies, processions
1363	Winchester, York	Expedition of Black Prince to Aquitaine; well-being of king and realm and good weather	Prayers
1366	Lincoln[c]	Peace, good weather and harvest	Prayers, masses, processions
1367	Lincoln, Canterbury, Salisbury[d]	Expedition and victory of Black Prince at Nájera, Spain	Prayers, processions, masses, psalms, litanies, almsgiving, bell-ringing
1369	Lincoln, Winchester	Peace and plague	Prayers, masses, processions, psalms, litanies, sermons
1370	Lincoln, Winchester	Peace; expeditions of Black Prince and John of Gaunt, duke of Lancaster, in France and Spain	Prayers, processions, masses, psalms, litanies
1372	Lincoln, Exeter, Winchester, Carlisle[e]	Peace negotiations with France; peace and well-being of king and realm; king's expedition to relieve La Rochelle	Prayers, processions, masses, psalms, litanies, fasts, vigils, almsgiving

[c] No date given, but probably 1366.
[d] No date given, but probably 1367.
[e] No date given, but probably 1372.

Year	Dioceses	Occasion	Response
1373	Winchester, Exeter	Expedition of John of Gaunt, duke of Lancaster, and William of Montagu, earl of Salisbury, to France	Prayers, processions, masses, fasts
1374	Lincoln, Ely, Exeter, Winchester	Peace and well-being of king and realm	Prayers, processions, masses, litanies, fasts
1375	Lincoln, Ely, Winchester, Exeter	Expedition overseas of Edmund of Langley, earl of Cambridge, and John of Montfort, duke of Brittany; peace and well-being of king and realm	Prayers, processions, masses, psalms, litanies, almsgiving, bell-ringing
1376	Lincoln	Peace of realm; convalescence of king; soul of Black Prince	Prayers, processions
1377	Lincoln, Winchester	Expedition of Thomas of Woodstock, earl of Buckingham, and John of Montfort, duke of Brittany, to Sluys, France	Prayers, processions, masses

Sources: Cambridge University Library, Ely Diocesan Records: G/1/1, Register Simon Montacute, fols. 69r.-70r., 84v.-85r., and Register Thomas de Lisle, fols. 58r.-59r., 68r.-69r., 73r.; G/1/2, Register Thomas Arundel, fols. 2v., 7r.; Borthwick Institute, York, Register 11 (John Thoresby), fols. 37v., 48r., 55v.; Wiltshire County Record Office, Trowbridge, Register Robert Wyvil, volume 1, fols. 75v.-76r., 212r., 228v.; Cumbria County Record Office, Carlisle, Carlisle Diocesan Records: DRC/1/2, Register Gilbert Welton, fols. 59-60; Register Thomas Appleby, fol. 253; *The Register of William Edington, Bishop of Winchester, 1346–1366*, ed. S. F. Hockey, 2 parts (Hampshire Record Series, 7, 8, 1986), 1:7–8; 2:3, 42–43, 49, 56; *Wykeham's Register*, ed. T. F. Kirby, 2 vols. (Hampshire Record Society, 1896–99), 2:82–83, 89–90, 105, 108–9, 116–17, 160, 171–72, 188, 192–93, 218, 233–35, 278, 576–77, 579, 585–86; *Registrum Johannis de Trillek, Episcopi Herefordensis, A.D. 1344–1361*, ed. J. H. Parry (Canterbury and York Society, 8, 1912), 65, 77–78, 149–50, 160, 242, 264–67, 273–74, 279–81, 318, 350–51; *A Calendar of the Register of Wolstan de Bransford, Bishop of Worcester, 1339–49*, ed. R. M. Haines (Worcestershire Historical Society, new ser., 4, 1966), 206, 286–87, 290, 296, 315, 321; *Registrum Simonis Langham, Cantuariensis Archiepiscopi*, ed. A. C. Wood (Canterbury and York Society, 53, 1956), 151–52, 161–63; *The Register of John Kirkby, Bishop of Carlisle, 1332–52*, and *The Register of John Ross, Bishop of Carlisle, 1325–32*, ed. R. L. Storey (Canterbury and York Society, 79, 81, 1993–95), 1:82–83, 110, 173; *The Register of Ralph of Shrewsbury, Bishop of Bath and Wells, 1329–1362*, ed. T. S. Holmes, 2 vols. (Somerset Record Society, 9, 10, 1896), 1:305–6, 334–36, 386–87, 400–401, 415, 2:571–78, 534–35, 602, 643–44, 685, 705; *Registrum Palatinum Dunelmense*, ed. T. D. Hardy, 4 vols. (Rolls Series, 62, 1873–78), 1:323, 499–501; *The Register of John de Grandisson, Bishop of Exeter (A.D. 1327–1369)*, ed. F. C. Hingeston-Randolph, 3 parts (London and Exeter, 1894–99), 2:66–67, 1158–59, 1173–74, 1190–91, 1200–3; *The Register of Thomas de Brantyngham, Bishop of Exeter (A.D. 1370–1394)*, ed. F. C . Hingeston-Randolph, 2 parts (London and Exeter, 1901–6), 1:186–87, 190–91, 199, 299–300, 342–44; Lincolnshire Archives Office: Episcopal Register 7, Thomas Bek, fols. 3v.-4v.; Episcopal Register 8, John Gynwell, fols. 65r.-v., 76r.; Episcopal Register 12, John Buckingham, fols. 34v., 41r.-v., 71r., 96v.-97r., 107r.-v., 125v., 128r., 133r.; A. K. McHardy, "Liturgy and Propanganda in the Diocese of Lincoln during the Hundred Years War," in *Studies in Church History: The Church and War*, ed. W. J. Sheils (Ecclesiastical History Society, 20, 1983), 225.

TABLE 5: CLERICAL MORTALITY, 1349

DIOCESE	PERCENT
Bath and Wells	47.6
Coventry and Lichfield	39.28
Ely	46.7
Exeter	48.8
Hereford	45.86
Lincoln	40.1
Norwich	48.8
Winchester	48.8
Worcester	48.8
York	38.97
Average	48.97

Sources: J. C. Russell, *British Medieval Population* (Albuquerque, N.M., 1948), 222; R. A. Davies, "The Effect of the Black Death on the Parish Priests of the Medieval Diocese of Coventry and Lichfield," *Bulletin of the Institute of Historical Research* 62 (1989): 87; J. Aberth, "The Black Death in the Diocese of Ely: The Evidence of the Bishop's Register, " *Journal of Medieval History* 21 (1995): 279.

TABLE 6: MORTALITY IN THE DIOCESE
OF HEREFORD, 1345–1400

Year	Deaths[a]	Non-residents[b]	Multiple[c] institutions	% total[d] benefices	% from York
1345	4	2		1.3	
1346	3	10		1.0	
1347	4	11		1.34	
1348	8	19		2.75	
1349	147	20	14	45.86	39.85
1350	22	16		7.48	
1351	15	17		5.12	
1352	14	15		4.75	
1353	20	15		6.78	
1354	2	11		0.67	
1355	10	11		3.34	
1356	8	10		2.67	
1357	6	11		2.0	
1358	2	16		0.68	
1359	7	15		2.37	
1360	incomplete				
1361	31	10		10.33	
1362	9	11	1	2.68	12.46
1363	13	5		4.26	
1364	6	2		1.95	
1365	3	2		0.97	
1366	10	3		3.26	
1367	12	7		3.96	
1368	12	9		3.99	
1369	40	7		13.2	12.39
1370	6	1		1.94	
1371	6	1		1.94	
1372	6	1		1.94	
1373	13	1		4.2	
1374	11	1		3.56	
1375	9			2.9	
1376					
1377	9	2		2.92	
1378	7	2		2.27	
1379	2	2		0.65	
1380	1	2		0.32	
1381	1			0.32	
1382	2			0.65	
1383	10	1		3.24	
1384	13	1		4.2	
1385	12	2		3.9	

TABLE 6 (continued)

Year	Deaths[a]	Non-residents[b]	Multiple[c] institutions	% total[d] benefices	% from York
1386	12	2		3.9	
1387	15	1		4.85	
1388	9	1		2.91	
1389	1			0.32	
1390	34	1		11.0	
1391	28	2	1	8.77	
1392	19	2		6.17	
1393	24	1	1	7.44	
1394	24	1		7.77	
1395	23	1		7.44	
1396	32			10.32	
1397	17			5.48	
1398	13			4.2	
1399	23			7.42	
1400	19			6.13	

[a] Figures adjusted in order to account for the probable death dates of incumbents, usually one month prior to the institution of successors.
[b] Includes all priests who had a licence for nonresidence for at least part of the given year.
[c] Benefices voided more than once in a given year are counted only once and the extra deaths are deducted from column 2.
[d] Taken from W. J. Dohar, *The Black Death and Pastoral Leadership: The Diocese of Hereford in the Fourteenth Century* (Philadelphia, 1995), 41. The total beneficiaries are 310, which represents a mean between Dohar's range of 301 to 319.

Sources: W. J. Dohar, *The Black Death and Pastoral Leadership: The Diocese of Hereford in the Fourteenth Century* (Philadelphia, 1995), 42; A. H. Thompson, "The Pestilences of the Fourteenth Century in the Diocese of York," *Archaeological Journal* 71 (1914): 132–34; *Registrum Ludowici de Charltone, Episcopi Herefordensis, A.D. 1361–1370,* ed. J. H. Parry (Canterbury and York Society, 14, 1914), 63–70; *Registrum Willelmi de Courtenay, Episcopi Herefordensis, A.D. 1370–1375,* ed. W. W. Capes (Canterbury and York Society, 15, 1914), 11–12; *Registrum Johannis Gilbert, Episcopi Herefordensis, A.D. 1375–1389,* ed. J. H. Parry (Canterbury and York Society 18, 1915), 115–22; *Registrum Johannis Trefnant, Episcopi Herefordensis, A.D. 1389–1404,* ed. W. W. Capes (Canterbury and York Society, 20, 1916), 174–84. Note that Thompson's figures represent averages taken from the four archdeaconries of the diocese of York and run respectively from March 25, 1349, 1362, 1369 to March 24, 1350, 1363, 1370.

TABLE 7: EXCHANGES, 1328–1400

Year	Exeter	Hereford	Winchester
1328	3	1	unavailable
1329	3	1	unavailable
1330	12		unavailable
1331	73		unavailable
1332	5	1	unavailable
1333	11	2	unavailable
1334	5	2	unavailable
1335	1	2	unavailable
1336	7	1	unavailable
1337	10		unavailable
1338	3		unavailable
1339	3	1	unavailable
1340	2	6	unavailable
1341	4	4	unavailable
1342	4	3	unavailable
1343	7	3	unavailable
1344	6	1	unavailable
1345	3	2	unavailable
1346	9	3	10
1347	3	4	12
1348	5	5	14
1349	3	6	20
1350	2	6	8
1351	3	5	12
1352	5	6	12
1353	2	3	14
1354	7	7	14
1355	3	6	10
1356	2	4	9
1357	5	9	11
1358	4	4	11
1359	3	3	6
1360	1	incomplete	8
1361	4	incomplete	6
1362	2	3	8
1363	5	3	9
1364		6	6
1365	1	1	10
1366	3	5	7
1367	5	4	7
1368	3	3	7
1369	incomplete	1	9
1370	incomplete	3	23
1371	18	7	17
1372	7	6	12
1373	10	3	10

TABLE 7 (continued)

Year	Exeter	Hereford	Winchester
1374	7	6	9
1375	8	1	6
1376	12		15
1377	13	4	16
1378	8	2	15
1379	6	8	8
1380	6	1	20
1381	13	6	17
1382	14	2	18
1383	7	8	17
1384	11	6	9
1385	14	7	11
1386	13	14	9
1387	17	7	15
1388	incomplete	4	19
1389	incomplete		5
1390	incomplete	14	15
1391	11	8	14
1392	18	7	9
1393	16	9	4
1394	18	14	18
1395	6	13	11
1396	10	6	16
1397	8	9	19
1398	6	6	6
1399	15	9	10
1400	13	6	17

Sources: *The Register of John de Grandisson, Bishop of Exeter,* A.D. *1327–1369,* ed. F. C. Hingeston-Randolph, 3 parts (London and Exeter, 1894–99), 3:1263–1507; *The Register of Thomas de Brantyngham, Bishop of Exeter,* A.D. *1370–1394,* ed. F. C. Hingeston-Randoph, 2 parts, London and Exeter, 1901–6), 1:13–137, 141–42, 155–56, 162, 171, 173–78, 413; *The Register of Edmund Stafford,* A.D. *1395–1419: An Index and Abstract of Its Contents,* ed. F. C. Hingeston-Randolph (London and Exeter, 1886), 140–220; *Registrum Thome de Charlton, Episcopi Herefordensis,* A.D. *1327–1344,* ed. W. W. Capes (Canterbury and York Society, 9, 1913), 83–84; *Registrum Johannis de Trillek, Episcopi Herefordensis,* A.D. *1344–1361,* ed. J. H. Parry (Canterbury and York Society, 8, 1912), 373–92, 404–10; *Registrum Ludowici de Charltone, Episcopi Herefordensis,* A.D. *1361–1370,* ed. J. H. Parry (Canterbury and York Society, 14, 1914), 66, 71–72; *Registrum Willelmi de Courtenay, Episcopi Herefordensis,* A.D. *1370–1375,* ed. W. W. Capes (Canterbury and York Society, 15, 1914), 11, 13–14; *Registrum Johannis Gilbert, Episcopi Herefordensis,* A.D. *1375–1389,* ed. J. H. Parry (Canterbury and York Society, 18, 1915), 115–26; *Registrum Johannis Trefnant, Episcopi Herefordensis,* A.D. *1389–1404,* ed. W. W. Capes (Canterbury and York Society, 20, 1916), 187–91; *Wykeham's Register,* ed. T. F. Kirby, 2 vols. (Hampshire Record Society, 1896–99), 1:5–230; 2:122, 444; *Registrum Simonis Langham, Cantuariensis Archiepiscopi,* ed. A. C. Wood (Canterbury and York Society, 53, 1956), 246–51; *The Register of William Edington, Bishop of Winchester, 1346–1366,* ed. S. F. Hockey, 2 parts (Hampshire Record Series, 7, 8, 1986), 1:17–251.

BIBLIOGRAPHY

Prologue

Medieval people's fascination with the millennium, Apocalypse, and the Antichrist has been explored by: N. Cohn, *The Pursuit of the Millennium: Revolutionary Messianism in Medieval and Reformation Europe and Its Bearing on Modern Totalitarian Movements,* 2nd ed. (New York, 1961); R. K. Emmerson, *Antichrist in the Middle Ages: A Study of Medieval Apocalypticism, Art, and Literature* (Seattle, 1981); and *The Apocalypse in the Middle Ages,* ed. R. K. Emmerson and B. McGinn (Ithaca and London, 1992). A study that focuses on apocalyptic prophecies as these relate to the Black Death is by R. E. Lerner, "The Black Death and Western European Eschatological Mentalities," *American Historical Review* 86 (1981):541–43, and repr. in *The Black Death: The Impact of the Fourteenth-Century Plague,* ed. D. William (Medieval and Renaissance Texts and Studies, 13, 1982).

Louis Heyligen's description of the plague was written in a letter that was incorporated into a Flemish chronicle, *Recueil des Chroniques de Flandre,* ed. J. J. De Smet, 4 vols. (Brussels, 1837–65). Other source quotations on the plague are taken from *The Black Death,* trans. and ed. R. Horrox (Manchester, 1994). "A Warning to Be Ware" is printed in *The Minor Poems of the Vernon MS,* ed. F. J. Furnivall, 2 parts (Early English Text Society, 117, 1901). Thomas Wimbledon's sermon is to be found in *Wimbledon's Sermon: Redde Rationem Villicationis Tue: A Middle English Sermon of the Fourteenth Century,* ed. I. K. Knight (Duquesne Studies: Philological Series, 9, 1967). John Wycliffe's fascination with the Apocalypse has been studied by M. Wilks, "Wyclif and the Great Persecution," in *Studies in Church History: Prophecy and Eschatology,* ed. idem (Ecclesiastical History Society Subsidia, 10, 1994). Two works that have explored apocalyptic themes in William Langland's *Piers Plowman* are: M. W. Bloomfield, *Piers Plowman as a Fourteenth-Century Apocalypse* (New Brunswick, N.J., 1961), and K. Kerby-Fulton, *Reformist Apocalypticism and Piers Plowman* (Cambridge, 1990).

Any reinterpretation of the later Middle Ages must start with the classic work by Johan Huizinga, *The Waning of the Middle Ages: A Study of the Forms of Life, Thought, and Art in France and the Netherlands in the Dawn of the Renaissance,* trans. F. Hopman (New York, 1924), and now available in a new

English translation as *The Autumn of the Middle Ages,* trans. R. J. Payton and U. Mammitzsch (Chicago, 1996).

Famine

The best general study of the Great Famine is by W. C. Jordan, *The Great Famine: Northern Europe in the Early Fourteenth Century* (Princeton, 1996). A study that focuses on the famine in England is by I. Kershaw, "The Great Famine and Agrarian Crisis in England, 1315–1322," in P*easants, Knights, and Heretics: Studies in Medieval English Social History,* ed. R. H. Hilton (Cambridge, 1976).

The debate about the link between famine and disease is explored in M. Livi-Bacci, *Population and Nutrition: An Essay on European Demographic History,* trans. T. Croft-Murray and C. Ipsen (Cambridge, 1991). Life spans of the well-fed monks of Christ Church and of the nobility are studied by: J. Hatcher, "Mortality in the Fifteenth Century: Some New Evidence," *Economic History Review,* 2nd ser., 39 (1986):19–38; and J. T. Rosenthal, "Medieval Longevity: The Secular Peerage, 1350–1500," *Population Studies* 27 (1973):287–93.

Mortality figures for England during the famine are conveniently summarized in: J. C. Russell, "The Preplague Population of England," *Journal of British Studies* 5 (1966):1–21; and R. M. Smith, "Demographic Developments in Rural England, 1300–48: A Survey," in *Before the Black Death: Studies in the "Crisis" of the Early Fourteenth Century,* ed. B. M. S. Campbell (Manchester and New York, 1991). Grain prices and yields in England during the famine decades are printed and discussed in: J. Z. Titow, *Winchester Yields: A Study in Medieval Agricultural Productivity* (Cambridge, 1972); D. L. Farmer, "Crop Yields, Prices, and Wages in Medieval England," *Studies in Medieval and Renaissance History,* new ser., 6 (1983):117–55; idem, "Prices and Wages," in *The Agrarian History of England and Wales: Volume 2: 1042–1350,* ed. H. E. Hallam (Cambridge, 1988). An important work on grain yields in the north of England is Ian Kershaw's *Bolton Priory: The Economy of a Northern Monastery, 1286–1325* (Oxford, 1973).

For in-depth research on what foods late medieval English peasants ate, see Christopher Dyer, "English Diet in the Later Middle Ages," in *Social Relations and Ideas: Essays in Honour of R. H. Hilton,* ed. T. H. Aston, P. R. Coss, C. Dyer, J. Thirsk (Cambridge, 1983); idem, *Standards of Living in the Later Middle Ages: Social Change in England, c. 1200–1520* (Cambridge, 1989); idem, "Changes in Diet in the Late Middle Ages: The Case of Harvest Workers," in idem, *Everyday Life in Medieval England* (London and Rio Grande, Ohio, 1994).

M. M. Postan first published his neo-Malthusian theory of the late medieval English economy in an article entitled "Some Economic Evidence of Declining Population in the Later Middle Ages," *Economic History Review,* 2nd ser., 2 (1950):221–46. A reevaluation of the Postan thesis has been conducted by B.

M. S. Campbell in a series of articles on medieval farming in County Norfolk. See B. M. S. Campbell, "The Regional Uniqueness of English Field Systems? Some Evidence from Eastern Norfolk," *Agricultural History Review* 29 (1981): 16–28; idem, "Arable Productivity in Medieval England: Some Evidence from Norfolk," *Journal of Economic History* 43 (1983):379–404; idem, "Agricultural Progress in Medieval England: Some Evidence from Eastern Norfolk," *Economic History Review,* 2nd ser., 36 (1983): 26–46; and idem and M. Overton, "A New Perspective on Medieval and Early Modern Agriculture: Six Centuries of Norfolk Farming, c. 1250–c. 1850," *Past and Present* 141 (1993): 38–105. Other regional studies that point to advances in late medieval English agriculture include: P. F. Brandon, "Demesne Arable Farming in Coastal Sussex during the Later Middle Ages," *Agricultural History Review* 19 (1971):113–34; C. Dyer, *Warwickshire Farming, 1349–c. 1520: Preparations for Agricultural Revolution* (Dugdale Society Occasional Papers, 27, 1981); M. Mate, "Medieval Agrarian Practices: The Determining Factors?" *Agricultural History Review* 33 (1985):22–31. On the important innovation of introducing horses into plow teams, see J. Langdon, *Horses, Oxen, and Technological Innovation: The Use of Draught Animals in English Farming from 1066 to 1500* (Cambridge, 1986). The role of marginal land in the medieval economy has been reexamined by Mark Bailey: "The Concept of the Margin in the Medieval English Economy," *Economic History Review,* 2nd ser., 42 (1989):1–17.

A work that studies medieval weather based on contemporary descriptions rather than the less reliable indicator of agricultural productivity is by P. Alexandre, *Le Climat en Europe au Moyen Age: Contribution à l'Histoire des Variations Climatiques de 1000 à 1425, d'après les Sources Narratives de l'Europe Occidentale* (L'École des Hautes Études en Sciences Sociales, Recherches d'Histoire et de Sciences Sociales, 24, 1987). Dendrochronolog- ical and other evidence of a "Little Ice Age" in Europe during the later Middle Ages is presented by: E. Le Roy Ladurie, *Times of Feast, Times of Famine: A History of Climate since the Year 1000,* trans. B. Bray (New York, 1971); H. H. Lamb, *Climate: Present, Past, and Future, Volume 2: Climactic History and the Future* (London, 1977); idem, *Climate, History, and the Modern World* (London and New York, 1982). Sea flooding of eastern England during the fourteenth century is discussed in M. Bailey, "*Per Impetum Maris:* Natural Disaster and Economic Decline in Eastern England, 1275–1350," in *Before the Black Death.*

Most of the information on Scottish devastation of the north of England is taken from C. McNamee, *The Wars of the Bruces: Scotland, England, and Ireland, 1306–1328* (East Lothian, Scotland, 1997), which is the best and most recent work on the subject. But see also R. A. Lomas, *North-East England in the Middle Ages* (Edinburgh, 1992).

The section on purveyance and its effect on peasant agriculture is largely based on my own research in the Public Record Office in London, particularly on the rolls recording the inquest of 1341 into the activities of purveyors in Lincolnshire and Nottinghamshire: JUST 1/521 and JUST 1/691. An important work that details the burden purveyance and taxation laid on fourteenth-century English peasants is by J. R. Maddicott, *The English Peasantry and the Demands of the Crown, 1294–1341* (*Past and Present* Supplement, 1, 1975). But see also: E. Miller, "War, Taxation, and the English Economy in the Late Thirteenth and Early Fourteenth Centuries," in *War and Economic Development: Essays in Memory of David Joslin,* ed. J. M. Winter (Cambridge, 1975); and W. M. Ormrod, "The Crown and the English Economy, 1290–1348," in *Before the Black Death.* In addition, purveyance is discussed in a recent book by James Masschaele, *Peasants, Merchants, and Markets: Inland Trade in Medieval England, 1150–1350* (New York, 1997).

War

A good, general book on war in the Middle Ages is by P. Contamine, *War in the Middle Ages,* trans. M. Jones (Oxford, 1984). A work that focuses on the medieval art of war in England is Michael Prestwich's *Armies and Warfare in the Middle Ages: The English Experience* (New Haven and London, 1996). For textbooks on the Hundred Years War, see: J. Favier, *La Guerre de Cent Ans* (Paris, 1980); C. Allmand, *The Hundred Years War: England and France at War, c. 1300–c. 1450* (Cambridge, 1988); R. Neillands, *The Hundred Years War* (London and New York, 1990); J. Sumption, *The Hundred Years War, Volume 1: Trial by Battle* (London, 1990); idem, *The Hundred Years War, Volume 2: Trial by Fire* (Philadelphia, 1999); A. Curry, *The Hundred Years War* (Basingstoke, Hampshire, and London, 1993).

A number of works lately have appeared on the military revolution debate: J. Black, *A Military Revolution? Military Change and European Society, 1550–1800* (1991); *The Military Revolution Debate: Readings on the Military Transformation of Early Modern Europe,* ed. C. J. Rogers (Boulder, Colo., and Oxford, 1995); *The Medieval Military Revolution: State, Society, and Military Change in Medieval and Early Modern Europe,* ed. A. Ayton and J. L. Price (London and New York, 1995); G. Parker, *The Military Revolution: Military Innovation and the Rise of the West, 1500–1800,* 2nd ed. (Cambridge, 1996). On some of the more technical aspects of late medieval warfare, such as the development of the longbow and gunpowder technology, the rise of infantry over cavalry, the changing use of warhorses, etc., see: H. J. Hewitt, *The Horse in Medieval England* (London, 1983); J. Bradbury, *The Medieval Archer* (Woodbridge, Suffolk, 1985); R. H. C. Davis, *The Medieval Warhorse: Origin, Development, and Redevelopment* (New York, 1989); R. Hardy, *Longbow: A Social and Military History,* 3rd ed. (1992); K. DeVries, *Medieval Military Technology* (Peterborough, Ontario, and Lewiston, N.Y., 1992); *Arms, Armies, and Fortifications in the Hundred Years War,* ed. A. Curry and M. Hughes (Woodbridge, Suffolk, 1994); A. Ayton, *Knights and Warhorses: Military Service and the English Aristocracy under Edward III* (Woodbridge, Suffolk, 1994); C. J. Rogers, "The Military Revolutions of the Hundred Years' War," in *Military Revolution Debate*; and relevant articles by A. Ayton, C. J. Rogers, and

M. Keen in *Medieval Warfare: A History,* ed. M. Keen (Oxford, 1999). In-depth analyses of the battles of Crécy and Agincourt are available in: J. Keegan, *The Face of Battle: A Study of Agincourt, Waterloo, and the Somme* (Harmondsworth, Middlesex, 1976); C. J. Rogers, "Edward III and the Dialectics of Strategy," *Transactions of the Royal Historical Society,* 6th ser., 4 (1994):83–102; K. DeVries, *Infantry Warfare in the Early Fourteenth Century: Discipline, Tactics, and Technology* (Woodbridge, Suffolk, 1996).

On the subject of chivalry and the laws of war during the later Middle Ages, see: M. G. A. Vale, *War and Chivalry: Warfare and Aristocratic Culture in England, France, and Burgundy at the End of the Middle Ages* (London, 1981); J. Vale, *Edward III and Chivalry: Chivalric Society and its Context, 1270–1350* (Woodbridge, Suffolk, 1982); M. H. Keen, *The Laws of War in the Late Middle Ages* (London, 1965); idem, *Chivalry* (New Haven and London, 1984); T. Meron, *Henry's Wars and Shakespeare's Laws* (Oxford, 1993). W. Matthews, *The Tragedy of Arthur* (Berkeley and Los Angeles, 1960) presents the thesis that the alliterative *Morte Arthure* is an allegorical criticism of Edward III's war policies during the fourteenth century. Matthews's interpretation, however, is somewhat contested by J. Barnie, *War in Medieval English Society: Social Values in the Hundred Years War, 1337–99* (Ithaca, N.Y., 1974). The exact date of the poem is also a matter of some debate.

On the subject of propaganda and nationalism as disseminated through the English chronicles, see: A. Gransden, "Propaganda in English Medieval Historiography," *Journal of Medieval History* 1 (1975):363–478; idem, "The Uses Made of History by the Kings of Medieval England," in *Culture et Idéologie dans la Genèse de l'État Moderne: Actes de la Table Ronde Organisée par le Centre National de la Recherche Scientifique et l'École Française de Rome, Rome, 15–17 Octobre 1984* (Collection de l'École Française de Rome, 82, 1985); T. Turville-Petre, *England the Nation: Language, Literature, and National Identity, 1290–1340* (Oxford, 1996). English campaign letters are discussed in K. A. Fowler, "News from the Front: Letters and Despatches of the Fourteenth Century," in *Guerre et Société en France, en Angleterre, et en Bourgogne, XIVe–XVe Siècle,* ed. P. Contamine, C. Giry-Deloison, and M. H. Keen (Centre d'Histoire de la Région du Nord et de l'Europe du Nord-Ouest, Collection "Histoire et Littérature Régionales," 8, 1991). The best and most evenhanded discussion of the alleged rape by Edward III of the countess of Salisbury is A. Gransden, "The Alleged Rape by Edward III of the Countess of Salisbury," *English Historical Review* 87 (1972):333–44.

For studies of English Church propaganda and array in support of the Hundred Years War, see: B. McNab, "Obligations of the Church in English Society: Military Arrays of the Clergy, 1369–1418," in *Order and Innovation in the Middle Ages: Essays in Honor of Joseph R. Strayer,* ed. W. C. Jordan, B. McNab, and T. F. Ruiz (Princeton, 1976); W. R. Jones, "The English Church and Royal Propaganda during the Hundred Years War," *Journal of British Studies* 19 (1979):18–30; A. K. McHardy, "Liturgy and Propaganda in the

Diocese of Lincoln during the Hundred Years War," and R. M. Haines, "An English Archbishop and the Cerberus of War," in *Studies in Church History: The Church and War,* ed. W. J. Sheils (Ecclesiastical History Society, 20, 1983). For the issue of papal diplomacy during the war, see: E. Déprez, "La Conférence d'Avignon, 1344: L'Arbitrage Pontifical entre la France et l'Angleterre," in *Essays in Medieval History Presented to Thomas Frederick Tout,* ed. A. G. Little and F. M. Powicke (Manchester, 1925); H. Jenkins, *Papal Efforts for Peace under Benedict XII, 1334–42* (London and Philadelphia, 1933); D. Wood, "*Omnino Partialitate Cessante:* Clement VI and the Hundred Years War," in *Studies in Church History: The Church and War.*

Some of the most important works, both English and French, on the fate of noncombatants and the destruction wrought in France by English chevauchées and the Free Companies during the Hundred Years War are the following: H. Denifle, *La Désolation des Églises, Monastères et Hopitaux en France pendant la Guerre de Cent Ans,* 2 vols. (Paris, 1897–99); C. T. Allmand, "The War and the Non-Combatant," in *The Hundred Years War,* ed. K. Fowler (Basingstoke, Hampshire, and London, 1971); idem, "War and the Non-Combatant in the Middle Ages," in *Medieval Warfare;* R. Boutruche, "The Devastation of Rural Areas during the Hundred Years War and the Agricultural Recovery of France," in *The Recovery of France in the Fifteenth Century,* ed. P. S. Lewis and trans. G. F. Martin (New York, 1971); P. Contamine, "Les Compagnies d'Aventure en France pendant la Guerre de Cent Ans," *Mélanges de l'École Française de Rome* 87 (1975):365–96; G. Bois, *The Crisis of Feudalism: Economy and Society in Eastern Normandy, c. 1300–1550* (Cambridge, 1984); N. Wright, *Knights and Peasants: The Hundred Years War in the French Countryside* (Woodbridge, Suffolk, 1998); C. J. Rogers, "By Fire and Sword: *Bellum Hostile* and 'Civilians' in the Hundred Years War," in *Civilians in the Path of War,* ed. M. Grimsley and C. J. Rogers (Lincoln, Neb., forthcoming). English scholars who debated the "costs" of the Hundred Years War to their country include: K. B. McFarlane, "War, the Economy, and Social Change: England and the Hundred Years War," *Past and Present* 22 (1962):3–13; M. M. Postan, "The Costs of the Hundred Years' War," *Past and Present* 27 (1964):34–53; A. R. Bridbury, "The Hundred Years' War: Costs and Profits," in *Trade, Government, and Economy in Pre-Industrial England: Essays Presented to F. J. Fisher,* ed. D. C. Coleman and A. H. John (London, 1976), and repr. in idem, *The English Economy from Bede to the Reformation* (Woodbridge, Suffolk, 1992); J. W. Sherborne, "The Cost of English Warfare with France in the Later Fourteenth Century," *Bulletin of the Institute of Historical Research* 50 (1977):135–50, and repr. in idem, *War, Politics, and Culture in Fourteenth-Century England,* ed. A. Tuck (London and Rio Grande, Ohio, 1994).

For accounts and discussions of Richard II's peace negotiations with France, see: J. J. N. Palmer, "The Anglo-French Peace Negotiations, 1390–1396," *Transactions of the Royal Historical Society,* 5th ser., 16 (1966):81–94; idem, "English Foreign Policy, 1388–99," in *The Reign of Richard II: Essays in*

Honour of May McKisack, ed. F. R. H. Du Boulay and C. M. Barron (London, 1971); idem, *England, France, and Christendom, 1377–99* (Chapel Hill, N.C., 1972); A. Tuck, "Richard II and the Hundred Years War," in *Politics and Crisis in Fourteenth-Century England,* ed. J. Taylor and W. Childs (Gloucester, 1990); N. Saul, *Richard II* (New Haven and London, 1997). For a survey of the pacifist movement so far as this can be traced in late medieval and early modern England, see B. Lowe, *Imagining Peace: A History of Early English Pacifist Ideas, 1340–1560* (University Park, Penn., 1997).

Plague

General textbooks on the Black Death include: P. Ziegler, *The Black Death* (New York, 1969); *The Black Death: A Turning Point in History?,* ed. W. M. Bowsky (New York, 1978); R. S. Gottfried, *The Black Death: Natural and Human Disaster in Medieval Europe* (New York, 1983); D. Herlihy, *The Black Death and the Transformation of the West,* ed. S. K. Cohn, Jr. (Cambridge, Mass., and London, 1997). An excellent source book for plagues throughout the second half of the fourteenth century is *The Black Death,* trans. and ed. R. Horrox. For works that focus on the Black Death in England, see: J. F. D. Shrewsbury, *A History of Bubonic Plague in the British Isles* (Cambridge, 1970); *The Black Death in England,* ed. W. M. Ormrod and P. G. Lindley (Stamford, Lincolnshire, 1996); C. Platt, *King Death: The Black Death and Its Aftermath in Late-Medieval England* (Toronto, 1996).

Modern medical knowledge and the epidemiological history of the disease are surveyed in: L. F. Hirst, *The Conquest of Plague: A Study of the Evolution of Epidemiology* (Oxford, 1953); S. R. Ell, "Interhuman Transmission of Medieval Plague," *Bulletin of the History of Medicine* 54 (1980):497–510; G. Twigg, *The Black Death: A Biological Reappraisal* (New York, 1984); O. J. Benedictow, *Plague in the Late Medieval Nordic Countries: Epidemiological Studies* (Oslo, 1992). For the contemporary medical response, see: A. M. Campbell, *The Black Death and Men of Learning* (History of Science Society Publications, 1, 1931); R. S. Gottfried, *Doctors and Medicine in Medieval England, 1340–1530* (Princeton, 1986); J. Arrizabalaga, "Facing the Black Death: Perceptions and Reactions of University Medical Practitioners," in *Practical Medicine from Salerno to the Black Death,* ed. L. García-Ballester, R. French, J. Arrizabalaga, and A. Cunningham (Cambridge, 1994).

With regard to the contribution of late medieval peasant housing to the spread of bubonic plague, there is considerable debate about when the long house gave way to a courtyard layout where animals were kept in separate buildings and pens. On this issue, see especially: J. G. Hurst and L. A. S. Butler, "Rural Building in England and Wales," in *The Agrarian History of England and Wales: Volume 2: 1042–1350;* H. E. J. Le Patourel and L. A. S. Butler, "Rural Building in England and Wales," in *The Agrarian History of England and Wales: Volume 3: 1348–1500,* ed. E. Miller (Cambridge, 1991); Dyer, *Standards of Living in the Later Middle Ages;* idem, "English Peasant Buildings in the Later Middle Ages (1200–1500)," in idem, *Everyday Life in Medieval England*.

The geographical origins and spread of the Black Death are examined in: É. Carpentier, "Autour de la Peste Noire: Famines et Épidémies dans l'Histoire du XIVe Siècle," *Annales: Economies, Sociétés, Civilisation* 17 (1962):1062–92; W. H. McNeill, *Plagues and Peoples* (New York, 1977); J. Norris, "East or West? The Geographic Origin of the Black Death," *Bulletin of the History of Medicine* 51 (1977):1–24. For demographic surveys of the effect of plague on late medieval English population, see: J. C. Russell, *British Medieval Population* (Albuquerque, N.M., 1948); T. H. Hollingsworth, *Historical Demography* (Ithaca, N.Y., 1969); J. Hatcher, *Plague, Population and the English Economy, 1348–1530* (London, 1977); idem, "Mortality in the Fifteenth Century: Some New Evidence," *Economic History Review*, 2nd series 39 (1986):19–38; R. S. Gottfried, *Epidemic Disease in Fifteenth-Century England: The Medical Response and the Demographic Consequences* (New Brunswick, N.J., 1978); R. M. Smith, "Demographic Developments in Rural England, 1300–48: A Survey," in *Before the Black Death*.

The following studies calculate plague mortality using episcopal registers: A. H. Thompson, "Registers of John Gynwell, Bishop of Lincoln, for the Years 1347–50," *Archaeological Journal* 68 (1911):301–60; idem, "The Pestilences of the Fourteenth Century in the Diocese of York," *Archaeological Journal* 71 (1914):97–154; R. A. Davies, "The Effect of the Black Death on the Parish Priests of the Medieval Diocese of Coventry and Lichfield," *Bulletin of the Institute of Historical Research* 62 (1989):85–90; J. Aberth, "The Black Death in the Diocese of Ely: The Evidence of the Bishop's Register," *Journal of Medieval History* 21 (1995):275–87; W. J. Dohar, *The Black Death and Pastoral Leadership: The Diocese of Hereford in the Fourteenth Century* (Philadelphia, 1995). The original mortality calculations by John Lunn in his 1930 Cambridge doctoral dissertation, "The Black Death in the Bishops' Registers," have been lost, but my attempts to recalculate mortality rates for several dioceses—Bath and Wells, Norwich, Winchester, and Worcester—yielded figures that were 5 to 10 percent higher than Lunn's. This leads me to agree with Davies that the 1291 *Taxatio Ecclesiastica Angliae* of Pope Nicholas IV tends to underestimate the number of benefices in a diocese. English coroner death rates from plague during the second half of the fourteenth century were presented by K. DeLange in an unpublished paper at the International Congress on Medieval Studies at Kalamazoo, Mich., in 1996.

Continental evidence of plague mortality is summarized in: J.-N. Biraben, *Les Hommes et la Peste en France et dans les Pays Européens et Méditerranéens*, 2 vols. (École des Hautes Études en Sciences Sociales, Civilisations et Sociétés, 35, 1975); P. Dollinger, *The German Hansa*, trans. and ed. D. S. Ault and S. H. Steinberg (Stanford, Calif., 1970); D. Herlihy, "Population, Plague, and Social Change in Rural Pistoia, 1201–1430," *Economic History Review*, 2nd ser., 18 (1965):225–44; idem and C. Klapisch-

Zuber, *Tuscans and Their Families: A Study of the Florentine Catasto of 1427* (New Haven and London, 1985); R. W. Emery, "The Black Death of 1348 in Perpignan," *Speculum* 42 (1967):611–23; W. P. Blockmans, "The Social and Economic Effects of Plague in the Low Countries, 1349–1500," *Revue Belge de Philologie et d'Histoire* 58 (1980):833–63; R. Gyug, "The Effects and Extent of the Black Death of 1348: New Evidence for Clerical Mortality in Barcelona," *Mediaeval Studies* 45 (1983):385–98; Bois, *Crisis of Feudalism*; É. Carpentier and M. Le Mené, *La France du XIe au XVe Siècle: Population, Société, Économie* (Paris, 1996).

General surveys of the economic impact of the Black Death in England during the later Middle Ages are available in: A. R. Bridbury, *Economic Growth: England in the Later Middle Ages* (London, 1962); Hatcher, *Plague, Population, and the English Economy;* idem, "England in the Aftermath of the Black Death," *Past and Present* 144 (1994):3–35; Bolton, "'The World Upside Down,'" in *The Black Death in England*. On medieval birth control, see: P. P. A. Biller, "Birth-Control in the West in the Thirteenth and Early Fourteenth Centuries," *Past and Present* 94 (1982):3–26; A. McLaren, *A History of Contraception from Antiquity to the Present Day* (Oxford, 1990); J. M. Riddle, "Oral Contraceptives and Early-Term Abortifacients during Classical Antiquity and the Middle Ages," *Past and Present* 132 (1991):3–32; idem, *Contraception and Abortion from the Ancient World to the Renaissance* (Cambridge, Mass., 1992). For the debate concerning late medieval English marriage patterns, consult the following works: Z. Razi, *Life, Marriage, and Death in a Medieval Parish: Economy, Society, and Demography in Halesowen, 1270–1400* (Cambridge, 1980); R. M. Smith, "Hypothèses sur la Nuptialité en Angleterre aux XIIIe–XIVe Siècles," *Annales: Économies, Sociétés, Civilisation* 38 (1983):102–36; L. R. Poos, *A Rural Society after the Black Death: Essex, 1350–1525* (Cambridge, 1991); P. J. P. Goldberg, "Marriage, Migration, and Servanthood: The York Cause Paper Evidence," in *Woman Is a Worthy Wight: Women in English Society, c. 1200–1500*, ed. idem (Stroud, Gloucestershire, 1992); idem, *Women, Work, and Life Cycle in a Medieval Economy: Women in York and Yorkshire, c. 1300–1520* (Oxford, 1992); M. E. Mate, *Daughters, Wives, and Widows after the Black Death: Women in Sussex, 1350–1535* (Woodbridge, Suffolk, 1998). These should be compared with evidence for the Continent, as presented in: D. Herlihy, "Deaths, Marriages, Births, and the Tuscan Economy (ca. 1300–1550)," in *Population Patterns in the Past,* ed. R. D. Lee (New York, 1977); and M.-Th. Lorcin, *Vivre et Mourir en Lyonnais à la Fin du Moyen Age* (Paris, 1981).

Some general works on the English Peasants' Revolt of 1381 include: *The English Rising of 1381,* ed. R. H. Hilton and T. H. Aston (Cambridge, 1984); and E. B. Fryde and N. Fryde, "Peasant Rebellion and Peasant Discontents," in *Agrarian History of England and Wales: Volume 3.* A good collection of primary documents concerning the revolt is available in *The Peasants' Revolt of 1381,* ed. R. B. Dobson, 2nd ed. (Basingstoke, Hampshire, and London, 1983). The role that the enforcement of the Statute of Labourers may have played in the revolt is explored in: B. H. Putnam, *The Enforcement of the Statutes of Labourers during the First Decade after the Black Death, 1349–1359* (Columbia University Studies in History, Economy and Public Law, 32, 1908); L. R. Poos, "The Social Context of Statute of Labourers Enforcement," *Law and History Review* 1 (1983):27–52; S. A. C. Penn and C. Dyer, "Wages and Earnings in Late Medieval England: Evidence from the Enforcement of the Labour Laws," *Economic History Review,* 2nd series, 43 (1990):356–76. The relationship between lords and peasants as another contributing factor to the revolt is discussed in: R. H. Hilton, *Bond Men Made Free: Medieval Peasant Movements and the English Rising of 1381* (London, 1973); idem, *The English Peasantry in the Later Middle Ages* (Oxford, 1975); idem, *Class Conflict and the Crisis of Feudalism: Essays in Medieval Social History* (London, 1985); J. Hatcher, "English Serfdom and Villeinage: Towards a Reassessment," *Past and Present* (1981):3–39; *The Brenner Debate: Agrarian Class Structure and Economic Development in Pre-Industrial Europe,* ed. T. H. Aston and C. H. E. Philpin (Cambridge, 1985); E. B. Fryde, *Peasants and Landlords in Later Medieval England* (New York, 1996).

J. W. Thompson's analysis of the sociological impact of the plague is available in his article, "The Aftermath of the Black Death and the Aftermath of the Great War," *American Journal of Sociology* 26 (1920–1):565–72. On the Flagellant movement, see: G. Leff, *Heresy in the Later Middle Ages: The Relation of Heterodoxy to Dissent, c. 1250–c. 1450,* 2 vols. (Manchester, 1967); R. Kieckhefer, "Radical Tendencies in the Flagellant Movement of the Mid-Fourteenth Century," *Journal of Medieval and Renaissance Studies* 4 (1974):157–76; F. Graus, *Pest-Geissler-Judenmorde: Das 14 Jahrhundert als Krisenzeit* (Veröffentlichungen des Max-Planck Institut für Geschichte, 86, 1987–8); M. Lambert, *Medieval Heresy: Popular Movements from the Gregorian Reform to the Reformation,* 2nd ed. (Oxford, 1992).

On the writings and influence of Joachim of Fiore, see: M. Reeves, *The Influence of Prophecy in the Later Middle Ages: A Study in Joachism* (Oxford, 1969); *Joachim of Fiore in Christian Thought: Essays on the Influence of the Calabrian Prophet,* ed. D. C. West (New York, 1975); M. Reeves, *Joachim of Fiore and the Prophetic Future* (New York, 1977); D. C. West and S. Zimdars-Swartz, *Joachim of Fiore: A Study in Spiritual Perception and History* (Bloomington, Ind., 1983); B. McGinn, *The Calabrian Abbot: Joachim of Fiore in the History of Western Thought* (New York, 1985); R. K. Emmerson and R. B. Herzman, *The Apocalyptic Imagination in Medieval Literature* (Philadelphia, 1992).

Medieval Christians' pogroms against the Jews during the plague are discussed in M. Breuer, "The 'Black Death' and Antisemitism," in *Antisemitism through the Ages,* ed. S. Almog and trans. N. H. Reisner (Oxford and New York, 1988); and Graus, *Pest-Geissler-Judenmorde.* For more general histories of medieval anti-Semitism, including works that focus on England, see: H. G.

Richardson, *The English Jewry under Angevin Kings* (London, 1960); C. Roth, *A History of the Jews in England,* 3rd ed. (Oxford, 1964); L. Poliakov, *The History of Anti-Semitism,* trans. R. Howard, N. Gerardi, M. Kochan, and G. Klim, 4 vols. (New York, 1965–85); P. R. Hyams, "The Jewish Minority in Mediaeval England, 1066–1290," *Journal of Jewish Studies* 25 (1974):270–93; G. I. Langmuir, *Toward a Definition of Antisemitism* (Berkeley and Los Angeles, 1990); idem, *History, Religion, and Antisemitism* (Berkeley and Los Angeles, 1990); Z. E. Rokéah, "The State, the Church, and the Jews in Medieval England," in *Antisemitism through the Ages;* K. R. Stow, *Alienated Minority: The Jews of Medieval Latin Europe* (Cambridge, Mass., 1992); S. T. Katz, *The Holocaust in Historical Context, Volume I: The Holocaust and Mass Death before the Modern Age* (Oxford, 1994); R. Chazan, *Medieval Stereotypes and Modern Antisemitism* (Berkeley and Los Angeles, 1997); R. R. Mundill, *England's Jewish Solution: Experiment and Expulsion, 1262–1290* (Cambridge, 1998).

Recruitment of English clergy during the later Middle Ages is discussed in: R. L. Storey, "Recruitment of English Clergy in the Period of the Conciliar Movement," *Annuarium Historiae Conciliorum: Internationael Zeitschrift feur Konziliengeschichts- forschung* 7 (1975):290–313; J. A. H. Moran, "Clerical Recruitment in the Diocese of York, 1340–1530: Data and Commentary," *Journal of Ecclesiastical History* 34 (1983):19–54; V. Davis, "Rivals for Ministry? Ordinations of Secular and Regular Clergy in Southern England, c. 1300–1500," in *Studies in Church History: The Ministry, Clerical and Lay,* ed. W. J. Sheils and D. Wood (Ecclesiastical History Society, 26, 1989). Two works that focus on the contributions that chantry priests and guild chaplains made to the overall service of the parish are: B. A. Hanawalt, "Keepers of the Lights: Late Medieval English Parish Gilds," *Journal of Medieval and Renaissance Studies* 14 (1984):21–37; and C. Burgess, "'For the Increase of Divine Service': Chantries in the Parish in Late Medieval Bristol," *Journal of Ecclesiastical History* 36 (1985):46–65.

Lately there has been much reassessment of late medieval English religion, most of which has tended to emphasize the continued vitality of Catholicism just prior to the Reformation. See in particular: L. G. Duggan, "The Unresponsiveness of the Late Medieval Church: A Reconsideration," *Sixteenth Century Journal* 9 (1978):3–26; C. M. Barron and C. Harper-Bill, *The Church in Pre-Reformation Society: Essays in Honour of F. R. H. Du Boulay* (Woodbridge, Suffolk, 1985); C. Harper-Bill, "English Church and Religion after the Black Death," in *The Black Death in England;* idem, *The Pre-Reformation Church in England, 1400–1530,* rev. ed. (London and New York, 1996); J. Hughes, *Pastors and Visionaries: Religion and Secular Life in Late Medieval Yorkshire* (Woodbridge, Suffolk, 1988); E. Duffy, *The Stripping of the Altars: Traditional Religion in England, c. 1400–c. 1580* (New Haven and London, 1992). Some local studies that make good use of wills left by the gentry and urban communities include: J. A. F. Thompson, "Piety and Charity in Late Medieval London," *Journal of Ecclesiastical History* 16 (1965): 178–95;

M. G. A. Vale, *Piety, Charity, and Literacy among the Yorkshire Gentry, 1370–1480* (Borthwick Papers, no. 50, 1976); N. P. Tanner, *The Church in Late Medieval Norwich, 1370–1532* (Pontifical Institute of Mediaeval Studies, Studies and Texts, 66, 1984); P. W. Fleming, "Charity, Faith, and the Gentry of Kent," in *Property and Politics: Essays in Later Medieval English History,* ed. T. Pollard (Gloucester and New York, 1984); P. Heath, "Urban Piety in the Later Middle Ages: The Evidence of Hull Wills," in *The Church, Politics, and Patronage in the Fifteenth Century,* ed. R. B. Dobson (Gloucester, 1984); C. Burgess, "'By Quick and by Dead': Wills and Pious Provision in Late Medieval Bristol," *English Historical Review* 102 (1987):837–58; idem, "Late Medieval Wills and Pious Convention: Testamentary Evidence Reconsidered," in *Profit, Piety, and the Professions in Later Medieval England,* ed. M. A. Hicks (Gloucester, 1990); R. Dinn, "Death and Rebirth in Late Medieval Bury St. Edmunds," in *Death in Towns: Urban Responses to the Dying and the Dead, 100–1600,* ed. S. Bassett (London and New York, 1992); A. D. Brown, *Popular Piety in Late Medieval England: The Diocese of Salisbury, 1250–1550* (Oxford, 1995).

The most recent scholarship on John Wycliffe and Lollardy, although continuing to explore the nature of their beliefs, nevertheless does not demonstrate a strong link between Lollardy and the Reformation. The exception is the Reformation historian A. G. Dickens, who, although revising his classic *English Refor- mation* in light of some of the new scholarship on late medieval religion, still seems to hold to his original position of 1964 that the English Reformation was irresistible. See: A. G. Dickens, *The English Reformation,* 2nd ed. (London, 1989); J. F. Davis, "Lollardy and the Reformation in England," *Archiv für Reformationsgeschichte* 73 (1982):217–36; M. Aston, *Lollards and Reformers: Images and Literacy in Late Medieval Religion* (London and Ronceverte, W. V., 1984); idem, *Faith and Fire: Popular and Unpopular Religion, 1350–1600* (London and Rio Grande, Ohio, 1993); A. Hudson, *Lollards and Their Books* (London and Ronceverte, W. V., 1985); idem, *The Premature Reformation: Wycliffite Texts and Lollard History* (Oxford, 1988); *Wyclif and His Times,* ed. A. Kenny (Oxford, 1986); Wilks, "Wyclif and the Great Persecution." For studies of late medieval popular piety on the Continent, see: J. Chiffoleau, *La Comptabilité de l'Au-Delà: Les Hommes et la Religion dans la Région d'Avignon à la Fin du Moyen Age, vers 1320–vers 1480* (Rome, 1980); and S. K. Cohn, Jr., *The Cult of Remembrance and the Black Death: Six Renaissance Cities in Central Italy* (Baltimore, 1992).

The best survey of English mysticism remains M. D. Knowles, *The English Mystical Tradition* (London, 1961). But the literature on female mysticism is large and growing. For surveys that include both English and Continental female mystics during the later Middle Ages, see: *An Introduction to the Medieval Mystics of Europe,* ed. P. E. Szarmach (Albany, N.Y., 1984); P. Dronke, *Women Writers of the Middle Ages: A Critical Study of Texts from Perpetua to Marguerite Porete* (Cambridge, 1984); *Medieval Women Writers,* ed. K. M. Wilson (Athens, Ga., 1984); R. Kieckhefer, *Unquiet Souls: Fourteenth-Century*

Saints and Their Religious Milieu (Chicago and London, 1984); E. Z. Brunn and G. Epiney-Burgard, *Women Mystics in Medieval Europe,* trans. S. Hughes (New York, 1989); F. Beer, *Women and Mystical Experience in the Middle Ages* (Woodbridge, Suffolk, 1992); E. A. Petroff, *Body and Soul: Essays on Medieval Women and Mysticism* (Oxford, 1994); J. Aberth, "Pseudo-Dionysius as Liberator: Influence of the Negative Tradition on Late Medieval Female Mystics," *Downside Review* no. 395 (1996):96–115. Numerous studies recently have appeared examining Julian's unique (but entirely orthodox) theology. See in particular: P. Molinari, *Julian of Norwich: The Teaching of a Fourteenth-Century Mystic* (London, 1958); B. Pelphrey, *Love Was His Meaning: The Theology and Mysticism of Julian of Norwich* (Salzburg, 1982); *Julian: Woman of Our Day,* ed. R. Llewelyn (London, 1985); G. Jantzen, *Julian of Norwich* (London, 1987); D. N. Baker, *Julian of Norwich's Showings: From Vision to Book* (Princeton, 1994). Translations of the long text of Julian's *Showings* are from the edition by E. Colledge and J. Walsh (New York and Ramsey, N.J., 1978).

Death

Works that explore death culture during the Middle Ages include: Huizinga, *Waning of the Middle Ages,* T. S. R. Boase, *Death in the Middle Ages: Mortality, Judgment, and Remembrance* (London and New York, 1972); P. Ariès, *The Hour of Our Death,* trans. H. Weaver (Oxford, 1981); M. Vovelle, *La Mort et l'Occident de 1300 à nos Jours* (Paris, 1983); J. Delumeau, *Sin and Fear: The Emergence of a Western Guilt Culture, 13th–18th Centuries,* trans. E. Nicholson (New York, 1990); M. Aston, "Death," in *Fifteenth-Century Attitudes: Perceptions of Society in Late Medieval England,* ed. R. Horrox (Cambridge, 1994); P. Binski, *Medieval Death: Ritual and Representation* (Ithaca, N.Y., 1996); M. Camille, *Master of Death: The Lifeless Art of Pierre Remiet, Illuminator* (New Haven and London, 1996). On the significance of the resurrection, particularly as it relates to the medieval body, see C. W. Bynum, *Fragmentation and Redemption: Essays on Gender and the Human Body in Medieval Religion* (New York, 1991); and idem, *Resurrection of the Body in Western Christianity, 200–1336* (New York, 1995).

For the section on Apocalypse manuscripts and tapestries, the following proved most useful: M. R. James, *The Apocalypse in Art* (London, 1931); R. Planchenault, *L'Apocalypse d'Angers* (Caisse Nationale des Monuments Historiques et des Sites, 1966); *L'Apocalypse d'Angers: Chef-d'Oeuvre de la Tapisserie Médiévale* (Paris, 1982–5); P. M. de Winter, "Visions of the Apocalypse in Medieval England and France," *Bulletin of the Cleveland Museum of Art* 70 (1983):396–417; N. Morgan, "The Burckhardt-Wildt Apocalypse," in *Art at Auction: The Year at Sotheby's, 1982–83* (Sotheby Publications, 1983); G. Henderson, "The Manuscript Model of the Angers 'Apocalypse' Tapestries," *Burlington Magazine* 127 (1985):209–18; *La Tenture de l'Apocalypse d'Angers,* 2nd ed. (Associations pour le Développement de l'Inventaire Général des Monuments et des Richesses Artistiques en Région des Pays de la Loire, Cahiers de l'Inventaire, 4, 1987); P. K. Klein, "Introduction: The Apocalypse in Medieval Art," in *The Apocalypse in the Middle Ages,* ed. R. K. Emmerson and B. McGinn (Ithaca, N.Y., and London, 1992). Penetration of the apocalyptic thought of Joachim of Fiore into England is discussed in: M. W. Bloomfield and M. E. Reeves, "The Penetration of Joachism into Northern Europe," *Speculum* 29 (1954):772–93; and R. Freyhan,"Joachism and the English Apocalypse," *Journal of the Warburg and Courtauld Institutes* 18 (1955): 211–44.

On the legend of the Three Living and the Three Dead, both in text and illustration, see: K. Künstle, *Die Legende der Drei Lebenden und der Drei Toten und der Totentanz* (Freiburg, 1908); *Les Cinq Poèmes des Trois Morts et des Trois Vifs,* ed. S. Glixelli (Paris, 1914); John Audelay, *The Poems,* ed. E. K. Whiting (Early English Text Society, 184, 1931); R. Van Marle, *Iconographie de l'Art Profane au Moyen Age et à la Renaissance et la Décoration des Demeures,* 2 vols. (La Haye, 1931–32); E. C. Williams, "Mural Paintings of the Three Living and the Three Dead in England," *Journal of the British Archaeological Association* 7 (1942):31–40; L. Guerry, *Le Thème du "Triomphe de la Mort" dans la Peinture Italienne* (Paris, 1950); E. W. Tristram, *English Wall Painting of the Fourteenth Century* (London, 1955); D. Gray, *Themes and Images in the Medieval English Religious Lyric* (London and Boston, Mass., 1972); P. Chihaia, *Immortalité et Decomposition dans l'Art du Moyen Age* (Madrid, 1988). Medieval ghost stories are exhaustively catalogued in J.-C. Schmitt, *Ghosts in the Middle Ages: The Living and the Dead in Medieval Society,* trans. T. L. Fagan (Chicago, 1998).

For the Danse Macabre, or the Dance of Death, I consulted the following: V. Dufour, *La Danse Macabre des Saints Innocents de Paris* (Paris, 1874); E. Male, *L'Art Religieux de la Fin du Moyen Age en France* (Paris, 1908); *The Dance of Death,* eds. F. Warren and B. White (Early English Text Society, 181, 1931); L. P. Kurtz, *The Dance of Death and the Macabre Spirit in European Literature* (New York, 1934); *La Danse Macabré des Charniers des Saints Innocents à Paris,* ed. E. F. Chaney (Manchester, 1945); J. M. Clark, *The Dance of Death in the Middle Ages and the Renaissance* (Glasgow, 1950); H. Rosenfeld, *Der Mittelalter- liche Totentanz* (Beihefte zum Archiv für Kulturgeschicte 3, 1954); E. Dubruck, *The Theme of Death in French Poetry of the Middle Ages and the Renaissance* (London and Paris, 1964); J. Brossollet, "L'Influence de la Peste du Moyen-Age sur le Theme de la Danse Macabre," *Pagine di Storia della Medicina* 13/3 (1969):38–46; J. Saugnieux, *Les Danses Macabres de France et d'Espagne et leurs Prolongements Littéraires* (Paris, 1972); P. Vaillant, "La Danse Macabre de 1485 et les Fresques du Charnier des Innocents," in *La Mort au Moyen Age* (Publications de la Société Savante d'Alsace et des Regions de l'Est, 25, 1975); P. Tristram, *Figures of Life and Death in Medieval English Literature* (New York, 1976); J. Batany, "Les 'Danses Macabre': Une Image en Negatif du Fonctionnalisme Social," in *Dies Illa: Death in the Middle Ages, Proceedings of the 1983 Manchester Colloquium,* ed. J. H. M. Taylor (Liverpool, 1984); I. le Masne de Chermont, "La Danse Macabre du Cimetière des Innocents," in *Les Saints-Innocents,* ed. M. Fleury and G.-M. Leproux (Paris, 1990).

The *Vado Mori* poems are discussed in: E. P. Hammond, "Latin Texts of the Dance of Death," *Modern Philology* 8 (1910–11):399–410; and Rosenfeld, *Mittelalterliche Totentanz*. For poems that pose a dialogue between the body and soul, see R. W. Ackerman, "The Debate of the Body and the Soul and Parochial Christianity," *Speculum* 37 (1962):541–65. *A Disputacioun betwyx the Body and Wormes* and *A Dysputacion betwyx the Saule and the Body when it Is Past oute of the Body* are contained in Additional MS 37049 in the British Library, London. For discussions of the text and illustrations, see: F. Wormald, "Some Popular Miniatures and their Rich Relations," in *Miscellanea pro Arte: Festschrift für Herman Schnitzler* (Dusseldorf, 1965); and M. M. Malvern, "An Earnest 'Monyscyon' and '[Th]inge Delectabyll' Realized Verbally and Visually in 'A Disputacion betwyx [th]e Body and Wormes,' a Middle English Poem Inspired by Tomb Art and Northern Spirituality," *Viator* 13 (1982):415–43.

A catalogue of known transi tombs is available in K. Cohen, *Metamorphosis of a Death Symbol: The Transi Tomb in the Later Middle Ages and the Renaissance* (Berkeley and Los Angeles, 1973). It should be noted, however, that Cohen omits at least twelve known transi tombs in Ireland. For these, see H. M. Roe, "Cadaver Effigial Monuments in Ireland," *The Journal of the Royal Society of Antiquaries of Ireland* 99 (1969):1–19. Other books and articles relating to tomb sculpture, and the transi tomb in particular, include: E. Panofsky, *Tomb Sculpture: Four Lectures on Its Changing Aspects from Ancient Egypt to Bernini* (New York, 1956); S. Lawson, "Cadaver Effigies: The Portrait as Prediction," *Bulletin of Celtic Studies* 25 (1974):519–23; P. M. King, "The English Cadaver Tomb in the Late Fifteenth Century: Some Indications of a Lancastrian Connection," in *Dies Illa;* idem, "The Cadaver Tomb in England: Novel Manifestation of an Old Idea," *Church Monuments: Journal of the Church Monuments Society* 5 (1990):26–38; B. Kemp, "English Church Monuments during the Period of the Hundred Years War," in *Arms, Armies, and Fortifications in the Hundred Years War.*

Shroud brasses are discussed in M. Norris, "Later Medieval Monumental Brasses: An Urban Funerary Industry and Its Representation of Death," in *Death in Towns*. For English resurrection monuments, see R. H. Bowdler, "Monuments of Decay and Resurrection: Themes of Mortality in 17th-Century English Church Monuments" (Ph.D. diss., Cambridge, 1991). Iconoclastic destruction of medieval art, including tomb sculpture, in England during the Reformation is chronicled in J. Phillips, *The Reformation of Images: Destruction of Art in England, 1535–1660* (Berkeley and Los Angeles, 1973).

Epitaph

The quotation of Simon Islip was taken from *The Black Death*, trans. and ed. Horrox. The English translation of Huizinga's *Waning of the Middle Ages* is from the 1924 edition by F. Hopman. The latest, 6th ed. of the textbook by Tierney and Painter was published in 1999.

INDEX

Earnest

Genealogical Table Showing the Interrelated Succession to the Crowns of England and France during the Later Middle Ages

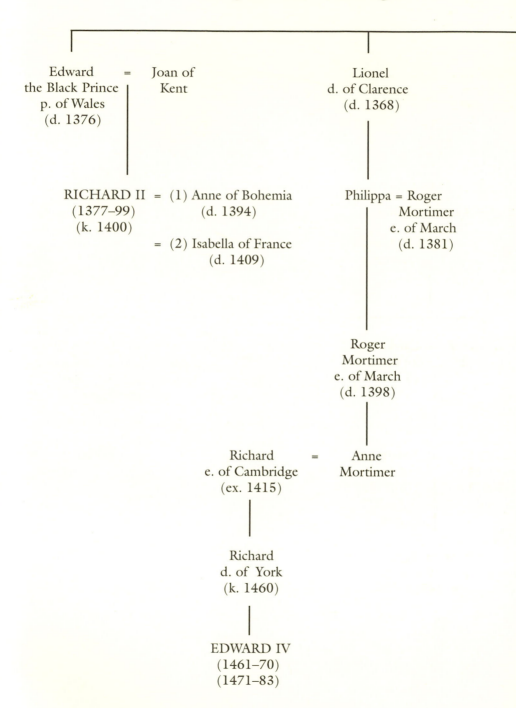